S0-DUU-614

DINO-GUIDE

The Saurian Source Book

By John C. Fredriksen, Ph. D.

Dollar Scholar Press
"Good stuff, cheap"

QE
861.95
.F74
1999

Copyright John C. Fredriksen, 1999
Artwork copyright David T. Hubbard, 1999

All rights reserved. Written permission must be secured from
the author to use or reproduce any part of this work.

Fredriksen, John C. *Dino-Guide: The Saurian Source Book.*
Salem, MA: Dollar Scholar Press, 1999. 228 pp.

Vol. 1 of *Reference Books for School and Public Libraries*

1. Dinosaurs. 2. Dinosaurs-Art. 3. Dinosaurs-Catalogs. 4. Dinosaurs-Collectibles. 5. Dinosaur
Paraphernalia-Directories. 6. Paleontology-Collectibles. 7. Popular Culture-Directories.
I. Title. II. Series.

LC 99-095676

ISBN 0-9674856-0-6

Available from: John C. Fredriksen
            461 Loring Ave.
            Salem, MA 01970 USA

Everyone remembers their first time. For me it was a stormy day in the fall of 1960, when a late season hurricane confined me and my sisters at home in Warwick, Rhode Island. The *good news* was that we had to miss school. However, to keep us occupied, my mother provided a welcome diversion by dipping into Christmas gifts hidden in the attic. Low and behold, I was suddenly recipient of the long-defunct Marx dinosaur set, replete with plastic fronds, cavemen, and a host of inexplicable beasts that I had never previously imagined. Set against the backdrop of this primeval weather, an appropriate prehistoric setting, the experience was pure magic. I readily played with and absorbed the mythical creatures of lore: *Trachodon*, *Triceratops*, and my favorite, *Tyrannosaurus*. So at the tender age of seven, I was smitten by paleontology and--forty years later--my passion continues unabated. The book you hold is very much a byproduct of that dark, tempestuous day, in many respects a defining moment in my life.

Why *Dino-Guide*? In the century and a half following their discovery, dinosaurs have been cast more as icons of popular culture than objects of scientific inquiry. This portrayal partly explains their tremendous and enduring popularity with children of all ages, and a good many adults. However, as a subject of inquiry, most attempts at reference literature have been restricted to the science end of the discipline. Moreover, where books about popular culture do exist, they invariably touch upon dinosaur "collectibles," namely, discontinued items no longer available on a commercial basis. As a reference librarian and a dinosaur aficionado, it always annoyed me that a topic this broad and popular lacked even a rudimentary buyer's guide. I concluded that it would be a shame-- and a disservice--to let the present century end or the new one begin without a bonafide dinosaur directory. My goal was to provide a tome that was exhaustive and easy to use, yet would confer intellectual respectability to the notion of dinosaurs as popular culture.

In designing this book, the sheer magnitude of dinosaur materials available posed *Brontosaurus-sized* problems of organization and utility. I therefore selected a two-pronged approach to convey this avalanche of information as quickly as possible, while keeping the book tidy and simple. The first section is 118-categories of products, divided alphabetically. These 1,200 entries are then subdivided alphabetically by *last* name. And, because we live in an information age, great care was taken to list websites and e-mail addresses to facilitate online inquiry. Whenever possible, phone and fax numbers are also appended, along with a brief description of items in question. Prices, where listed, are naturally subject to change and should be used as reference points only. The appendix, or 'Bestiary,' was in many respects the most difficult feature to conceive, but also the most rewarding. Here I collate products available on a *species-by-species* basis. Dinosaurs and other extinct reptiles are arranged alphabetically and listed *downward*, smallest to largest, by size (basically, snout to tail, but flying creatures are by wingspan). Headings *across* the page denote size, artist, price, source with catalog number, if known, and commentary, if relevant. Bronze items are further delineated by **bold** type. In fairness to all our deceased ancestors, an identical scheme is also provided for mammals and other extinct vertebrates. Between the two, 439 animals types are listed, representing over 2,000 items. Thus situated, *Dino-Guide* should direct users to the products they covet most. If you find what you're looking for, it has exceeded my highest expectations.

The compiler acknowledges the help of several individuals in the dinosaur community, without whose assistance *Dino-Guide* would have been all the poorer: Art Crecca of *Link and Pin Hobbies*, Allen Debus and Gary R. Williams of *Dinosaur World*, Mike Evans of the *Alchemy Works*, Mike Fredericks of *Prehistoric Times*, Dan LoRusso of the *Dinosaur Studio*, plus Steve Brusatte, Mike Howgate, John Lanzendorf, Steve Telleria, and Dean Walker. Special thanks also to David T. Hubbard for gracing these pages with his enticing art. I wish all my work could be this rewarding.

Dino-Guide...more fun than a barrel of raptors. Safer, too!

TABLE OF CONTENTS

Introduction, i
Animation, 1
Ant farms, 1
Art, 1
Artists, 3
Asteroids, 14
Auctions, 15
Banks, 15
Banking, 15
Books, 16
Bread Molds, 17
Cakes, 17
Calenders, 18
Candy, 18
Caps, 19
Cards, 20
Casting, 20
CD-Rom Holders, 20
Ceramics, 20
Cereal, 21
Chess, 21
Children, 22
Clip Art, 24
Clocks and Watches, 25
Clothes and Fabrics, 25
Coins, 26
Collectibles, 27
Coloring Books, 28
Comics, 28
Cookies, 29
Costumes, 29
Creationism, 30
Cropolites, 31
Cyber Pets, 31
Decals, 32
Digs and Tours, 32
Dinner Sets, 35
Dinotopia, 35
Door Knobs, 35
Educational, 35
Films, 38
Fine Arts, 38
Fonts, 38
Fossil Preparation, 39

Fossil Replicas, 40
Fossils, 43
Furniture, 51
Games, 51
Gifts, 54
Globes, 56
Golf, 56
Holograms, 57
Inflatables, 58
Jewelry, 58
Jumpers, 59
Kit Building, 60
Lectures, 61
Life-sized Models, 62
Light Switches, 64
Magnets, 64
Medals, 64
Mobiles, 64
Models and Sculpture, 64
Mouse Pads, 69
Mugs, 69
Museum Displays, 70
Music, 69
News, 71
Organizations, 71
Painting, 74
Paleontology Courses, 74
Paper Dinosaurs, 76
Parks, 77
Party Supplies, 79
Pet Supplies, 81
Pewter, 81
Picture Frames, 82
Pinatas, 83
Place Mats, 83
Plaques, 83
Plastic Figures, 85
Posters, 86
Publications, 88
Puppets, 91
Puzzles, 91
Recipes, 93
Reference, 94
Research, 96

Restaurants, 96
Rockers, 97
Rubber Stamps, 97
Sand Boxes, 98
Screen Savers, 98
Sculpting, 99
Silhouettes, 99
Signs, 99
Sleeping Bags, 100
Soap, 100
Sounds, 100
Special Effects, 100
Sports, 100
Stamps, 100
Stationary, 102
Stencils, 103
Stickers, 103
Stuffed Dinosaurs, 104

Swings, 104
T-shirts, 105
Tatoos, 107
Three-dimensional, 107
Topiary, 107
Toys, 108
Tracks, 112
Travel bags, 113
Traveling Acts, 112
Video, 113
Vitamins, 119
Wooden Toys, 120
Writing Utensils, 121

BESTIARY

Dinosaurs and Extinct Reptiles, 124
Extinct Mammals and Others, 213

To Hannah Landes,
The *Jewish* Velociraptor

ANIMATION

Animation Factory
T 605/339-4722
F 605/335-1554
sales@animationfactory.net
www.animfactory.net
> Download a year's worth of dino animation for only $29.95!

ANT FARMS

ExploraToy
16941 Keegan Ave.
Carson, CA 90746 USA
T 800/995-9290
scitoys@exploratoy.com
www.exploratoy.com
> Sells "Antasaurus", a big, glow-in-the-dark Stegosaurus with a transparent belly.

ART

Beri's Dinosaur World
geocities.com/CapeCanaveral/Lab/1638/index.html
> A stunning site showcasing the works of Berislav Krzic. A wide assortment of topics is covered.

Candi's Dinoart
www3.memlane.com/troodon/candi.html
> Some very good artwork for sale as 17 x 11" prints.

Center Stage Illustrations
www.centerstage-musicals.com/illustr/i.html
> Showcases the dinoart of Joe Heller.

Dann's Dinosaur Reconstruction
www.geocities.com/CapeCanaveral/4459
> Australian artist Dann Pigdon's display of dinosaurs "down under," accompanied by a useful text.

Dawn of Time Gallery
home.earthlink.net/~joedasso/
> A small selection of works by Mark Hallet, Doug Henderson, Karl Huber, and Todd Lorbecki; all items are for sale with prices posted.

Dino Don's Art Gallery
www.dinodon.com/dinosaurs/gallery.html
> This innovative site features a series of notable artists on a monthly, rotating basis.

Dino Russ's Collection of Dino Gifs
www.isgs.uiuc.edu/dinos/art.html
> Highlights 44 drawings from various sources, including the fine-dot pictures of Brenner Fishman.

Dinoart
www.indyrad.iupui.edu/public/jrafert/dinoart.html
> One of the best sites on the web with sections for kits, artists, galleries, and reader art.

Dinobase
palaeo.gly.bris.ac.uk/dinobase/picturesJS/dinopicturesJS.html
> A very impressive collection of artwork by Britain's John Sibbick.

Dinosaur Art by Josef Moravec
www.prehistory.com
> The site of one of the profession's most prolific and accomplished artists. Many items for sale.

Dinosaur Illustrated Magazine
illustrissimus.virtualave.net/dimfront.html
> Another intriguing site by Berislav Krzic, with wonderful dinosaur art, the latest news, and much, much more! Drop by and unwind.

Dinosaur Illustration and Animation
members.aol.com/WileE81/index.html
> *An impressive collection by artist/animator Frank J. DeNota; check out those tyrannosaurs.*

Dinosaur Illustrations
web.syr.edu/~dbgoldma/pictures.html
> *The ultimate dinosaur picture site, hosted by David Goldman. Many, many species are listed alphabetically, frequently with more than one illustration. Superb!*

Dinosaur Man
www.dinosaur-man.com/gallery.html
> *Featuring a gallery by artist Richard Penny and several exciting confrontations. The "courting T. rexes" reminds me of a blind date!*

Dinosauria Online
www.dinosauria.com/gallery/gallery.htm
> *Jeff Poling's informative site also features a gallery of art by Michael Rusher, Chris Srnka, Kelley Taylor, and Joe Tucciarone.*

Dinosauricon
dinosaur.umbc.edu
> *With 24 artists and 508 illustrations, this is one of the best dino sites around.*

Dinosaur's Square
www.comlink.ne.jp/~raptor/en/index.html
> *A medium-sized display of Sunao Mochizuki's fine black and white artwork.*

Early Mass Published Prehistoric
home.twcny.rr.com/dbg/prehistoric/dinosaurs/index.html
> *A black and white collection of some early notable art, mostly by the legendary Charles Knight.*

Earth History Illustrations
gallery.in-tch.com/~earthhistory/index.html
> *An extensive site with painting depicting life in its various stages across time. Featuring the work of Doug Henderson and an engaging text. Slow to load because the extent of artwork but worth the wait!*

Jurassic Gallery
www3.justnet.ne.jp/~mshiraishi/
> *A wonderful Japanese site featuring innumerable works by Mineo Shiraishi.*

La Galerie des Dinosaures
www.chez.com/fucci/journal.html
> *A nice, if largely black & white site, hosted by French 'Dino-gal' Diana Fucci.*

Lost Worlds: The Paleolife of Brian Franczak
www.geocities.com/~lostworlds/contents.html
> *Large and diverse site subdivided into several sections, including theropods, Tyrannosaurus, and new dinosaurs.*

Luis V. Rey's Art Gallery
www.ndirect.co.uk/~luisrey
> *Showcases one of the most accomplished paleoartists today, with sevral speculative paintings about "dinobirds."*

Mesozoic Fauna in Pen and Ink
www.eskimo.com/~stevew/dinoart/dinoart.htm
> *Proffers some charming black & white dinosaur drawings for children. Items are for sale and suitable for coloring purposes.*

Natural History Museum
owen.nhm.ac.uk/cgi-bin/browsing/piclib.pl
> *Huge collection of 518 drawings, paintings, and photographs of various*

creatures, alphabetically arranged. An essential resource!

Oceans of Kansas Paleontology
www.oceansofkansas.com/
A fascinating site—one of my favorites—featuring the artwork of Dan Varner and Doug Henderson. Contains more mosasaurs than should be allowed by law!

Paleo-Art
www.fossilhut.com/paleo-art.htm
A site, maintained by Bill Hessin, showcases the works of Dan Boewn, Robert Lundquist, Sue Grannerman, and Shelley Penner, all of which are for sale as prints.

Paleomod
www.u-net.com/~paleomod/
A nice assortment of animal sculpture and drawings by leading British artist Richard Hammond.

Paper Dinosaurs
www.lhl.lib.mo.us/pubserv/hos/dino/welcome.htm
An intriguing collection of early dinosaur illustrations as displayed at the Linda Hall Library.

Shinzen Takeuchi
www.niji.or.jp/home/shinzen/
Shinzen maintains a nice site full of his impressive dinosaur sculptures.

Vertebrate Phylogeny Page
www.geocities.com/CapeCanaveral/Hall/1636/
Jack Conrad's excellent site features his skeletal diagrams and reconstructions. A detailed history of animals with backbones, accompanied by an informative text.

Walters & Kissinger
www.dinoart.com
Featuring art and sculpture by Robert F. Walters, Tess Kissinger, Paul Sorton, and Bruce J. Mohn.

The World of Model Dinosaurs
village.infoweb.ne.jp/~dinodino/index.htm
A fantastic review of the sculpted wonders of Japanese artist Kazunari Araki. The subjects are simply gorgeous in detail!

ARTISTS

Alden, David
83 Brook Rd.
Weston, MA 02195 USA
T 781/647-4906

Alderson, Bruce A.
68 Wilmarth Bridge Rd.
Rehoboth, MA 02769 USA
T/F 508/336-5298

Anton, Mauricio
C. Los Yebenes 56 3-C
28047 Madrid SPAIN
T/F 34-1-7194222
MANTON@santandersupernet.com

Araki, Kazunari
1-22-7 Ymate-higashi
Kyotanabe City, Kyoto
610-0357 JAPAN
dinodino@mb.infoweb.ne.jp
village.infoweb.ne.jp/~dinodino/

Auger, Jean-Guy
265 Dubois St.
Breckenridge, Quebec
J0X 2G0 CANADA
T 819/682-5212
marty0069@hotmail.com

Battan, Russel
33 Wedgewood Dr.
Longlevens, Gloucester
Gloucestershire, ENGLAND
T 011-44-1542-311265

Barlowe, Wayne D.
6 Oakwood Lane
Rumson, NJ 07760 USA
T 908/758-1035

Baugh, Bryan
421 14th St.
Santa Monica, CA 90420 USA
T 310/395-5061

Berdak, Keith
621 Twillman Dr.
St. Charles, MO 63301 USA
T 314/946-3526
F 314/332-5626

Bindon, John
1241 Nottingham Ave.
Burlington, Ontario
L7P 2R5 CANADA
T/F 905/319-3977
bindon@affirmative.com
www.bindonillustrations.on.ca/portfolio.htm

Bowman, Bruce
2111 NE 23rd #2
Portland, OR 97212 USA
T 503/281-1516
bbow@teleport.com

Boydston, James S.
1019 SW 6th St.
Topeka, KS 66606-1403 USA
T 913/357-7769

Brady, Joseph
7026 Thomas Blvd.
Pittsburgh, PA 15208 USA
T 412/826-2765

Braginetz, Donna
Quail Studio Paleographics
PO Box 305, Rd 25 E
Bellvue, CO 80512 USA
F 970/484-0275
quailspg@frii.com

Braund, Matthew
Surrey TW10 6SH
ENGLAND
T 011-41-71-735-7644

Buchholz, Peter
2827 14th Ave. W #4
Seattle, WA 98119 USA
Tetanurae@aol.com

Burgess, Jerry
3514 W. Carla Vista Dr.
Chandler, AZ 85226 USA
T 480/786-5382
F 480/786-6449
jcburgess@az.rmci.net
home.rmci.net/jcburgess/

Burris, John
537 Cooper Ave.
Milford, OH 45150 USA
T 513/831-0242
dinoart@earthlink.net
*John does an incredible series of pen
and ink dinosaur portraits.*

Bush, George A.
570A Church Lane Rd.
Reading, PA 19606 USA
gabush@bellatlantic.net
www.third-wave.com/gabush

Carpenter, Kenneth
Denver Museum of Natural History
2001 Colorado Blvd.
Denver, CO 80205-5798 USA
T 303/331-6492

Carr, Karen
2612 Cross Bend
Plano, TX 75023 USA
T 972/867-9636
karencarr@ont.com
www.karencarr.com

Carroll, Michael
6280 W. Chestnut Ave.
Littleton, CO 80128 USA
T 303/933-1645
spaceart@power-online.com

Castellano, Juan Jose Rosado
Dos de Mayo N53 4b
28934 Mostoles (Madrid) SPAIN
junajocast@yahoo.com

Choo, Brian
2 Sierra Close
Leeming 6149 West Australia
AUSTRALIA
bchoo@cyllene.uwa.edu.au

Clark, Rachel K.
RaptorRKC@aol.com
members.aol.com/raptorrkc/sketchbook.htm#di
nosaurs

Cole, Michael E.
4280 Latham St., Ste. L
Riverside, CA 92501-1737 USA
T 909/683-3749
F 909/683-1604

Coles, Philip
The Vicarage, St. Mildres Rd.
Minster, Romsgate, Kent
CT12 4DE ENGLAND
T 01843-821250

Compton, Michael W.
2151 West Fair Ave., Ste. 184
Lancaster, OH 43130 USA
T 614/654-8293

Conti, Kevin
6125 Good Fortune Rd.
Peyton, CO 80831 USA
T 719/683-5818

Cooley, Brian
6727 Silverview Rd NW
Calgary, Alberta
T3B 3L5 CANADA
T 403/247-0581
F 403/269-3097
Cooley@cadvision.com
www.ignitionM2.com/

Courtland, Chad
241 4th Ave. #8
Venice, CA 90291 USA
T 310/450-6277

Cox, Sharon S.
656 Honey Locust Way
Lexington, KY 40503 USA
T 606/277-9237
ssc@bestcreaturefeatures.com
www.bestcreaturefeatures.com

Cunningham, Betty
PO Box 370876
Montara, CA 94037 USA
resume@flyinggoat.com
www.flyinggoat.com

Czerkas, Stephan and Sylvia
6350 S. Hwy 191
Monticello, UT 84535 USA
T 435/587-2094
F 801/587-2054
www.dinosaur-museum.org/

Dasso, Joe
23710 El Toro Rd., Ste. C
Lake Forest, CA 92630 USA
F 714/586-4615
joedasso@msn.com

Davies, Jim
14543-52 Street
Edmonton, Alberta
T5A 4N1 CANADA

DeVito, Joseph
115 ShadyHill Dr.
Chalfort, PA 18914-2029 USA
T 215/822-3002

Davis, Buddy
1040 Henpeck Rd.
Utica, OH 43080 USA
T 614/668-3321

Dixon, Dougal
55 Mill Lane
Wareham, Dorset
BH20 4QY ENGLAND
T011-44-929-556005

Dollak, Nicholas
116 Lewis Lane
Fairhaven, NJ 07704 USA
T 732/741-9194
jdollak@momouth.com

Eisner, Glen
12154 Spring Trail
Kagel Canyon, CA 91342 USA
T 818/899-8262

Ellis, Tommy
2293 N. March Rd.
Murfreessboro, TN 37129 USA
T 615/890-9415
paleoart@ccast.com
www.ccast.com/paleo

Felder, Larry
33 Stillwater Ct.
Bridgewater, NJ 08807 USA
T 908/218-1638

Florides, George
11 Korinthiakov P/SSA
1048 Nicosia CYPRUS
T 357-2-337911

Ford, Tracy
13503 Powers Rd.
Poway, CA 92074 USA
tlford@ix.netcom.com

Foulkes, Shane
8420 Craig Hill
St. Louis, MO 63123 USA
T 314/849-9754

Franczak, Brian
117 Roslyn Dr.
New Britain, CT 06052 USA
T 860/224-0484
F 860/225-7074
franzak@ntplx.net
www.geocities.com/~lostworlds/contents.html

Fucci, Diana
Chemin de la Maladiere
01630 Perm FRANCE
fucci.diana@wanafoo.fr
www.chez.fr/fucci

Garner, Truett
2901 Piney Grove
Wilbon Rd.
Holly Springs, NC 27540 USA
T 919/557-2289
Dinoboy@worldnet.att.net

Gaston, Robert
1943 K Rd.
Fruita, CO 81521 USA
T 970/858-4785
gastondesign@compuserve.com

Geraghty, Paul
Box 358
Avonlea, Saskatchewan

S0H 0C0 CANADA
grantg@compusmart.ab.ca

Geraths, Dana
2431 C. Coral Ave. NE
Salem, OR 97305 USA
T 503/581-3216
paleoart@navicom.com

Giest, Donna
1409 W. Magnolia
Burbank, CA 91506 USA
T 818/848-3770

Glazer, Bruce A.
48-958 Greenwood Lane
Palm Desert, CA 92260 USA
T 619/346-9302

Greb, Stephen
228 MMR Bldg.
University of Kentucky
Lexington, KY 40506-0107 USA
T 606/ 257-5500
F 606/257-1147

Green, John G.
2955 Sylvia St.
Bonita, CA 91902-2139 USA
T 619/475-4939
F 619/224-6775

Groman, James
13464 Clifton Rd.
Lakewood, OH 44107-1431 USA
T 216/228-1042

Groves, Alan
6 Godolphin Rd.
London W12 8JE
ENGLAND
DRAUTTO@hotmail.com

Gurche, John
c/o Karen Ashley

1304 Olive St.
Denver, CO 80220 USA
T 303/370-8365

Gurney, James
PO Box 693
Rhinebeck, NY 12572 USA
T 914/876-7746
F 914/876-2030
www.dinotopia.com

Hallet, Mark
5052 Halls Ferry Rd. South
Salem, OR 97302 USA
T 503/585-7056
F 503/585-8131

Hammond, Richard P.
2 Grin Close, Harpur Hill
Buxton, Derbyshire
SK17 9NR ENGLAND
T 011-44-1298-72478
hammond@paleomod.u-net.com
www.u-net.com/~paleomod/

Harder, Rolf
273-A Bord du Lac
Pointe-Claire, Quebec
H9S 4L1 CANADA
T 514/426-9181
F 514/426-9188

Hawley, Russell J.
1900 South Missouri, Apt. 2736
Casper, WY 82609 USA
T 307/235-4780

Hays, James T.
8036 Park Ridge Circle
Morris, AL 35116 USA
T 205/647-1456

Headden, Jamie
238 Delaware Ave., Apt. #40
Nampa, ID 83651 USA

qilongia@usc.edu
http://members.tripod.com/~Qilong/

Henderson, Doug
117 Mackkowski Lane
Whitehall, MT 59759 USA
T 406/287-3731

Holgate, Doug
23 Woodbine Ave.
Normanhurst, NSW 2076 AUSTRALIA
douggie52@hotmail.com

Holmes, Graeme
PO Box 38510
Howick, Auckland
NEW ZEALAND
homepages.ihug.co.nz/~smilodon

Holmes, John W.
"The Croft," 23 St. Stephen Rd.
Sticker, St. Austell, Cornwall
PL26 7HA ENGLAND
T 01726-75630

Howard. Walter K.
115 NW 84th
Seattle, WA 98117 USA
T 206/784-4240
F 206/942-5611

Hubbard, David T.
29827 Country Rd. 22 West
Elkhart, IN 46517 USA
T 219/295-6081
jhubbard@michiana.net

Huber, Karl
Rt. 6, Box 14
Santa Fe, NM 87501 USA
T 505/474-2917

Johnson, Arri
100 Birchwood Rd.
St. Anne's, Bristol

BS4 4QT ENGLAND
T/F 0117-997-2107

Jones, Mike
2034 Brighton, Apt. D
Burbank, CA 91504 USA
T 818/845-3379

Keesey, T. Michael
Severn 112
1000 Hilltop Circle
Baltimore, MD 21250 USA
T 443/612-7166
tkeese1@gl.umbc.edu

Kelley, Scott
1237 Fort Hunter Rd.
Schenectady, NY 12303 USA
T 518/355-7958
Aimages@nycap.rr.com

Kirk, Steven
Egerton House Cottage
Egerton, North Ashford
Kent TH27 9BD ENGLAND
T 011-44-1233-756700

Kish, Ely
RR 1, Lavigne Rd. 1861
Hammond, Ontario
K0A 2A0 CANADA
T/F 613/487-3348

Kissinger, Tess
2634 Parrish St.
Philadelphia, PA 19130 USA
T/F 215/765-1123
bobtess@dinoart.com

Klausmeyer, John
Museum of Natural History
University of Michigan
1109 Geddes Ave.
Ann Arbor, MI 48109-1079 USA
T 313/747-1383

Koroshetz, Paul
630 Van Buren St.
Pueblo, CO 81004-1861 USA
T 719/543-0829

Kozinvich, Klim
185 12th St.
Brooklyn, NY 11215 USA
T 718/788-8329
F 718/369-1934

Krb, Vladimir
#706 4th St SW
Drumheller, Alberta
T0J 0Y6 CANADA
T 403/823-4950
F 403/823-6720
sunshine@das.magtech.ab.ca

Krejsa, Vera
Black Hills Institute
PO Box 643
Hill City, SD 57745 USA
T 605/574-4289

Krzic, Berislav
Cesta 9 Augusta 8d
1410 Zagorje ob Savi SLOVENIA
T/F 38660161569
veselinka.stanisavac@silo.net
www.geocities.com/CapeCanaveral/Lab/
1638/index.html

Lilpob, Martin
Im Bruch 2
66399 Mandelbachtal GERMANY
T 01149-6803-3838
F 01149-6803-3636
rzdlil@med-rz.uni-sb.de

Linder, Staffan
Box 230 66
104 35 Stockholm SWEDEN
swede-creations@the-lair.com
www.swedecreations.com/index.htm

Lorbecki, Todd A.
313 N. 95th St #137
Milwaukee, WI 53226 USA
T 414/454-0109
fantasy@execpc.com
www.execpc.com/~fantasy

LoRusso, Daniel A.
116 Bowdoin St.
Medford, MA 02155 USA
T 781/396-8066
F 781/396-8177
webmaster@dinosaurstudio.com
www.dinosaurstudio.com/artistsdl.html#loruss
ob

Lowe, Alexander
The Hayes Cottage, Bibstone
Cromhall, Wotten-under-Edge
Gloucestershire GL12 8AD
ENGLAND
T 0454-0260155

McGrady, Charlie
600 N. Adams St.
Gillespie, IL 62033 USA
T 217/839-2593
F 217/839-2558
paleoart@ccast.com
www.cmstudio.com

Malicki, Michael
Academy of Natural Sciences
1900 Benjamin Franklin Pkwy
Philadelphia, PA 19103-1195 USA
T 215/299-1154
F 215/299-1028

Marrs, David
309 4th Ave. #203
San Francisco, CA 94118 USA
T 415/626-4768
F 415/252-0924

Matsumura, Shinobu
6-10 Tonoshima-cho
Kadoma-shi, Osaka JAPAN
T 01-81-6-909-1051
F 011-81-6-909-1334

Merrithew, Tony
PO Box 66435
Portland, OR 97236 USA
T 503/775-5270

Milbourne, Michael
3478 Godspeed Crt.
Davidsonville, MD 21035 USA
T 410/721-7772
F 410/956-9492

Miller, D. W.
PO Box 1921
Bellingham, WA 98227 USA
T 360/734-8792
F 360/734-1423

Miller, Ralph W.
307 Lexington Dr.
Menlo Park, CA 94025-2911 USA
T 415/329-8119

Milochau, Eric
10 rue de Bretonnerie
95300 Pontoise FRANCE
milochau.eric@wanadoo.fr
www.perso.wanadoo.fr/eric.milochau/Eric-
Dinosaurs.html

Mohn, Bruce J.
2634 Parrish St.
Philadelphia, PA 19130 USA
T/F 215/765-1123

Morales, Bruno Hernandez
Nicanor Fajardo #1115
Villa Sta. Barbara, Renca
Santiago CHILE
T 562/-6412951

F 562/2251186

Moravec, Josef
5650 Westfield St.
Yorba Linda, CA 92887 USA
T 714/970-1128
F 714/970-2780
www.prehistory.com

Mullane, John P.
49A Edgewater Park
Bronx, NY 10465 USA
T 212/486-9644
F 212/486-9646

Mullins, Gerald L.
269 Main St.
Hinton, WV 25951 USA
T 304/466-2367

Munn, William
13654 Norris Ave.
Sylmar, CA 91342 USA
T 818/833-1873
F 818/899-5684

Murphy, Lee M.
17814 Cantara St.
Reseda, CA 91335 USA
T 818/343-2922

Murtha, Sean R. J.
154 Baltic St.
Brooklyn, NY 11201 USA
T 718/855-3286

Musy, Mark
PO Box 1143
Hayesville, NC 28904-1143 USA
T 818/389-3491
www.voicenet.com/~redassoc/musy

Nagle, Shawn
648 Jasmine Way South
St. Petersburg, FL 33705 USA

T 813/906-9284
nagleworks@aol.com
members.aol.com/crom357/nagleworks.htm

Neill, Jonathan
3854 N. Orchard Lane., Apt. A
Calabasas, CA 91302 USA
Neilopolis@aol.com
www.Neillfineart.com

Nissen, Elaine
2803 38th Ave. S
Minneapolis, MN 55406 USA
T 612/832-1727
F 612/722-6396

O'Brian, Patrick
300 Chestnut Ave.
Studio 6
Baltimore, MD 21211 USA
T 410/243-5113
Panda.Obrien@prodigy.net

Oda, Takashi
1-350-#102 Shinmatsudo-minami
Matsudo-City 270-0035 JAPAN
d-oda@MX2.nisiq.net

Ortega, Pat M.
c/o J. M. B. Productions
2531 Sawtelle Blvd., Ste. 58
Los Angeles, CA 90064 USA
T 310/472-7603
F 310/476-3603

Paul, Gregory
3109 N. Calvert St., Side Apt.
Baltimore, MD 21218 USA

Penny, Richard
1212 Lujan St.
Santa Fe, NM 87505 USA
T 505/471-0705
talktous@dinosaur-man.com
www.dinosaurman.com/

Penkalski, Paul
The Geology Museum
1215 W. Dayton St.
Madison, WI 53706 USA
T 608/256-0741

Peters, David
12812 Wood Valley Crt.
St. Louis, MO 63131-2051 USA
T/F 314/821-8701

Postma, Bren C.
903 Crandall Ave.
Salt Lake City, UT 84106 USA
T 801/463-4666
Bren.postma@dsw.com

Pulara, Dino
399 Melville Ave.
Maple, Ontario
L6A 2N8 CANADA
Dpulero@better.net

Redman, Patrick D.
2980 Euclid Ave. Apt. 2
Boulder, CO 80303 USA
T 303/444-5732
zma535a@prodigy.com

Rey, Luis V.
8 Aldham House
79 Malpas Rd., London
SE4 1DP ENGLAND
T/F 011-44-181-6910318
luisrey@ndirect.co.uk
www.ndirect.co.uk/~luisrey

Richard, John J. and Carolyn E.
3575 Highway 11
Hazel Green, WI 53811 USA
T 608/748-4530

Robert, Frank
c/o Melissa Turk
The Artist Network

9 Babbling Brook Lane
Suffern, NY 10901 USA
T 914/368-6806

Rothman, Michael
62 East Ridge St.
Ridgefield, CT 06877 USA
T/F 203/438-4954
/02060.3434@compuserve.com

Sardinha, Richard
204 Van Buren St.
Warwick, RI 02888-2720 USA
T 401/781-5481
oasis42@earthlink.net
www.greenwater.com

Saville, Alethea
Palaeo Replicas
84 Tor-o-moor Rd.
Woodhall Spa
Lincolnshire LN10 6SB
ENGLAND

Schellenbach, Jennifer
Gaston Design
1943 K. Road
Fruita, CO 81521 USA
T 970/858-4785

Shea, Shannon
164 San Francisco St.
Anaheim, CA 92807-3917 USA
T 714/998-0409

Shiraishi, Mineo
11-34 Myouken-cho
Susaki-shi, Kouchi-ken
785-0042 JAPAN
mshiraishi@ma3.justnet.ne.jp
www3.justnet.ne.jp/~mshiraishi/jurassicGallale
y.htm

Shouten, Peter
152 Denison St.

New Town, NST 2042
AUSTRALIA
T 011-2-50-1803

Sibbick, John
6 Bloomfield Ave.
Bath BA2 3AB ENGLAND
T/F 44-0-1225-422011

Sillin, William B.
34 S. Main St.
Sunderland, MA 01375 USA
T413/665-4238

Skrepnik, Michael
215 Hunter's Place
Okotoks, Alberta
T0C 1T4 CANADA
T 403/938-6274

Smith, Anthony F.
1414 Lynnview Dr.
Houston, TX 77055 USA
T 713/827-7203

Solvak, Jan
Ste. 1910
355 4th Ave. SW
Calgary, Alberta
T2P 0J1 CANADA

Sorton, Paul
2011 Mount Vernon St.
Philadelphia, PA 19130 USA
T 215/763-5129

Spears, Rick C.
1220 Katie Lane
Watkinsville, GA 30677 USA
T 706/310-0582
tyrannorix@hotmail.com

Srnka, Christopher
353 E. 13th Ave., Apt. 2A
Columbus, OH 43201 USA

T 614/291-7542
theclaw@sprintmail.com

Stieninger, Earl W. & Sue
549 W. 5th St.
Dubuque, IA 52001 USA
T 319/582-5071

Stout, William
1468 Loma Vista St.
Pasadena, CA 91104-4709 USA
T 626/798-6490

Strasser, Keith
15 Sandal Wood Dr.
Smithtown, NY 11787 USA
T 516/345-6825

Swerver, Leonid
PO Box 296
34 N. Rochdale Ave.
Roosevelt, NJ 08555 USA
T 609/448-2221
F 609/448-6433

Tanimoto, Masahiro
Higashi 3-249, Yurigaoka
Nabari, Mie 518-04
JAPAN
T 011-81-595-639715

Taylor, Kelley
1174 Englewood Ave.
St. Paul, MN 55104 USA
T 651/645-3483
F 651/645-2212
Annede@real-time.com

Tedesco, John A.
533 Union Hill Rd.
Englishtown, NJ 07726 USA
T 908/536-3443
jtedesco@pluto.skyweb.net

Thomas, David A.
3205 Alcazar NE
Albuquerque, NM 87110 USA
T 505/883-8061

Train, Hall
258 Adelaide St. East
Toronto, Ontario
M5A 1N1 CANADA
T 416/955-9007
F 416/955-9388

Trammell, Tony J.
3031 Cashion Place
Oklahoma City, OK 73112 USA

Trcic, Michael
245 Roca Roja
Sedona, AZ 86336 USA
T 520/284-0619
trcic@sedona.net

Trusler, Peter
9 White Horse Rd.
Blackburn, Victoria 3130
AUSTRALIA
T 011-2-877-7882

Tucciarone, Joseph
2403 W. Friday Circle
Cocoa, FL 32926 USA
members.aol.com/Dinoplanet/joe.html

UiBreaslin, Seaghan
PO Box 152
Laramie, WY 82070 USA
T 307/742-7630

Vaughan, Vicki
RT. 5, Box 276E
Rutherfordton, NC 28139 USA
T 704/286-8116

Venish, Shaun M.
385 Westwind Crt.

Berne, IN 46711 USA
T 219/589-3045

Walters, Robert F.
2634 Parrish St.
Philadelphia, PA 19130 USA
T 215/765-1123
www.dinoart.com/

Walthall, Jeffery
2031 Rockingham St.
McLean, VA 22101 USA
T 703/538-2738

Wenzel, Greg
5 High St.
Maynard, MA 01754 USA
T/F 508/897-3636
www.dinosaurstudio.com/artistsgw.html#wenz
elb

Wessels, Kenneth
724 N. Dodge St.
Iowa City, IA 52245 USA

Whitcraft, James
LRC c/o IPFW
2101 E. Coliseum Blvd.
Ft. Wayne, IN 46805 USA
219/482-6139
whitcraj@IPFW.edu

White, Steve
Clockwork Studios
38S Southwell Rd.
London SE5 9PG ENGLAND
T 0171-924-0921
F 0171-738-3743

Whitfield, Colin
PO Box 1381
East Orleans, MA 02543 USA
T 508/255-1310

Whitley-Bolton, Neil
Prinseneiland 79N
Amsterdam 1013 LM
NETHERLANDS
T 011-31-206274425

Wilson, Dennis J.
Pangea Designs
4505 E. Harvard Ave.
Denver, CO 80222 USA
T 888/772-6423

Wilson, Jared T.
352 W 46th St., Apt. 1C
New York, NY 10036 USA
T 212/265-0170

Winkley, Buckey
Box 22072
Anchorage, AK 99502-0792 USA
T 907/248-7571
F 907/243-8047

Wroblewald, Anton
1662 Coughlin St.
Laramie, WY 82070 USA
T 307/745-6045

Yeager, Shannon S.
RR5, Box 378
Bloomfield, IN 47424 USA
T 812/825-6989

Zeidler, Ulrich
Niehler Str. 3E
50670 Cologne GERMANY
T 011-221-739-1531

ASTEROIDS

Bamboole, Inc.
PMB 102
1702-H Meridian Ave.
San Jose, CA 95125 USA
T 408/723-2635

feedback@danddvd.com
www.CDandDVD.com
> *Sells the CD-ROM entitled Impact:*
> *Ground Zero.*

AUCTIONS

Discovery Channel Fossil Auction
www.discovery.com/exp/fossilzone/auction.ht
ml

eBay
www.ebay.com
> *According to Dave Goldman, "Just do a*
> *search for 'dinosaur' and you'll never*
> *leave the computer; you'll go broke, but*
> *at least you'll have a houseful of*
> *incredible dinosaur things!" Nuff said.*

Fossil Auction.com
Extinctions Fossil Company
PO Box 2222
Ada, OK 74821 USA
T 580/265-9550
custserv@extinctions.com

Gavel International
15-348 Zephyr Ave.
Ottawa, Ontario
K2B 6A1 CANADA
T 613/829-9183
F 613/829-4710
gavel@resudox.net
www.gavelnet.com

Natural History Auctions
PO Office Drawer J
Ithaca, NY 14851 USA
T 607/257-5349
F 607/266-7904
director@naturalhistory.auction.com
www.naturalhistoryauction.com

Philips Auctioneers
406 E. 79th St.

New York, NY 10021 USA
T 212/570-4830

BANKS

D. D. Sales
29 South Wagner Ave.
Stockton, CA 95215 USA
T 209/462-5345
F 209/464-2459
cookiejarsplus@ddsales.com
www.ddsales.com/banks.html
> *A very cute, musical ceramic*
> *Triceratops bank, #308.*

Frick and Frack
1470 Rt. 23 N
Wayne, NJ 07470 USA
T 973/696-8266
ffgift@aol.com
www.frickandfrack.com/Images/Dinobanks.gif
> *A big wooden dino with a see-through*
> *belly!*

Reed & Barton
144 W. Brittania St.
Taunton, MA 02780 USA
T 801/221-5805
information@reedbarton.com
www.reedandbarton.com
> *A silver plated Stegosaurus.*

BANKING

Dino-mite Savings Club
First National Bank
2421 Whitetail Dr.
Cedar Falls, IA 50613-4478 USA
T 319/266-2000
F 319/266-4478
bank@fnbcedarfalls.com
fnbcedarfalls.com/kidsclub.htm
> *Hosted by Dexter, the T-rex!*

BOOKS

Baldwin's Scientific Books
Boars Tyre Rd.
Silver End, Whittam
Essex 6M8 3QA ENGLAND
T 44-01376-583502
F 44-01376-585960
stuart@fossilbooks.co.uk
www.fossilbooks.co.uk
> *Stuart has one the biggest and finest collections anywhere, including many English-language translations.*

Bibliofind
www.bibliofind.com
> *An extensive online site with a huge collection of older titles, reasonably priced.*

DK Multimedia
95 Madison Ave.
New York, NY 10016 USA
T 212/213-4800
F 212/213-5202
www.dkonline.com
> *A fantastic source for some of the most numerous and lavishly produced dinosaur books around!*

GeoScience Books
319 Mineral Ave.
Libby, MT 59923 USA
T 406/293-2982
F 406/293-2983
mdc@geoscience.com
www.geosciencebooks.com
> *Mike Cohan stocks a huge collection of used and out of print earth science books.*

Paul Gritis Books
PO Box 4298
Bethlehem, PA 18018 USA
T 610/954-0466

> *Paul stocks many older titles on dinosaurs and prehistoric life.*

The Incredible Fossil Online Bookstore
fossils@levins.com
levins.com/dinosaurbooks.html
> *A lavish site featuring many of the latest releases. In conjunction with Amazon.com.*

Natural History Books
PO Box 1004
Cottonwood, AZ 86326 USA
T 520/634-5016
F 520/634-1217

Natural Science Bookclub
300 Cindel Dr.
Delran, NJ 08370-0001 USA
> *Home of the Fossil Hunter's Library.*

Paleobook
www.paleobook.com
> *Really extensive site with sections on fiction and non-fiction literature.*

Ed Rogers Rare and Out of Print Geoscience Books
PO Box 455
Poncha Springs, CO 81242 USA
T 719/539-4113
F 719/539-4542
erogers@lynx.sni.net
www.sni.net/erogers
> *A huge listing of old paleontology books at reasonable prices.*

Dr, Frank Rudolph
Verlag und Versandbuchhandel
Bahnhof Str. 26.
D-24601 Wankendorf GERMANY
T/F -49-04326-2205
fossilbuch@t-online.de
www.geocities.com/CapeCanaveral/Hangar/75
18/dinosaur.htm

Big German-language site with several English text for sale.

Science Nook
2277 S. Tennyson St.
Denver, CO 80219 USA
info@sciencenook.com
www.sciencenook.com/books
Tim Herrod's fine site, in conjunction with Amazon.com.

Anthony F. Smith, Bookseller
1414 Lynnview Dr.
Houston, TX 77055 USA
T 713/827-7203
Rare books, prints, and fine art.

Troodon Productions
355 4th Ave., Ste. 1910
Calgary, Alberta T2P 0J1 CANADA
troodon@cadvision.com
www.troodonproductions.com
The source for a series of well-illustrated books for children.

BREAD MOLDS

Dino-Mo
PO Box 5218
Bradford, MA 01835 USA
T 978/469-0706
F 978/469-0706
rsitro@netway.com
www.dinomo.com
Use Dino-Mo stainless steel bake ware to fashion a free standing Tyrannosaur or Apatosaur bread sculpture!

CAKES

Edward R. Hamilton, Bookseller
Falls Village, CT 06031-5000 USA
www.hamiltonbook.com
Sells the 80-page book Dinosaur Cakes by Jacqui Hine for only $4.95.

Ginny Cakes
T 703/590-4943
cakeinforeq@fichten.com
www.fichten.com/ginnycakes/
This firm in Dale City, Virginia, offers a big dino birthday cake.

Schroeder's Bakery
212 Forest Ave.
Buffalo, NY 14213 USA
T 716/882-8424
bakery@schroedersbakery.com
www.schroedersbakery.com/frames/bdaycakes1.html
Sells an impressive Jurassic Park raptor cake, and wonderful dinosaur cake candles.

Sugarcraft
1143 S. Eric Blvd.
Hamilton, OH 45011 USA
F 800/289-5552
proicer@one.net
www.sugarcraft.com/

Wilton Industries
98 carrier Dr.
Etobicoke, Ontario
M9N 5R1 CANADA
T 416/679-0790
F 416/679-0798
info@wilton.com
www.wilton.com
The source for the 16 x 10" Partysaurus cake pan, #2105-1280.

John Wright
PO Box 266
Silver Springs, PA 17575 USA
T 800/444-9364
johnwright@jwright.com
Where to find dinosaur muffin pans.

CALENDERS

Dinotreker
2005 Palos Verde Ave. #171
Long Beach, CA 90815 USA
Dinotreker@aol.com
home.earthlink.net/~dinotreker/products/
*Michael Rusher hawks calenders based
upon his fine dinosaur dioramas.*

CANDY

Ala Carte Gifts
3425 Foot Hill Blvd.
La Crescenta, CA 91214 USA
marie@alacartegifts.com
www.alacartegifts.com/
*Where else can you find a giant 21-
pound chocolate dinosaur egg?!*

Cake Emporium
1051 Bryant Way #F
Bowling Green, KY 42103 USA
T 502/782-0552
Don@cakeemporium.com
www.cakeemporium.com
Dinosaur-shaped candy molds.

Candy Warehouse
375 S. Marengo Ave.
Pasadena, CA 91101 USA
T 626/359-5622
info@candyware.com
www.candywarehouse.com
*Where to buy Dinosaur Eggs, Dinosaur
Buddies, and a whole line of
Cretaceous confectionaries.*

Candyland
Ismail Industries
17, Banglore Town
Main Shara-e-Faisal
Karachi-75350 PAKISTAN
sales@Candyland1.com
www.candyland.org

Markets Dinosaur bubblegum!

Chewits
www.chewits.com
*A Finnish site hosted by the
"Chewitsaurus," along with games and
other activities for children. The
product looks tasty, too.*

Chocolate Gallery
5705 Calle Real
Goleta, CA 93117-2315 USA
T 800/426-4796
F 805/967-1895
tjohnsen@chocolategallery.com
chocolategallery.com/tcg.dinosaurs.html
*A small herd of chocolate dinosaurs
and dino-pops.*

Fifth Avenue Chocolatiere
510 Madison Ave.
New York, NY 10022 USA
Sitereview@mindspring.com
members.aol.com/fifthchoc/choc.htm
Yummy-looking chocolate dinosaur.

Gardners Candies
Tyrone Industrial Park, PO Box E
Tyrone, PA 16686 USA
T 800/800-24-CANDY
info@gardnercandies.com
www.gardnerscandies.com
More chocolate dino dessert!

Hanna Krause Candy
Rt. 17 South
Paramus, NJ 07662 USA
T 888/6-KRAUSE
F 201/291-5388
Hkrause@aol.com
www.hannakrausecandy.com/
*Chocolate Apatosaurus, Triceratops,
and Tyrannosaurus pops.*

Light Vision Confections
8 Faneuil Hall
Boston, MA 02109 USA
T 513/469-0330
F 513/489-8222
holo@lightvision.com
www.lightvision.com/
*Can you believe it? Holographic
dinosaur lollipops! Check this out!*

Lollipop Tree
c/o K-Merchandise
1691 Linden Blvd.
Vineland, NJ 08361 USA
sjtilden@aol.com
A source for dinosaur lollipop molds.

Magic Spatulas
PO Box 801
East Hampton, MA 01027 USA
T 413/529-9125
www.magic-spatulas.com
A half-dozen chocolate dino pops.

Marvin's Candy Kitchen
1997 NE 150th St.
North Miami, FL 33181 USA
T 305/949-5552
www.candykitchen.com/
*Three chocolate "Jurassic–saurs,"
307-309.*

Material Things
PO Box 18532
Tucson, AZ 85731-8532 USA
T 520/733-0009
mckcs10341@aol.com
material-things.com/candy.htm
Dinosaur lollipop molds.

Sarris Candies
511 Adams Ave.
Canonsburg, PA 15317 USA
T 800/255-7771
F 412/745-5643
order@sarriscandies.com
www.sarriscandies.com
Nice chocolate Apatosaurus.

Thornton's Chocolate Heaven
Thornton Park, Somercotes
North Alfreton, Derby
DE55 4XJ ENGLAND
T 44-870-160-1911
Thorncsrv@Prolgistics.co.uk
www.thorntons.co.uk
*Item #2347 is a chocolate
Tyrannosaurus!*

United Gummi Bears, Inc.
Hwy 34 East
Creston, IA 50250 USA
T/F 515/523-2093
Kens@mddc.com
www.mddc.com/gummi_b
Bags and bags of sticky little dinos.

CAPS

Camelot's Castle
2039 Regency Rd. #7
Lexington, KY 40503 USA
T 606/276-4266
F 606/276-3565
lisau@lex.infi.net
www.castleviewmall.com/clothing.html
*"Extreme Dinosaurs" cartoon
characters.*

Copy Caps
PO Box 284
Provinceton, MA 02657 USA
T 508/349-1300
F 815/361-1160
Zapmail@copycaps.com
www.copycaps.com/index1.html
*A large variety of 22 full-color dino
designs.*

Jewish Bazaar.com
24 Redding Ridge Road
North Potomac, MD 21878 USA
T 301/738-6486
F 301/738-6486
sales@ipol.com
www.ipol.com/BAZAAR/
Suede dinosaur kipahs? Such a thing!

CARDS

De Jankins
3151 Bethania Ridge Rd.
Pfafftown, NC 27040-9573 USA
T 336/922-1542
deanosaurs@aol.com
Dean Walker markets nine sets of colorful "Deanosaur" trading cards for only $6.50 a set. A tremendous value.

Cottage Cards
8-A Village Loop Rd.
Pomona, CA 91766 USA
Offers a series of Pterosaur cards.

Creation Sensation
2619 Donald Circle
Benton, AK 72015 USA
T 501/776-3147
hardwick@creationsensations.com
www.creationsensation.com/
A set of 18 3-D dinosaur cards with a Christian perspective.

Dinocardz Company
146 5th Ave.
San Francisco, CA 94118 USA
T 415/751-5805
F 415/751-3629
dinoz@earthlink.com
The ultimate dinosaur card set, both colorful and accurate. By many of the world's leading dino artists.

Mable's Card Shop
PO Box 331
Old Greenwich, CT 06870 USA
T 800/554-6175
Sells "The Age of Dinosaurs" card set.

Monstrosities
PO Box 1024
North Baldwin, NY 11510 USA
T 516/378-1338
monstrosities@mcimail.com
www.monstrosities.com
Here find ye Michael Barsons' Dinosaur Nation Trading Cards, which highlights those cheezy dinosaur movies we love so much.

CASTING

The Alchemy Works
PO Box 773
Cleburne, TX 76033 USA
T 817/517-5968
F 817/556-2541
a0001979@airmail.net
Mike Evans can meet a wide variety of your resin figure casting needs.

Dream Master Creations
1352 Mary Dr.
Edwardsville, IL 62065 USA
T 618/659-9478
DREAMMASTCRE@iw.edwpub.com
Russ Muller is one of the best custom casters around!

CD-ROM HOLDERS

Quick Gift.com
PO Box 4025
La Mesa, CA 91944 USA
T 619/253-7705
support@quickgift.com
www.quickgift.com/dino.htm
Offers "Tyranno Rack," a three foot-

tall wooden skeleton!

CERAMICS

Dinosaur Dirt Farm
3841 Gossburg Rd.
Beechgrove, TN 37018-3004 USA
T 931/394-3262
dirtfarm@hotcom.net
www.hotcom.net/ddf
A good source for abstract clay sculptures, platters, and book ends. Anybody for a Santa-saurus?

C & W Ceramicraft
9 Dalrymple Place
Barden Ridge, NSW 2234
AUSTRALIA
T 02-95439591
ceramics@rivernet.com.au
Colin and Wendy make several charming and functional dino designs, including a dinosaur soap holder and tooth-paste dispenser. Must haves!

The Jewish Bride..and More!
PO Box 26341
Tamarac, FL 33320 USA
F 954/724-9696
F 800/864-1390
Chana@jewishbride.com
www.jewishbride.com/products/creative-gifts/index2.html
Dinosaur Tzedakah boxes? Oy vey!

Magma Terra
656 Rue Martineau
Levis, Quebec
G6W 1K3 CANADA
A complete line of scale dinosaurs.

Maksim Krivelev
2445 W. Bancroft #4
Toledo, OH 43607 USA
T 419/531-0807
F 419/474-0603
maximdecor@hotmail.com
www.geocities.com/WallStreet/Floor/4515/dinos/
Some Russian wonderful designs; a Styracosaurus knife holder (!), an Ankylosaurus jewelry box, and a large Tarbosaurus, elaborately decorated.

Millie's Plastercraft
294 N. Fulton Ave.
Lindenhurst, NY 11757 USA
T 516/888-0608
F 516/888-8615

Rainfall
10141 Mason Dixon Circle
Orlando, FL 32821 USA
artsncrafts@rainfall.com
www.rainfall.com/Carole/dinosaur/htm
Carole Anthony sells a cute baby Stegosaurus.

Three Sisters Antiques and Collectibles
1157 State
Augusta, KS 67010 USA
T 316/775-6845
F 316/775-2782
info@3sis.com
www.3sis.com/index.html
Item BG-1 is a glass Tyrannosaurus.

CEREAL

Quaker Oatmeal
quaker-dinoeggs.com
Home of "Dinosaur Eggs"–just add water and find a Stegosaurus in your bowl!

CHESS

American River Games
PO Box 1810
Fair Oaks, CA 95628 USA

Maker of Dinosaur Chess

JaMar Galleries
T 877-823-0218
info@jamar.com
jamar.com/cat.html#fantasy
> *A wonderful, hand-decorated dino chess set, A169.*

Spirit Games
98 Station Street
Burton on Trent, Staffordshire
DE14 1BT ENGLAND
T/F 01283-511293
salnphil@spiritgames.u-net.com
www.spiritgames.co.uk/classic.html

ZDNet's Software Library
shareware.gamespot.com/board/0004kd.html
> *Download Fantasy Chess for Windows, $9.95*

CHILDREN

Aristoplay, Inc.
450 S. Wagner Rd.
Ann Arbor, MI 48103 USA
T 734/995-4353
F 734/995-4611
info@aristoplay.com
www.aristoplay.com
> *Dinosaurs & Things is a colorful game that teaches children to identify shapes and objects.*

Cape Fear Images
5621 Athens Lane
Wilmington, NC 28405 USA
T 888/755-0550
www.cfimages.com
> *Where to buy Dinosaur Land, a child's personalized name dinosaur book.*

Cascoly CD-ROMS
4528 36th NE

Seattle, WA 98105 USA
cascoly.com
> *Source of several educationally based dinosaur products including Jurassic Challenge: Trivia and Database.*

Computer Information Enterprises
2091 Business Center Dr., Ste. 100
Irvine, CA 92612 USA
T 949/263-0910
F 949/263-0337
dlt@compinfo.com
www.compinfo.com
> *They sell the Draw to Learn: Dinosaur Edition CD-Rom.*

Dinosaur Adventure Software
9801 Dupont Ave. S. #465
Bloomington, MN 55431 USA
DinosaurInfo@web-dock.com
www.dinosauradventure.com
> *A online source for you to download Dinosaur Memory Watch, Dinosaur Math, and the Dinosaur Coloring Book Creator.*

Discis Knowledge Research, Inc.
90 Sheppard Ave. E
7th Floor
Toronto, Ontario
M2N 3A1 CANADA
T 416/250-6537
F 416/250-6540
discis@goodmedia.com
www.goodmedia.com/discis
> *The Dinosaur CD-ROM will help answer dozens of questions by exploring five different species.*

DK Multimedia
95 Madison Ave.
New York, NY 10016 USA
T 212/213-4800
F 212/213-5202
www.dk.com

*An excellent CD-ROM for children,
Dinosaur Hunter.*

Dynotech Software
1105 Home Ave.
Waynesville, MO 65583-2231 USA
T 577/774-5001
F 573/774-3052
dynotech@msn.com
www.dynotech.com
*Buy or download the following, award-
winning software programs: Dino
Cards, Dino Math, Dino Numbers,
Dino Spell, and Dino Tiles.*

Harperkids Interactive
News America
10 E 53rd St.
New York, NY 10022 USA
T 212/207-7000
F 800/424-6234
*They sell the children's activity CD-
ROM Danny and the Dinosaur.*

Knowledge Adventure, Inc.
1311 Grand Central Ave.
Glendale, CA 91201 USA
T 818/246-4400
F 818/246-5640
george_niklas@adventure.com
www.adventure.com
*Makers of the exciting 3-D Dinosaur
Adventure for imparting the basics of
geology, biology, and paleontology.*

The Learning Company
6493 Kaiser Dr.
Fremont, CA 94555 USA
T 510/713-6081
F 510/713-6072
dgaldin@learingco.com
www.learningco.com
*Markets DinoPark Tycoon CD-ROM
for teaching management skills to
children.*

Legends and Lore
1501 Pine Heights Dr.
Rapid City, SD 57709-8046 USA
T 800/888-1495
*Suppliers of cute dinosaur "Tub
Buddies" to help keep the kiddies clean.*

Microsoft Corporation
One Microsoft Way
Redwood, WA 98052 USA
T 206/882-8080
F 206/931-7329
*Markets a Mrs. Frizzle CD-ROM, The
Magic School Bus Explores: The Age of
Dinosaurs.*

MultiMedia
2019 Eight Ave., 3rd Floor
Seattle, WA 98101 USA
T 206/622-5530
F 206/622-4380
pr@m-2k.com
Sells the Dandy Dinosaur CD-ROM.

Nordic Software
6911 Van Doren St.
Lincoln, NE 68506-0007 USA
T 402/488-5086
F 402/488-2914
info@nordicsoftware.com
www.nordicsoftware.com
*Makers of the skill-oriented CD-ROM
Dinosaur Kids.*

Panasonic Interactive Media
4701 Patrick Henry Dr., Ste. 101
Santa Clara, CA 95054 USA
T 408/653-1898
*Find the book-based Theo the Dinosaur
CD-ROM here.*

New Media School House
Market Plaza Bldg.
Box 390, Westchester Ave.
Pound Ridge, NY 10756 USA

The Talking First Mac Dinosaur Reader.

Pro One Software
PO Box 16317
Las Cruces, NM 88004 USA
T 505/523-6200
F 505/523-6600
> *A multimedia dinosaur coloring book in CD-ROM format.*

Roaring Mouse Entertainment
1800 Bridgegate St., Ste. 103
Westlake Village, CA 91361 USA
themouse@roaringmouse.com
roarmouse.com
> *Buy the Dinosaur Explorers CD-ROM!*

Softdisk
PO Box 30008
Shreveport, LA 71130-0008 USA
T 318/221-8718
F 318/221-8870
sdwletters@softdisk.com
www.downloadstore.com
> *Download "Picture-Me Dinosaurs" coloring program.*

Theron Wienga
PO Box 595
Muskegon, WI 49443 USA
T 847/854-0489
F 847/854-0489
twiereng@remc4.k12.mi.us
www.novagate.com/~wierenga
> *Here we find the coloring guide, Bert's Dinosaurs for Windows, 5.0.*

CLIPART

Aztech New Media Corp.
1 Scarsdale Road
Don Mills, Ontario
M3B 2R2 CANADA
T 416/449-4787

F 416/449-1058
www.aztech.com
> *The Jurassic Dinosaur CD-ROM sports 96 royalty-free dinosaur art images by photographer Al Copley.*

Computer Support Corporation
15926 Midway Rd.
Dallas, TX 75244 USA
T 972/661-8900
F 972/661-5429
www.arts-letters.com/dino/dinosaur.html
> *Download Jurassic Art, a 1,000 image clip art database, for only $29.95.*

Corel Corporation
1600 Carling Ave.
Ottawa, Ontario K92 8R7
CANADA
T 613/728-8200
F 613/761-9176
www.corel.ca:80/
> *The Dinomania CD has 1,000 images.*

Educational Images
PO Box 3456, Westside Station
Elmira, NY 14905-0456 USA
T 607/732-1090
F 607/732-1183
edimages@edimages.com
> *Item #CDR-1505 is a Clip-art CD featuring over 800 prehistoric images.*

M & M Software
PO Box 15769
Long Beach, CA 90815-0769 USA
T 800/642-6163
F 562/420-2955
mmsoft@aol.com
www.mm-soft.com/
> *Sells a dinosaur clipart CD.*

Microverse Computer Services
1, Paras, Near Dr, Baliga Nursing Home
S. U. Road, Goregaon (West)

Mumbai 400 062 INDIA
T 872/97-25
F 91-22-872-74-46
Karim@mwcdrom.com
mwcdrom.com
Sells Dragons and Dinosaurs CD-ROM.

CLOCKS AND WATCHES

Alpharetta Pocketwatches
7330 Dew Dr.
Cumming, GA 30040 USA
Alphadino@mindspring.com

Country Clocks and Gifts
7772 Princeton-Glendale #22
Cincinnati, OH 25246 USA
T 513/860-2295
F 513/860-2294
www.country-gifts.com/

D. C.'s Clock Shop
662 Main St.
Lafayette, IN 47901 USA
T/F 765/423-1908
A roaring voice alarm dino with glowing eyes!

Dible Industrial Co., Ltd.
Room 820, 8th Floor, No. 1
Hung to Road, Kwun Tong
Kowloon HONG KONG
T 852/2759-9366
F 852/2757-9393
info@dible.com.hk
www.dible.com.hk/product/393.htm
Three cute watches to choose from!

ExploraToy
16941 Keegan Ave.
Carson, CA 90746 USA
T 800/995-9290
scitoys@exploratoy.com
www.exploratoy.com
Three colorful designs.

Foreign Dimension
1901 Manley Commercial Bldg.
367-375 Queens Rd. Central
Hong Kong, CHINA
T 852/2542-0282
F 852-2541-6011
sales@dimension.com.hk
www.dimension.com.hk/dinosaur.htm
Offers hologram dino wrist watches.

Opane.com
40-36 Union St.
Flushing, NY 11354 USA
T 718/358-5539
opane@yahoo.com
www.opane.com/opane/dinglowcloc.html
Neat dino clock, CE-635.

Rick's Wood Products
56 Hunt Rd.
Oakham, MA 01068 USA
T 508/882-3313
rickswood@udwt.com
Very nice, blue Bronto clock.

CLOTHES AND FABRICS

Cygnet Education
1507 E. 53rd St. #301
Chicago, IL 60615 USA
T 773/288-2366
F 773/288-2477
information@cygneis.com
www.cygneis.com/dbf/sweaters.htm
Assorted clothes including a blue bronto sweater for children, #S-1.

Dinosaur Hill
306 E. 9th St.
New York, NY 10003 USA
T 212/473-5850
A large assortment of children's clothing.

Dragon Dreams
112 High meadow Dr.
Moncton, New Brunswick
E1G 2C4 CANADA
T 250/721-4034
F 250/721-4023
dragondr@nbnet.nc.ca
www.antibe.com/westview/DD07.html
    *Featuring a cross-stitched pillow
    design, "Tooth-a-saurus" for teething
    children, #DD07.*

Fun N' Folly
13223 Black Mountain Rd.
San Diego, CA 92129 USA
T 619/277-4622
her-llo@funfolly.com
funfolly.com/
    *A dino-child back-pack carrier for your
    prehistoric papoose, #JDIN2CH.*

Karen Land Cross Stitch Designs
9 The Fairway
Darlington County, Durham
DL1 1ES ENGLAND
T 01325-262980
Kland1@compuserve.com
ourworld.compuserve.com/homepages/kland1/
    *Featuring Dino-Bet, alphabetical
    embroidery with a dinosaur in each
    letter (!), and cross stitch designs of
    Allosaurus, Brachiosaurus, and
    Veliociraptor.*

Quilt Shop
Hatchery Business Center
301 Main St., PO Box 88
Wakefield, NE 68784 USA
T 402/287-2325
F 402/287-2045
quiltshop@thenetpages.com
www.thenetpages.com/quiltshop/catalog.htm
    A large, attractive baby quilt blanket.

Warp 10 Fibers
3003 Wakefield Dr.
Carpentersville, IL 60110 USA
F 847/836-2058
mail@warp10fibers.com
warp10fibers.com/
    Sixteen different embroidery patterns.

COINS

Hoffman Mint
PO Box 896
Carmel, CA 93921 USA
T 831/625-5333
F 831/649-3318
Sales@hoffmanmint.com
hoffmanmint.com/
    An impressive set of bronze coins.

Maddy's Treasure Chest
197 Woodland Pkwy., Ste. 104-227
San Marcos, CA 92069-3021 USA
T 760/738-9093
sales@maddys-treasure.com
www.maddys-treasure.com/
    *A good choice of foreign coins,
    reasonably priced.*

Mathematical.com
www.mathematical.com/coinsdinosaurs.html
    *The source for a series of 13 large coins
    issued by different governments.*

Red Rock Design Studio
Kingston, WA 98346-0129 USA
T 360/638-2987
F 360/638-2909
www1.tagonline.com/Ads/RedRock/slammerpage1/html
    *A series of copper and silver
    "slammers" adorned by skull designs*

Westminster Coin and Jewelry
3489 West 72nd Ave., Ste. 100
Westminster, CA 80030-0276 USA

T 303/428-9175
sales@4preciousmetals.com
westminsterpublishing.nu/specialty.htm
Four Jurassic Park design coins.

COLLECTIBLES

Joe DeMaroo
1145 Lebanon School Rd.
West Mifflin, PA 15122 USA
T 412/466-8018
mmmu39a@prodigy.net
Specializes in Marx dinosaurs.

Dinosaur Collectible's Club
71 Hoppers Road
London N21 3LP ENGLAND
An interesting newsletter by Mike Howgate; $20.00 in bills per year membership.

Fun House Toy Company
PO Box 444
Warrendale, PA 15086 USA
T 724/935-1392
www.funhouse.com
A good source for Marx dinosaur sets.

Dean Hannotte
151 First Ave. #200
New York, NY 10003 USA
T 212/674-5848
dhannotte@msn.com
geocities.com/~dhannotte/Dinos.htm
One of the biggest collections anywhere.

John Lanzendorf
T 312/751-1101
John is probably the greatest dinosaur fine arts collector in the universe, an authority on the subject and a friendly person to boot!

Jim Murphy
565 N. Kansas
Edwardsville, IL 62025 USA
T 618/692-1945

Kenneth Proffitt
1156 Riverside Dr.
Lanexa, VA 23089 USA
T 804/966-9325
Buys, sells, and trades old and new dinosaur toys, including plastic and pewter.

Stephan Pickering
4950 Capitola Rd.
Capitola, CA 95010 USA

Prehistoric Times
145 Bayline Circle
Folsom, CA 95630-8077 USA
members.aol.com/pretimes
The source for the book Dinosaur Collectibles (1999) by Mike Fredericks and Dana Cain, only $30.00, ppd. This sumptuously illustrated tome is a "must-have" for all serious collectors!

Dean Walker
3151 Bethania Ridge Rd.
Pfafftown, NC 27040-9573 USA
T 336/922-1542
Dean is a major collector of figurines and an all-purpose neat guy to do business with.

Gary R. Williams
436 Paliament, St. 1
Toronto, Ontario
M5A 3A2 CANADA
T 416/922-7539
Buys and sells all manner of paper materials on dinosaurs and prehistoric life, including museum displays and guide books. Another great contact!

COLORING BOOKS

Amazing Experiences Press
1908 Keswick Lane
Concord, CA 94518 USA
T 925/691-5204
order@booksptinted.com
www.booksprinted.com/kids.htm

Colorado Geological Survey
1313 Sherman St., Rm 315
Denver, CO 80203 USA
T 303/866-2611
F 303/866-2461
*Sells a small assortment of dinosaur
coloring books.*

Creation Science Fellowship, Inc.
PO Box 99303
Pittsburgh, PA 15233-4303 USA
T 412/341-4908
csf@trfn.clpgh.org
trfn.clpgh.org/csf/csfbooks.html

P. S. I. Associates
13322 SW 128th St.
Miami, FL 33186 USA

Resources For Reading
PO Box 5783
Redwood City, CA 94063 USA
T 650/299-1067
F 650/747-0141
info@abcstuff.com
www.abcstuff.com/assets/items/bk039.html

COMICS

Comic Connection
16519 Wilderness Rd.
Poway, CA 92064 USA
T 858/592-6526
F 858/592-6586
orders@comic-connection.com
www.comic-connection.com

*Your best source for Cavewoman
Comics and action figures. Eat your
heart out, too!*

Steve R. Bissette
PO Box 442
Wilmington, VT 05363 USA
www.insv.com/tyrant
*Where you can subscribe to Tyrant, one
of the best dinosaur comics ever!*

Dark Horse Comics
10956 SE Main St.
Milwaukie, OR 97222 USA
A source for Delgardo lithographs.

Devil Dinosaur
www.fantasy.com/devildinosaur/1/
*A site dedicated to the late, great Jack
Kirby and his nine-episode series.*

Family Comics & Cards
505 Park Ave. N #207
Winter Park, FL 32789 USA
orders@comics2read.com
*Features six volumes of the Japanese
comic Gen by Masashi Tanaka.*

James Van Hise
57754 Onaga Trail
Yucca Valley, CA 92284 USA
T 760/365-5836
*Jim draws the serial Tyrannosaurus
Tex, with several volumes available.*

Youth Academy Books, Ltd.
11 All State Pkwy, Ste. 410
Markham, Ontario
L3R 9T8 CANADA
info@tyrannosaurus-rex.com
www.tyrannosaurus-rex.com/tales.htm
*Sells four volumes of W. Howard
Stuart's exciting T-rex! comic.*

COOKIES

Artistic Sweets
7636 Edinder Ave.
Huntington Beach, CA 92647 USA
T 714/841-0151
F 714/841-0352
artswts@gte.net
www.artisticsweets.com/artswt_art/dinobday_b
ig.jpg
> *A big basket of colorful dino cookies for your birthday!*

Buylink.com
info@buylink.com
www.buylink.com/
> *The online source for Dino Cookie Mix.*

Compliments
PO Box 170
Varna, IL 61375 USA
T 309/463-2033
deborah@gourmetreats.com
www.gourmetreats.com/
> *Decorated metal tins with Tyrannosaurus or Triceratops on the outside and different flavors on the inside.*

Concept 2 Bakers
7350 Commerce Lane
Minneapolis, MN 55432 USA
T 612/586-6200
custserv@c2b.com
c2b.com/cookies.htm
> *Custom dino-shaped cookies baked with any flavored dough of your choice!*

Cookie Garden
1508 Miner St.
Des Plaines, IL 60016 USA
T 847/582-9191
F 800/550-2032
webmaster@cookiegarden.com
www.cookiegarden.com/dinosaur_tin.html

> *Dispenses a colorful metal tin hosting half a dozen cookies and 22 plastic dinosaurs.*

Happycooker.com
243 Sixth St.
Holliston, CA 95023 USA
T 831/637-6444
F 831/637-5274
dmcnett@happycookers.com
www.happycookers.com/
> *Cookie cutter 1-12917 is a Triceratops.*

Kitchen Collectibles
8901 J St., Ste. 2
Omaha, NE 68127-1416 USA
T 888/593-2436
info@kitchengifts.com
www.kitchengifts.com/animals.html
> *Copper cookie stamps shaped like a Tyrannosaurus, Triceratops, and Apatosaurus.*

COSTUMES

Creative Costumes
PO Box 266
Weathervane Mall
Blue Star Hwy
Douglas, MI 49423 USA
T 616/857-1614
F 616/857-8453
fun@creativecostumes.com
www.creativecostumes.com/
> *Features a green satin dino outfit for toddlers.*

Fun N' Folly
13223 Black Mountain Rd.
San Diego, CA 92129 USA
T 888/267-9271
hello@funfolly.com
www.funfolly.com
> *A large, velvet Tyrannosaur costume.*

Funtastic Events
1650 Smith St.
N. Providence, RI 02911 USA
T 401/353-4700
F 401/353-2990
funtastic.com
Offers a 10 foot inflatable dino costume for rent.

Gamemaster Sports
PO Box 19130
San Diego, CA 92159 USA
T 619/444-8133
F 619/444-9585
sales@gamemaster.com
www.gamemaster.com
Rents out colorful Tyrannosaurus and Triceratops costumes.

A Harlequin Costume
9589 Foothill Blvd.
Rancho Cumamonga, CA 91730 USA
T 909/948-2950
info@costumemagic.com
costumemagic.com
Rent out a large Tyrannosaurus mask; why wait until morning to look like Hell?

Inflatable Design Group
9545 Pathway St., Ste. C
Santee, CA 92071 USA
T 619/596-6100
F 619/596-8399
idguy@aol.com
inflatabledesigngroup.com/costuminf/dino.htm
Nice, rather rotund inflatable T-rex costume.

Mardi Gras
269 Aldborough Road South
Ilford, Essex IG3 8JB ENGLAND
T 0181-503-8080
F 0181-220-0777
www.scoot.co.uk/mardi_gras/costume.htm

Offers a generic costume for rent.

Marylen Costumes
5 Corning Crt.
Medford, OR 97584 USA
T 800/628-6417
F 541/734-0025
arf@marylen.com
www.marylen.com
Offers a big selection of somewhat "Barneyesque" designs and a reasonably serious T. rex.

Star Design Costumes, Inc.
2708 W. Sylvania Ave.
Toledo, OH 43613 USA
T 419/473-2584
F 419/473-9650
mike@starcostumes.com
www.starcostumes.com/
Rent three different green velvet dinos, including Rex.

Triumph Enterprises Online
PO Box 1011
Prospect, KY 40059-1011 USA
T 5032/228-7850
F 502/228-9248
info@triumph-ent.com
www.triumph-ent.com/
Comical brown and green design with large open mouth.

CREATIONISM

The Ark Foundation
PO Box 33071
Dayton, OH 45433-0071 USA
www.arky.org/index.htm
The source for several Christian-oriented dino books and games.

Creation Education Center
405 Coloma St.
Folsom, CA 95630 USA

T/F 916/351-0250
Markdisbrow@Christian-internet.com
www.Christian-internet.com/

Creation Resource Foundation
PO Box 570
El Dorado, CA 95623 USA
T 916/626-8509
> *Author Dennis Peterson offers and extensive lecture series on VHS tape.*

Creation Science Evangelism
28 Cummings Rd.
Pensacola, FL 32503 USA
T 850/479-3466
F 850/479-8562
dinos@drdino.com
www.drdino.com/
> *Offers an extensive series of books, videotapes, and fossil replicas.*

Creation Science Fellowship, Inc.
PO Box 99303
Pittsburgh, PA 15233-4303 USA
csf@trfn.clpgh.org
trfn.clpgh.org/csfl

Creation Science Resources
5 Great Castle Court
Greensboro, NC 27455 USA
T 336/288-7935
liebech1@ix.net.com.com
www.sixdaycreation.com/

Creation Sensation
2619 Donald Circle
Benton, AR 72015 USA
T 501/776-3147
hardwick@creationsensation.com
www.creationsensation.com
> *Sells the CD-ROM Dinosaurs and the Creation Story.*

Creation Store
PO Box 74

Lebanon, TN 37088 USA
T 888/55GENESIS
www.projection.org/creation.htm
> *Offers an extensive selection of adult and children's books, with fossils.*

Creation Truth Foundation
PO Box 1435
Noble, OK 73068 USA
T 405/872-9856
F 405/872-7500
ctf@creationtruth.com
creationtruth.com/

Institute for Creation Research
PO Box 2667
El Cajon, CA 92021 USA
T 619/448-0900
F 619/448-3469

CROPOLITES

Dino Dung Enterprises
1140 W. 1500 S.
Vernal, UT 84078 USA
T 435/781-0270
F 435/789-1542
arnswood@easilink.com
www.dinodung.com
> *Get the poop on gifts for the people who think they have "everything..."*

CYBER PETS

Aardvark Pet
3647 India St.
San Diego, CA 92103 USA
T 800/298-2358
service@aardvarkpet.com
www.aardvarkpet.com
> *"Dinkie Dinos" by the bushel.*

DER, Inc.
212 N. W. 4th St.
Hallendale, FL 33009 USA

T 954-458-7505
F 954/458-8554
www.tonetmedia.com/babydino/
Buy Kute Pets "My Baby Dinosaur."

Expert Software
802 Douglas Rd.
North Tower, Ste. 600
Coral Gables, FL 33134-4506 USA
T 800/759-2562
F 305/443-0786
www.expertsoftware.com/rex.htm
This firm markets a wonderful CD-ROM called Rex! Your Interactive Dinosaur, which actually consists of five different animals, each with its own unique personality. At $12.95, highly recommended.

Golden Autumn, Inc.
PO Box 527686
Flushing, NY 11352-7686 USA
T 718/229-8300
F 718/229-2866
info@goldenautumn.com
www.goldenautumn.com/dinosaur.html
Item #1009t is a baby Tyrannosaur!

Maximum Value Merchandising Corporation
PO Box 30035
Saanich Center, Victoria
British Columbia V8X 5E1
CANADA
T 250/384-6854
F 250/384-6894
maxual@islandnet.com

Sehl Productions, Inc.
2580 Hadley Valley Rd.
Rochester, MN 55906 USA
T 507/289-2119
F 507/289-7613
sales@sehl.com
www.sehl.com/zoeydin.html

PPD-001 is "Zoey the Dinosaur."

DECALS

Dino-Friends
301 Breesport
San Antonio, TX 78216 USA
T 210/402-3666
scent@connecti.com
www.scentchips.com/dftyrannosaurus.html
Offers several simple designs at $1.00 each.

DIGS AND TOURS

Bighorn Basin Foundation
Wyoming Dinosaur Center
PO Box 71
Thermopolis, WY 82443 USA
T 307/864-2259
bones@wyodino.org
www.wyodino.org

Cincinnati Museum Center
Dr. Glenn Storrs
1302 Western Ave.
Cincinnati, OH 45203 USA
T 513/345-8507
Storrsw@email.uc.edu

Digs By Mail
Fossil Image, Inc.
PO Box 398
Pleasant View, TN 37146 USA
T 615/746-4182
digsbymail@aol.com
members.aol.com/digsbymail/

Dinamation's Dinosaur Discovery Expeditions
550 Jurassic Crt.
Fruita, CO 81521 USA
T 970/858-7282
F 970/858-3532
dis@gj.net

www.digdino.org

Dino Dig
Fort Worth Museum of Natural History
1501 Montgomery St.
Ft. Worth, TX 76107 USA
T 817/732-1631, Ex. 405

Dinosaur Diggers of America
Box 479
Baker, MT 59313 USA
T 406/778-3267
henson@midrivers.com
www.dinodiggers.com/

Dinosaur Dreaming
Department of Earth Sciences
Monash University
Melbourne, Victoria 3168
AUSTRALIA
T 03-9905-4879
F 03-9905-4903

Dinosaur Expedition
Museum of Western Colorado
248 South 4th St.
Grand Junction, CO 81502 USA
T 970/242-0971
F 970/242-3960
museum@mwc.mus.co.us
www.dinodigs.org/dig-it/

Dinosaur Productions
9520 Owensworth Ave., Unit 5
Chatsworth, CA 91311 USA
T 877/346-6366
Dinodon@aol.com
www.dinodon.com

Dinosaur Research Expeditions
Montana State University, Northern
Hagener Science Center
PO Box 7751
Havre, MT 59501 USA
T 800/662-6132, Ex. 3716

clousev@yahoo.com
labrat3.nmclites.edu/dinosaurs/digs.html-ssi

Earthwatch Institute
680 Mt. Auburn St, Box 9104
Watertown, MA 02471-9104 USA
T 617/926-8532
F 617/926-8532
info@earthwatch.org

FACT
PO Box 570
El Dorado, CA 95623 USA

Geo Tours Africa
Box 521
Newlands 0049 SOUTH AFRICA
www.geotoursafrica.com/english/home.htm

Grand River Museum
211 1st Ave. West
Lemmon, SD 57638 USA
T 605/374-3911
www.grandrivermuseum.org

Judith River Dinosaur Institute
Box Y
Malta, MT 59538 USA
T 406/654-2323

Jurassic Digs
Rene Quammen
PO Box 94
Otto, WY 82434 USA
T 307/762-3290
dinoguy@hotmail.com
www.angelfire.com/wy/jurassicdigs/

Jurupa Mountains Cultural Center
7621 Granite Hill Dr.
Riverside, CA 92509 USA
T 909/685-5818

Mesalands Dinosaur Museum
Mesa Technical College

911 South 10th St.
Tucumcari, NM 88401 USA
T 505/461-4413

Museum of Geology
South Dakota School of Mines and Technology
501 E. St. Joseph St.
Rapid City, SD 57701 USA
T 800/544-8162, Ex. 2467

Nomadic Expeditions
1095 Cranbury-South River Rd., Ste 20A
Jamesburg, NJ 08831 USA
T 609/860-9008
F 609/860-9608
nomadic@idt.net
www.Nomadicexp.com
        *Specializing in Gobi Desert trips and
        Mongolian digs!*

Old Trail Museum
823 N. Maine Ave.
Choteau, MT 59422 USA
T 406/466-5332

Paleo Impressions
PO Box 321
New Meadows, ID 83654 USA
T/F 208/347-2507

Paleontology Field Program
Museum of the Rockies
Montana State University
Bozeman, MT 59717-0272 USA
T 406/994-6618
museum.montana.edu/

Point Lookout State Park
Calvert Cliffs
Box 48
Scotland, MD 20687 USA
T 301/872-5688

Passport In Time Clearing House
CEHP, Inc.

PO Box 18364
Washington, DC 20036 USA
T 212/293-0922
F 202/293-1782

Research Expeditions Program
University of California, Davis
One Shields Ave.
Davis, CA 95616 USA
T 530/752-0692
F 530/752-0681
urep@ucdavis.edu
urep.ucdavis.edu

Royal Tyrrell Museum Explorers Digs
PO Box 7500
Drumheller, Alberta T0J 0Y0
CANADA
T 403/823-7707
F 403/823-7131

Sahara Sea Collection
PO Box 15083
Sarasota, FL 34277 USA
T 941/378-5000
F 941/378-5840

Smithsonian Associates
Research Expeditions
MRC 933
490 L'Enfant Plaza SW, Ste. 4210
Washington, DC 20078-5642 USA

Southwest Paleontological Society
Mesa Southwest Museum
53 N. MacDonald St.
Mesa, AZ 85201-7325 USA
T 602/982-2314

Tate Geological College
123 College Dr.
Casper, WY 82601 USA
T 307/268-2890
F 307/268-2514
ksundell@acad.cc.whecn.edu

www.cc.whecn.edu/tate/webpage.htm

Timescale Adventures
PO Box 356
Choteau, MT 59422 USA
T 406/466-5410
dtrexler@3rivers.net

U-Dig Fossils
350 E. 300 South
PO Box 113
Delta, UT 84624 USA
T 801/864-3638
F 801/864-4294

Western Interior Paleontological Society
Denver Museum of Natural History
PO Box 200011
Denver, CO 80220 USA
aam421@ecentral.com
www.wipsppc.com/

Western Paleo Safaris
PO Box 1042
Laramie, WY 82072 USA
T 888/875-2233
jpc@westernpaleo.com
www.westernpaleo.com/

Wyoming Dinosaur Safaris
1 Lynnes Way
East Bridgewater, WY 02333 USA
T 508/378-7081

Wyoming Dinamation International Society
301 Thelma Dr. #503
Casper, WY 82609 USA
T 877-WYO-DINO

DINNER SETS

Trade Union International
#1 Topline Plaza
Montclair, CA 91763 USA
T 909/628-7500

F 909/628-0382
info@tradeunion.com
www.tradeunion.com/dino_din_set.htm
> *A five piece "Extreme Dinosaurs: set and sports bottles.*

DINOTOPIA

Dinotopia
www.dinotopia.com
> *The official site for James Gurney's sprawling tale. The store function sells calenders, tape cassettes, maps, trading cards, and post cards based on the series.*

DOOR KNOBS

Porcelain Knob Shop
PO Box 3069
El Segundo, CA 90245 USA
T 310/640-9422
www.pknobs.com
> *Six different and very colorfully painted porcelain doorknobs for children.*

EDUCATIONAL

Andrews & McMeel
4520 Main St. #700
Kansas City, MO 64111 USA
T 816/932-6700
> *Makers of "Perfect Little Dinosaurs," which consist of a model skeleton and educational literature. Chose from Stegosaurus, Brachiosaurus, Leptoceratops, Velociraptor, Hypacrosaurus, Tyrannosaurus, Triceratops.*

Ira Cooper, Inc.
PO Box 2137
Woodinville, WA 98072 USA
T 206/720-6264
F 206/720-6317

Manufactures the instructional <u>Fossil</u>
<u>Excavation Kits</u>.

Countertop
15443 NE 95th St.
Redmond, WA 98052 USA
T 425/895-9811
  Sells the <u>World of Dinosaurs</u>, a boxed.
  5 CD-ROM set featuring such titles as
  <u>3D-Dinosaur Adventure</u>, <u>I can Be A</u>
  <u>Dinosaur Finder</u>, <u>Smithsonian</u>
  <u>Institution Dinosaur Museum</u>, <u>Primeval</u>
  <u>Giants</u>, and <u>Multimedia Dinosaurs</u>. A
  terrific value!

Dinocards
E5298 Margaret St.
Ironwood, MI 49938 USA
T 906/932-0617
www.nconnect.net/~mwendt/dinocards.html
  This is an award-winning set of cards
  using dinosaurs to illustrate and
  describe 180 different occupations. A
  wonderful tool for young children!

Dinosaurs live!
www.onlineclass.com/dinosaurs/home.htm
  Features an ongoing, interactive
  classroom for children K-6. Excellent
  for inquiring young minds.

Educational Images
PO Box 3456, Westside Station
Elmira, NY 84905-0456 USA
T 607/732-1090
F 607/-732-1183
edimages@edimages.com
www.educationalimages.com/
  Distributes an extensive series of slide
  packets on a number of paleontological
  subjects.

Educational Insights
16491 Keegan Ave.
Carson, CA 90746 USA

T 800/995-4436
F 310/886-8858
service@edin.com
www.edin.com
  Item EL8749-9P is the GeoSafari
  Electronic Learning CD-ROM about
  dinosaurs. They also market the <u>Animal</u>
  <u>Growth Charts</u>, <u>Dino Bingo</u>, <u>Dino</u>
  <u>Sound Station</u>, and <u>Dinosaurs &</u>
  <u>Fossils</u>.

Fossils as Arts
Box 980069
Houston, TX 77098 USA
T 281/250-2574
F 713/529-2447
fossils@fossils-as-art.com
www.fossils-as-art.com
  A source for the excellent "Digging into
  the Past" classroom fossils kits.

Learning Links
2300 Marcus Ave., Dept. A 99
New Hyde Park, NY 11042 USA
T 800/724-2616
F 516/437-5392
www.learninglinks.com
  Carries an extensive thematic study unit
  for eight or more primary students,
  consisting of books, board games,
  puzzles, and card games.

Learning Resources
380 N. Fairway Dr.
Vernon Hills, IL 60061 USA
T 847/573-8400
F 847/573-8425
info@learningresources.com
www.learningresources.com/Shop.lasso
  Markets several educationally-based
  dinosaur puzzles and games for very
  young children including <u>Problem</u>
  <u>Solving with Dinos</u> and <u>Dino Math</u>
  <u>Tracks</u>.

Light Bright Ideas
7809 Raintree Dr.
Ypsilanti, MI 48197 USA
T 734/480-4341
karen@lightbolt.com
www.lightbright.com
>   Featuring *Dig Those Dinosaurs!*, a
>   thematic study unit for young children.

Natural Curiosity
2595 W. 9545 South
S. Jordan, UT 84095-9409 USA
T 877/466-6418
F 801/466-6413
questions@naturalcuriosity.com
www.naturalcuriosity.com
>   A good source for Fossil Excavation
>   Kits, puppets heads, and other
>   educational toys.

Pan Terra
PO Box 556
Hill City, SD 57745 USA
T/F 605/574-4760
curator@pconline.com
www.wmnh.com
>   They sell a 38 x 28" correlated wall
>   chart of earth history, with special
>   reference to animal evolution.

Prehistoric Products
PO Box 1151
Happy Camp, CA 96039 USA
T 530/493-5178
dino@finishingfirst.com
www.finishingfirst.com/Dino
>   Makers of the "Museum in A Box," an
>   assortment of 19 fossil reproductions
>   for teachers and budding curators.

Science Matters
PO Box 383310
Waikoloa, HI 96738 USA
T 808/883-9404
ScienceMatters@JUNO.com

>   *Ann H. Scanlon has designed a high-*
>   *school level game called* Dinosaur Trek
>   *based upon 55 clue cards. Highly*
>   *recommended.*

Science Stuff
1104 Newport Ave.
Austin, TX 78753-4019 USA
T 512/837-6020
www.sciencestuff.com/
>   *Distributes small collections of fossils*
>   *and literature for classroom instruction.*

Science Text and Boreal Labratories
777 East Park Dr.
Tonawanda, NY 14150 USA
T 800/828-7777
F 800/828-3299
sk@sciencekit.com
www.sciencekit.com
>   *Lavish catalog contains fossil tracking*
>   *and footprint casting kits, posters, and*
>   *some plastic dinosaurs.*

Smith Studios
PO Box 8342
Bozeman, MT 59771 USA
T 406/587-4057
info@discoverykit.com
www.discoverykit.com
>   *Miniature excavation and casting kits*
>   *for the amateur paleontologist.*

Sound Source Interactive
26115 Mureau Rd.
Calabasas, CA 91302-3126 USA
T 800/877-4778
soundsource@ssiimail.com
www.soundsourceinteractive.com
>   *Sells five different* Land Before Time
>   *CD-ROMS for teaching math and*
>   *cognitive skills in young children.*

Skullduggery, Inc.
624 South B St.

Tustin, CA 92780 USA
T 800/336-7745
F 714/832-1215
skulduggery.com
> They manufacture <u>Dinoworks</u> kits to
> cast and paint miniature skeletons of
> Tyrannosaurus, Triceratops, and
> Velociraptor.

Steck-Vaughn
PO Box 690789
Orlando, FL 32819-0789 USA
T 800/531-5015
F 800/699-9459
www.steck-vaughn.com
> Sells the <u>Message in a Fossil:</u>
> <u>Uncovering the Past</u> (# 0-8172-8075-8)
> a CD-Rom for young children, K-8.

Twin Sister Productions
1340 Home Ave., Ste. D
Akron, OH 44310 USA
T 800/248-4946
F 800/480-8946
twinsisters@twinsisters.com
www.twinsisters.com
> They market the book and cassette set
> <u>I'd Like to Be A Paleontologist</u> for
> young children.

FILMS

Milestone Films and Video
275 W 96th St. #286
New York, NY 10025 USA
T 800/603-1104
> Distributes several black and white
> dinosaur classics.

Movies Unlimited
3015 Darnell Rd.
Philadelphia, PA 19154 USA
T 800/668-4344
F 215/637-2350
search@moviesunlimited.com
www.moviesunlimited.com
> A great source for dinosaur.movies
> currently available on video; search the
> word 'dinosaur' and hand onto your
> seat!

Creepy Classics Video
PO Box 213
Ligonier, PA 15658 USA
T 724/238-6436
www.abulsme.com/creepy
> Another good tool for finding hard-to-
> find dino flicks. Many old titles
> available.

FINE ARTS

Dino Art
11 Riggs Rd.
Gloucester, MA 01930 USA
T 978/283-7186
dinoart@jimedia.com
www.jimedia.com/dinoart/

Dinosaur Gallery
1327 Camino Del Mar
Del Mar, CA 92014 USA
T 619/794-4855
F 858/505-0260
aeba@jps.net

Fine Arts Publishing
130 N. Marengo Ave.
Pasadena, CA 91101-1759 USA
T 626/449-3840
F 626/577-7578
blueone@earthlink.net
www.fineartpublishing.com
> A source for William Stout artwork.

A Former World
48-958 Greasewood Lane
Palm Desert, CA 92260 USA
T 619/346-9302

Mother Nature's Trading Co.
336 Hwy 179, Tlaquepaque, B218
Sedona, AZ 86339 USA
T 520/282-5932

Scheele Fine Arts
PO Box 18869
Cleveland Heights, OH 44118 USA
T 216/421-0600

FONTS

P22 Type Foundry
PO Box 770
Buffalo, NY 14213 USA
T 716/885-4482
F 716/885-4482
P22@P22.com
www.p22.com/products/dinosaur.html
> *Dinosaur is a CD-ROM that imparts really cool dino drawings and fonts onto your computer.*

FOSSIL PREPARATION

Karen Alf
1355 Niagara St.
Denver, CO 80220 USA
T 303/322-2536
karenalf@aol.com

American Association of Paleontological Suppliers
400 Western Ave. N
St. Paul, MN 55103 USA
T 651/227-7000
www.aaps.net
> *A very large and reputable concern.*

Archmat
PO Box 1418
Merrimack, NH 03054-1418 USA
T 603/429-1300
F 603/429-1310
Archmat@aol.com

members.aol.com/ARCHMAT/catalog/archmat.index.html

Marc Behrendt
421 S. Columbus St.
Somerset, OH 43783-9503 USA
T 614/743-2818
Fossilprep@aol.com
members.aol.com/fossilprep

J-P Cavigelli
4318 Gray's Gable Rd.
Laramie, WY 82072 USA
T 307/742-4651
jpc@westernpaleo.com

Custom Paleo
PO Box 348
Hill City, SD 57745 USA
T 605/574-4188
global-expos.com/custompaleo/default.htm

The Fossil Hunter
mperona@iwaynet.net
www.iwaynet.com/%7emperona/
> *An excellent online site for fossil books, safety tips, rules and regulations.*

Global Expos
174 Broad St., PO Box 305
Glen Falls, NY 12801 USA
T 510/745-4139
F 510/793-4467
george@global-expose.com
www.global-expos.com/paleobond.htm/
> *A large selection of precision hand tools.*

Carlo Godel
2873 Unaweep Ave.
Grand Junction, CO 81503-2160 USA
regiaero@gj.net
www.gj.net/~regiaero/dino diggies.html
> *Hand-made digging tools for the discriminating paleontologist.*

MissingLink Fossil Enterprises
833 Poplar Way
Qualicum Beach, British Columbia
V9K 1X8 CANADA
T 250/252-3979
F 250/752-8130
fossil@fossilhut.com
www.fossilhut.com

St. Petersburg Paleontological Laboratory
Arkadiy Evdokimov
Podvoyskogo 24149
193231 St Petersburg RUSSIA
fossils@mail.nevalinl.ru
www.paleoart.com/russian_fossils/

Uncommon Conglomerates
400 Western Ave. N
St. Paul, MN 55103-2257 USA
T 651/227-7000 ·
F 651/227-6526
uncommonconglomerates@bitstream.net
www.global-expos.com/paleo-bond.html
        The makers of Paleobond glue, the
        paleontologist's best friend!

FOSSIL REPLICAS

Anatomics
PO Box 4012
Eight Mile Plains
Queensland 4113 AUSTRALIA
T 61-7-3364-0776
F 61-7-3364-0786
anatomics@qmi.asn.au
www.qmi.asn.au/anatomics

Antiquarian Fossils
3217 Patten Way
Bakersfield, CA 93308 USA
T 800/249-5512
feedback@fossils.com
www.fossils.com

Ants
PO Box 9208
Albuquerque, NM 87119 USA
T 800/642-9267
F 505/842-9195
www.ants-inc.com

Black Hills Institute of Geological Research
217 Main St.
Hill City, SD 57745 USA
T 605/574-4289
F 605/574-2518
marionz@bhigr.com
www.bhigr.com

Bone Clones
21416 Chase St. #1
Canoga Park, CA 91304 USA
T 818/709-7991
F 818/709-7993
kronen@boneclones.com
www.boneclones.com

Bone Room
1569 Solano
Berkeley, CA 94707 USA
T 510/526-5252
evolve@boneroom.com
www.boneroom.com

Cameron Campbell
8707 Eagle Mtn. Circle
Ft. Worth, TX 76135 USA
T 817/237-2039
F 734/758-7031
ccampbell@spindle.net
www.spindle.net/cteel/Paw_skull.htm

Creations E. T.
261-E. Kennedy Blvd.
Beauceville, Beauce
Quebec G0S 1A0 CANADA
T/F 418/774-3188 (French)
T 514/875-1910 (English)
Creation@creationset.com

www.creationset.com

Cretaceous Creations
265 Dubois St.
Breckinridge, Quebec
J0X 2G0 CANADA
marty0069@hotmail.com
www.microplus.ca/dino/

Dino Lab
PO Box 9415
Salt Lake City, UT 84109-0415 USA
T/F 801/272-2409

Dinosaur Foundry
559 Sperling Rd.
Nanaimo, British Columbia
V9R 5T6 CANADA
dino@nanaimo.ark.com
www.dinosaurfoundry.com/

Dino Productions
PO Box 3004
Englewood, CO 80155 USA
T 303/741-1581

Dinosaur Productions
9520 Owensworth Ave., Unit 5
Chatsworth, CA 91311 USA
T 877/346-6366
Dinodon@aol.com
www.dinodon.com/dinosaurs/stuff.html

Earth Lore
94 Durand Rd.
Winnipeg, Manitoba
R2J 3T2 CANADA
F 204/654-1018
elore@earthlore.mb.ca
www.earthlore.mb.ca

Fossilnet, Inc.
1517 Greentree Lane
Garland, TX 75042 USA
T 972/494-3443

docpaleo@home.com
www.fossilnet.com/Cast/cast.htm

Ron Gaston Designs
1943 K Road
Fruita, CO 81521 USA
T 970/858-4785
gastondesign@compuserve.com

Geological Enterprises, Inc.
PO Box 996
Ardmore, OK 73402 USA
T 580/223-8537
F 580/223-6965
geoent@ardmore.com

GEOU
Department of Earth Sciences
The Open University, Walton Hall
Milton Keynes MK7 6AA
ENGLAND
geou@open.ac.uk
geou.open.ac.uk/Fossils/fossilmain.html

Gondwana Studios
Queen Victoria Museum
Wellington St.
Launceston, Tasmania 7250
AUSTRALIA
T 03-63-951437
F 03-63-233790
gondwana@microtech.com.au
www.microtech.com.au/gondwana

Mesozoic Research Institute
PO Box 3157
Pueblo, CO 81005-3157 USA
M_R_Inst@nestacpe.net
www.aculink.net/~mri

Mt. Blanco Company
PO Box 559
Crosbyton, TX 79322 USA
T 806/675-2421
F 806/675-7777

entrophy9@hotmail.com
www.mtblanco.com

Natural Canvas
1419 Speers Ave.
San Mateo, CA 94403 USA
T 650/638-2512
F 650/345-3692
ncanvas@aol.com
members.aol.com/ncanvas

Northeastern Geologic
291 Sheppler St.
Rochester, NY 14612 USA
F 716/663-0005
gartland@frontiernet.net
www.frontiernet.net/~gartland/

John Payne Studios
140-C Roberts St.
Asherville, NC 28805 USA
sculpsteel@circle.net
www.circle.net/~sculpsteel/comm.html

Prehistoric Products Co.
Box 1151
205 Indian Creek Rd.
Happy Camp, CA 96039 USA
T 530/493-5178
dino@finishingfirst.com
www.finishingfirst.com/Dino/

Robert Reid Studios
1709 Tremont Ave.
Fort Worth, TX 76107 USA
T 817/723-2140
F 817/737-9297

Research Casting International
4902 Union Rd.
Beamsville, Ontario
L0R 1B4 CANADA
T 905/563-9000
F 905/563-8787
pmay@recast.com

www.rescast.com

Safari, Ltd.
1400 NW 159th St.
Miami, FL 33169 USA
T 305/621-1000
F 305/621-6894
www.safariltd.com

Rudolfo Salas Gismondi
Labrotorio de Paleontologia de Vertebrados
Casa Honorio Delagdo-UPCH
Av. Armendaris 445-Miraflores
Lima PERU
F 0051-1-4450164
paleovert@hotmail.com

Second Nature
PO Box 45
New Prague, NM 56071-0045 USA
T 800/815-3466
F 612/758-2323

Skullduggery
624 South B. St.
Tustin, CA 92780 USA
T 800/336-7745
F 714/832-1215
skullduggery.com

Skulls of Antiquity
PO Box 227
Calistoga, CA 94515 USA
T 707/942-5292

Skulls Unlimited
PO Box 6741
Moore, OK 73153 USA
T 800/659-skul
info@skullsunlimited.com
www.skullsunlimited.com

Smith Studios
122 East Park St.
Livingston, MT 59047 USA

T/F 406/222-8340
exhibithall@mcn.net
lwl.ycsi.net/museum/dino2

Taylor Studios
1320 Harmon Dr.
Rantoul, IL 61866 USA
T 217/893-4874
F 217/893-1998
taylor@shout.net
www.taylorstudios.com

Triebold Paleontology
1365 Kings Crown Rd.
Woodland Park, CO 80863 USA
T 719/686-1495
F 719/686-1499
triebold@pcisys.net
www.pcisys.net/~triebold/

Two Guys Minerals and Fossils
1 Lynne Way
E. Bridgewater, MA 02333 USA
T/F 508/370-7081
app@twoguysfossils.com
www.twoguysfossils.com

Valley Anatomical Reproductions
9520 Owensmouth Ave., Unit 5
Chatsworth, CA 91311 USA
T 818/700-8020
F 818/998-6218
vaprep@worldnet.att.net

Vintage Reproductions
18200 Yorba Linda Blvd., Ste. 109F
Yorba Linda, CA 92686 USA
F 714/572-8617

Western Paleo Labs
1038 N. Industrial Park Dr.
Orem, UT 84057 USA
T 801/226-5330
F 801/226-5382
western@itsnet.com

www.itsnet.com/~western/casts.html

Wiccart
420 St. Augustine Dr.
Oakville, Ontario
L6K 3E9 CANADA
www1.centtel.com/wiccart/index.htm

FOSSILS

Ackley's Rock and Stamps
3230 N. Stone Ave.
Colorado Springs, CO 80907 USA
T 719/633-1153

Ambercraft
40 Oak Ave.
Tuckahoe, NY 10707 USA
T 914/337-1252
F 914/337-1261
ambercraft@cyburban.com
www.ambercraft.com/

Ammonites
Gerhard-Hauptmann Str. 4
38372 Buddenstedt GERMANY
F 049-05352-6139
Fossilien.Heine@t-online.de
www.ammonites.de/

Ancient Earth
PO Box 441
Hurricane, UT 84737 USA
T/F 435/635-5060

Arts By God
3705 Biscayne
Miami, FL 33137 USA
T 800/940-4449
Artsbygod@netside.net

Big Jim's Fossils
PO Box 114
Wylie, TX 75096 USA
T 972/442-7303

bigjimsfossils@compuserve.com
www.bigjimsfossils.com

Bitner's
42 W. Hatcher
Phoenix, AZ 85121 USA
T 602/870-0075

Black Hills Institute of Geological Research
217 Main St.
Hill City, SD 57745 USA
T 605/574-4289
F 605/574-2518
marionz@bhigr.com
www.bhigr.com

The Bone Room
1569 Solano
Berkeley, CA 94707 USA
T 510/526-5252
evlove@boneroom.com
www.boneroom.com

Bonznstonz
Michael R. Fellenz
8 Niagara Mobile Park
Tonawanda, NY 14150 USA
Bonznstonz@aol.com
www.bonznstonz.com/dinosaur.html
An excellent source for teeth!

Bryson's Rock Shop
326 Washington
Ogden, UT 84404 USA
T 801/399-2838
F 801/399-4109
silver-bear@brysonrockshop.com
www.brysonsrockshop.com/

Caddo Trading
1010 Caddo Dr.
Murfreesboro, AR 71958 USA
T 870/285-3736
http://www.caddotc.com

Canada Fossils
536-38 A Ave. SE
Calgary, Alberta
T2G 1X4 CANADA
T 403/287-0299
F 403/243-3959
info@canadafossils.com
www.canadafossils.com

Casablanca Imports
PO Box 1494
Arlington, VA 22210 USA

Cierra Company
c/o Daniel Quint
502 Perry Way
Sparks, NV 89431 USA
T 775/673-5918
dquint@gowbway.com
192.215.22.73/

Collectibles Online
7613 Blueberry Lane
Powell, TN 37849 USA
T 423/938-6822
csvc@collectiblesnetwork.com

Collector's Corner
PO Box 1211
Dandendong, Victoria 3175
AUSTRALIA
T 61-3-9798-5845
F 61-3-9706-1425
webmaster@collectorscorner.com.au

Custom Paleo
PO Box 348
Hill City, SD 57745 USA
T 605/574-4188

Days Gone By
45-3 Ave. West
Drumheller, Alberta
T0J 0Y0 CANADA
T 403/823-4921

Dinosaur Bone.com
1841 Cotton Ave.
Levelland, TX 79336 USA
sales@dinosaur.bone.com
www.dinosaurbone.com/

Dinosaur Gallery
1327 Camino Del Mar
Del Mar, CA 92014 USA
T 619/794-4855

The Dinosaur Store
26664 Seagull Way, Ste. B-117
Malibu, CA 90265 USA
T 800/634-6672
F 310/589-6199

The Dinosaur Store
936 Hatch St.
Cincinnati, OH 45202 USA
T 513/929-0146
us21.worldpages.com/513-929-0146/index.html

Discount Agate House
3401 N. Dodge
Tucson, AZ 85716 USA
T 520/323-0781

East-West Development, Inc.
5380-B Naiman Pkwy.
Solon, OH 44139 USA
T 440/349-1433
F 440/349-1769
eastwet80@aol.com

Ebersole Lapidary Supply, Inc.
11417 West Hwy 54
Wichita, KS 67209 USA
T 316/722-4771

Extinctions
PO Box 7
Clarita, OK 74535 USA
T 405/478-3220

Extinctions Fossil Comapny
PO Box 1040
Walsenburg, CO 81089 USA
T 719/738-1870
www.extinctions.com/catalogs

Extinctions.Com
PO Box 2222
Ada, OK 74821 USA
T 580/265-9550
custserv@extinctions.com
www.dinostore.com

Famous Fossils
Mulberry Lane, 4 Heritage Cottages
Harper Lane, Radlett
WD7 9HL ENGLAND
T/F 44-1727-826071
ianj@ukonline.co.uk
web.uk.online.co.uk/members/ian.j/index.htm

Fossil Collector Forum Archive
www.gtlsys.com/FossilForum/Archive/FossilForum.html
> *An impressive discussion list of what's for sale and where to get it!*

The Fossil Company
PO Box 1339
El Cerrito, CA 94530-1339 USA
F 510/232-5614
sales@fossil-company.com
www.fossil-company.com

Fossil Finds
PO Box 35
Pilot Hill, CA 95664-0035 USA
T 916/622-9375
fossils@fossilfinds.com
www.fossilfinds.com

Fossil Record
1083 Vine St.
PO Box 152
Heraldsburg, CA 95448 USA

T 707/473-0316
carl@fossilrecord.com
www.fossilrecord.com

The Fossil Shop
61 Bridge St.
Drumheller, Alberta
T0J 0Y0 CANADA
T 403/823-6774
F 403/823-6774

Fossils as Art
Box 980069
Houston, TX 77098 USA
T 281/250-2574
F 713/529-2447
fossils@fossils-as-art.com
www.fossils-as-art.com

Fossilnet, Inc.
1517 Greentree Lane
Garland, TX 75042 USA
T 972/494-3443
docpaleo@hojme.com
www.fossilnet.com

Fossilsource
47 W. 1670 S
Orem, UT 84058-7496 USA
T/F 801/225-5546

Geological Enterprises, Inc.
PO Box 996
Ardmore, OK 73402 USA
T 405/223-8537
F 405/223-6965
geoent@ardmore.com

Glenn's Fossils
1706 Evergreen Dr.
Baltimore, MD 21222 USA
T 410/282-7519
zfossils@glenns-fossils.com
www.glenns-fossils.com

Global Treasures Fossil Page
1224 N. E. Walnut, Ste. 370
Roseburg, OR 97470 USA
global@orcote.com
www.orcote.com/~global/welcome.html

Great South Gems and Minerals
38 Bend Dr.
Ellenwood, CA 30294 USA
T 888/933-4367
F 770/474-4507
ray@greatsouth.net
www.greatsouth.net/FP971.html

Hal Bach's Rock Shop
137 Marne Rd.
Cheektowage, NY 14215 USA
T 800/568-6888

Hammer & Hammer Paleotek
260 Dutchman View Dr.
Jacksonville, OR 97530-9731 USA
T 541/899-1864
F 541/899-6815
paleotek@cdsnet.net
www.global-expos.com/paleotek

Paul Hanks
1042 E. Fort Union Ave. #405
Midvale, UT 84047 USA
T 801/944-0121
F 801/562-1144
phanks@lgcy.com

Hanman's Fossils and Minerals
PO Box 2606
Cedar City, UT 84721-2606 USA
T 435/867-0891
info@hanmasfossils.com
www.hanmansfossils.com

Henskens Fossils
Witte Hoeflann 69
5343 EG Oss NETHERLANDS
theo@henskensfossils.nl

www.henskensfossils.nl

George Heslep Fossils
PO Box 51212
Colorado Springs, CO 80949 USA
T 719/632-2983

Highland Rock and Fossil
509 Raritan Ave.
Highland, NJ 08904 USA
T 732/819-7900
F 732/545-5802
orius.com@cwix.com
www.orius.com/fossils/dinosaur.htm

Simon M. Hmani
PO Box 18997
Tucson, AZ 85731 USA
T 520/721-2992
F 520/721-4028

Holger Knebel
Am Steg 1
58089 Hagen GERMANY
F 01149-2331-303770

House of Onyx
Aaron Bldg.
120 N. Main St., Box 261
Greenville, KY 42345-0261 USA
T 502/338-2363
F 502/338-9605
onyx@muhlon.com
www.houseofonyx.com

Charles Isbon
PO Box 431701
Houston, TX 77243-1701 USA

J & S Fossils
17 Jeff Rd.
Largo, FL 34644 USA
T 813/595-2662
home1.gte.net/fossils/jaws.htm

Jeanne's Rock & Jewelry
5420 Bissonet
Bellaire, TX 77401 USA
T 713/664-2988

Jungle Intrigue
6520 Platt Ave.
West Hills, CA 91307 USA
T 818/346-5680
jungle@jungleintrigue.com
jungleintrigue.com/jungle/dino.html

Jurassic Creations
PO Box 12082
Mill Creek, WA 98082-0082 USA
F 630/839-3046
james@jurassiccreations.com
www.jurassiccreations.com/bone.html

Jurupa Mountains Cultural Center
7621 Granite Hill Dr.
Riverside, CA 92509 USA
T 909/685-5818
F 909/685-1240

K. B. V. Fossils and Minerals
PO Box 394
Northampton, PA 18067 USA
T 800/628-8089
Kbv1@enter.net
www.kbv-minerals.com/

R. A. Langheinrich Meteorites & Fossils
290 Brewer Rd.
Ilion, NY 13357 USA
T/F 732/764-0879
orders@nyrockman.com
www.nyrockman.com

Lifestones Fossil Co.
3639 14th Ave. S
Minneapolis, MN 55407-2711 USA
kevin@lifstonefossilco.com
www.lifestonefossilco.com

Lou-Ben Gems & Rocks
Lake Barcroft Plaza
6341 Columbia Pike
Bailey's Crossroads, VA 22041 USA
T 703/256-1084

McCarthy's Fossils
3585 Passfield Law
Mt. Pleasant, SC 29464 USA
T/F 803/881-0064

McCullough Fossils
1397 Corte de Primavera
Thousand Oaks, CA 91360 USA
T 805/523-1541
mccullough1@earthlink.net
home.earthlink.net/~mccullough1/
    A good source for Mesosaurs.

Ken Mannion
59, Barrow Rd.
Barton upon Humber
N. Lincolnshire DN18 6AE
ENGLAND
T 01652-634827
F 01652-660700
fossils@btinternet.com
www.kenmannion.co.uk/

Maxilla & Mandible
451 Columbus Ave.
New York, NY 10024 USA
T 212/724-6173
F 212/721-1073

Mineral Enterprises
PO Box 313
Weimar, CA 95736 USA
T 530/637-4325
F 530/389-8774
vision@foothill.net

Missing Link Fossils
833 Poplar Way
Qualicum Beach, British Columbia

V9K 1X8 CANADA
T 604/752-3979

Montana Fossils
820 4th St., Apt. 107
Havre, MT 59501 USA
T 406/265-4760
boucher@hi-line.net
www.hi-
line.net/~boucher/montanaf/montanaf.htm

Moroccan Imports
PO Box 2661
Carlsbad, CA 92018 USA
T 460/438-3467

Moussa Direct, Ltd.
Unit 16
Cave Ind. Estate
Fen Road, Cambridge
CB4 1UN ENGLAND
T 44-223-424870
F 44-223-242869

Natural Canvas
1419 Speers Ave.
San Mateo, CA 94403 USA
T 650/638-2512
F 650/345-3692
ncanvas@aol.com
members.aol.com/ncanvas

Natural Expressions
13802 E. Williams Field Rd.
Gilbert, AZ 85296 USA
T 602/963-6552
F 602/963-4180

Natural History Supply House
12419 Coronet Dr.
Sun City West, AZ 85375 USA
T 520/283-6872

The Nature Source
423 Ridge Rd.

Queensbury, NY 12804 USA
T 518/761-6702
F 518/798-9107
mammoth357@aol.com
www.nature-source.com

Nature's Gifts
South Plains Mall
6002 Slick Rd. #68342
Lubbock, TX 79414 USA
T 806/791-1265

Nature's Treasures
1163 E. Ogden Ave.
Naperville, IL 60513 USA
T 708/983-5504

Newell Paleontology
Rt. 1, Box 103B
Newell, SD 57760 USA
T 605/456-0152
dinosaur_57760@yahoo.com

Older Than Dirt
Box 371
Moorpark, CA 93020 USA
sjbn@ix.netcom.com

Richard Owens
3174 ½ Bookcliff
Grand Junction, CO 81504 USA
T 970/434-8153

Paleo Park
ronbuckley@fuse.net
home.fuse.net/paleopark/
    Lots and Tyrannosaur teeth.

Paleo Place
60 E. Fox Meadow Rd.
Leominster, MA 01453 USA
T 978/537-3614
rand50@tiac.net
www.tiac.net/users/rand50/

Paleosearch, Inc.
PO Box 621
Hays, KS 67601 USA
T 785/625-2240
F 785/625-2235
rockers@paleosearch.com
www.paleosearch.com

Don and Sara Parsons
2808 Eden Lane
Rapid City, SD 57703 USA
T 605/348-0937
F 605/341-2568
www.enetis.net/~dparsons

Phoenix Fossils
6401 E. Camino De Los Ranchos
Scottsdale, AZ 85254 USA
T 602/991-5246
F 602/991-0679

Pike's Peak Rock Shop
451 Forest Edge Rd.
Woodand Park, CO 80863 USA
T 800/347-6257

Prehistoric Journeys
PO Box 3376, Dept. 4
Santa Barbara, CA 93130 USA
T 805/563-2404
F 805/682-2309

Prehistoric Treasures
1060 N. Oakmont Lane
Provo, UT 84604 USA
T 801/375-9251
provobell@burgoyne.com
www.riviera.fr/din1.htm

Jim Ray
3324 W. University Ave.
Box 321
Gainesville, FL 32607 USA
F 352/595-4721

Renaissance Fossils
217 E. Linda Dr.
Garland, TX 75041-1941 USA
rfossils@hotmail.com
www.renaissance-fossils.com/

Ron Roble Enterprises
639 J. Street
San Diego, CA 92101 USA
T 619/234-1428

Sahara Sea Collection
7080 Weber Rd.
Sarasota, FL 34277 USA
T 941/378-5000
F 941/378-5840

Schooler's Minerals and Fossils
PO Box 1032
Blue Springs, MO 64013 USA

Seven Seas Trading Company
60-B Terra Cotta Ave.
PMB 14
Crystal Lake, IL 60014 USA
T 815/459-5060
inquiry@7cs.com
www.7cs.com/fossils

Sin-Am Bridge
609 Daisy St.
Escondido, CA 92027 USA
T/F 760/737-3022
fossil@sin-am.com
www.sin-am.com

Skolta Enterprises
947 McIvere Rd.
Great Falls, MT 59404 USA

Somewhere in Time
1921 S. Hall St.
Allentown, PA 18103 USA
T 610/791-9198

Sphere's to You
PO Box 1270
Agoura Hills, CA 91376-1270 USA
T 818/991-5143
F 818/207-3543
spheres@iswest.com
www.spherestoyou.com

Mary Stephenson
Rt. 2, Box 34
Hamilton, TX 76531 USA
T 817/386-8363

Stone Company
PO Box 18814
Boulder, CO 80308 USA
T 303/581-0670
F 303/581-0490
stoneco@aol.com
www.stonecompany.com

Stone Jungle.com
1609 E. 1220 N.
Logan, UT 84341 USA
T 435/772-3971
webmaster@stonejungle.com
www.stonejungle.com

Stones & Bones
7334 Quail Run Rd.
Lizella, GA 31052 USA
T 800/720-9624
sales@stonesbones.com
www.stonesbones.com

Treasures of the Earth
PO Box 510
Hollsopple, PA 15935 USA
T 814/479-7661
F 814/479-4816
treasure@ctcnet.net
www.ctcnet.net/treasure

Trilobite Treasures
PO Box 232D

Thompson, CT 06277 USA

Twin Crystal Rock Shop
43 Broadway
Saranac Lake, NY 12983 USA
T 518/891-2170

Two Guys Minerals and Fossils
1 Lynne's Way
E. Bridgewater, MA 02333 USA
T/F 508/378-7081
app@twoguysfossils.com
www.twoguysfossils.com

Ulrich's Fossil Gallery
Fossil Station #508
Kemmerer, WY 85101 USA
T 507/877-6466
F 507/877-3289

Warfield Fossil Quarries
2072 Muddy String Rd.
Thayne, WY 83127 USA
T/F 307/803-2445
warfosq@cyberhighway.net

Western Paleo Laboratories
1038 N. Industrial Park Dr.
Orem, UT 84057 USA
T 801/226-5330
F 801/226-5382
western@itsnet.com
www.itsnet.com/~western/dinosaur.html

What on Earth Naturally
6250 Busch Blvd.
Columbus, OH 43229 USA
T 614/436-1458

Wonders of the World & Beyond
1460 Lincoln Blvd.
Santa Monica, CA 91401 USA
T 310/393-4700

X-Fossil
PO Box 431701
Houston, TX 77243-1701 USA
T 713/849-5951
F 713/937-1998
xfossil@wt.net
www.xfossil.com

FURNITURE

Craig Nutt
1305 Kingston Springs Rd.
Kingston Springs, TN 37082 USA
T 615/952-4308
cnutt@mindspring.com
www.mindspring.com/~cnutt
> *Craig sells a seven-foot coffee table with raptor legs!*

GAMES

Academic Software, Inc.
331 W. 2nd St.
Lexington, KY 40507 USA
T 606/233-2332
F 606/231-0725
asistaff@acsw.com
www.acsw.com
> *Manufacturer of Dino-GAMES software, including Dino-Maze, Dino-Find, Dino-Like, and Dino-Dot.*

Acclaim Studios
1 Acclaim Plaza
Glencove, NY 11542-2708 USA
> *The source for the ultra-realistic Turok: Dinosaur Hunter and Turok 2: Seeds of Evil CD-ROM games.*

Alive Software
PO Box 4004
Santa Clara, CA 95056 USA
T 408/982-0109
F 408/982-0780
webmaster@alivesoft.com

www.alivesoft.com
*Download Dinosaur Predators, a
matching game for young children.*

American Sports and Hobbies
2921 Fulton St.
Berkeley, CA 94705 USA
T 510/540-8788
www.ashon.line.com/jurassicjeopardy/
*Sells the colorful 32-card game
Jurassic Jeopardy.*

Aristo Pals
450 S. Wagner
Ann Arbor, MI 48103 USA
T 888/GR8-GAME
F 734/995-4611
info@aristoplay.com
*They market an cassino-type game
called Dinoslot for children, with rocks
for coins and dinosaur questions.*

BMG Interactive Entertainment
1540 Broadway
New York, NY 10036-4098 USA
*Makers of the Bermuda Syndrom CD-
ROM game.*

CapCom Entertainment
475 Oakmead Pkwy.
Sunnyvale, CA 94086 USA
F 408/774-3994
*Makers of the ultra-violent, ultra-
realistic Dino-Crisis CD-ROM game
for adults, and the Magical Dinosaur
Tour for young children.*

Cheapass Games
2530 E. Miller St.
Seattle, WA 98112 USA
T 206/324-6728
ernest@speakeasy.org
*As the title implies, Bitin' off Hedz is a
simple and inexpensive card game.*

Cybernetic Research Labs, Inc.
3625 E 42nd St.
Tucson, AZ 85713 USA
T 520/571-8065
*A source for the CD-ROM game Dino
Park.*

Dinotopia
PO Box 391
Red Hook, NY 12571-0391 USA
webmaster@dinotopia.com
www.dinotopia.com
*Markets the few remaining copies of the
Dinotopia CD-ROM game by Turner
Interactive.*

Dreamworks Interactive
640 N. Sepulveda Blvd.
West Hollywood, CA 90049 USA
*Home of the most lavish, most realistic
dinosaur CD-ROM games anywhere:
Lost World: Jurassic Park Trespasser,
Chaos Island: The Lost World; The Lost
World: Special Edition, and Warpath.*

Educational Insights
16941 Keegan Ave.
Carson, CA 90746 USA
T 310/884-2000
service@edin.com
www.edin.com
*Among other things, plastic dino sets,
Dino Checkers, and Dino Bingo for
young children.*

Electronic Arts
1450 Fashion Island Blvd.
San Mateo, CA 94404-2064 USA
T 415/571-7171
F 415/571-6375
sdyssegard@ea.com
www.ea.com
*Another source for Jurassic Park Lost
World: Special Edition and Trespasser:
Jurassic Park.*

Finnish Evolutionary Enterprises
Mellunmaenraito 2 E 50
00970 Helsinki FINLAND
*These gents sell an interesting product
called The Evolution Game for around
$33.00.*

Fractal Dimensions
17 Main St., Ste. 316
Cortland, NY 13045 USA
T 607/753-9246
http://shareware.gamespot.com/adventure/000o
7l.html
*Another unusual game to download,
Escape from Dinosaur Island.*

Games People Play
1100 Massachusetts Ave.
Cambridge, MA 02138 USA
T 617/492-0711
Sells "Dino dice" game.

Hasbro
1027 Newport Ave.
Pawtucket, RI 02861 USA
T 401/431-5075
www.hasbro.com
*Makers of Dig N' Dinos Monopoly
game.*

Hodges & Reed Services
PO Box 23504
Stanley, KS 66283 USA
T 887/888-1604
webmaster@hrweb.com
www.ierc.com/educinst/i0003029.htm
*Where to buy the colorful Dino Jump-a-
saurus, a variation of Chinese checkers.*

Interplay Productions, Inc.
16815 Von Karman Ave.
Irvine, CA 92606 USA
T 714/553-6655
F 714/553-1406
info@interplay.com

www.interplay.com/evolution/index.html
*These folks offer the exciting CD-ROM
Evolution: The Game of Intelligent Life,
which more politicians should play.*

Steve Jackson Games
Box 18957
Austin, TX 78780 USA
T 512/447-7886
F 512/447-1144
sigames@ic.com
www.sjgames.com/dinohunt
*The source for Dinohunt, another high
excitement quality game with excellent
graphics and factoids.*

Latz Chance Games
PO Box 251
Lutsen, MN 55612 USA
T 888/524-4263
F 218/663-8131
lcgayal@msn.com
www.latzchancegames.com/
*Manufacturers of Survival or
Extinction, one of the best dino card
games ever developed.*

The Learning Company
1 Athenaeum St.
Cambridge, MA 02142 USA
T 612/494-5700
F 617/494-5998
www.learningco.com
*They sell the CD-ROM game DinoPark
Tycoon for teaching management skills
to young children.*

Maritime Trading Company
5687 West St., Ste. 270
Halifax, Nova Scotia
B3K 1H6 CANADA
T 800/461-3361
F 902/492-8770
www.pangeeah.com
Makers of Super Continent Pan-Gee-

Ah: The Dinosaur Game. Neat stuff!

Professor Smarty Games, Inc.
PO Box 2043
Davidson, NC 28036 USA
T 800/763-6722
F 704/331-7598
Info@professorsmarty.com
professorsmarty.com/
> *DinoZoo is an exciting and colorful time travel adventure game!*

Rio Grande Games
PO Box 45715
Rio Rancho, NM 87174 USA
T 505/771-8813
F 505/771-8967
cafejay@aol.com
www.riograndegames.com.htm
> *Distributor of the games Fossil, designed by Herr Goldsieber, and T-rex a fast playing egg-capture card game, by Hanno and Wilfred Kuhn.,*

Safari, Ltd.
PO Box 527812
Miami, FL 33152-7812 USA
T 800/554-5414
F 305/624-9433
> *The source for children's card games, Dino Lotto, Dino Pick Up Pairs, Dino Quiz, and Dinosaur Rummy.*

Science Matters
PO Box 383310
Waikoloa, HI 96738 USA
> *They sell Dinosaur Tracks card game.*

Sierra Madre Games
3438 N. Appleseed Dr.
Tucson, AZ 85712 USA
Phileklund@aol.com
www.io.com/~wasson/smg/amf.html
> *Here you can obtain American Megafauna, which pits primitive*

mammals against dinosaurs in a game of survival.

Wizard Works
2155 Niagara Lane N., Ste. 150
Plymouth, MN 55447 USA
T 800/229-2714
F 612/249-7676
www.wizworks.com/carnivores.htm
> *Makers of the 3D, hyper-realistic Carnivore and Carnivore 2 CD-ROM games. You hunt the dinosaurs–or do they hunt you?*

GIFTS

A. Boyd.com
PO Box 4568
Jackson, MS 39296 USA
campbab@netdoor.com
www.aboyd.com/toys/dinostore.html
> *A good source for skeleton kits, models, and action figures.*

Bearz Creations
PO Box 3386
Batte, MI 59702-3386 USA
T 406/782-0764
bearz@griz.com
www.griz.com/dinosaurs.htm
> *Where to obtain sone surreal dinosaur figurines.*

Dakota Dinosaur Museum
200 Museum Dr.
Dickson, ND 58601 USA
T 701/225-DINO
dinomusuem@dickinson.ctcel.com
www.ctctel.com/dino/
> *A well-stocked giftshop with T-shirt, jewelry, and toys.*

Dinoland
Box 3
241 21 Eslov SWEDEN

T 0413-155-76
F 0413-156-33
Kundtjanst@dinoland.nu
Probably the northern-most source for dino toys in the world.

Dinosaur Depot
330 Royal Gorge Rd.
Canon City, CO 81212 USA
T 719/268-7150

Dinosaur Farm
1514 Mission St.
South Pasadena, CA 91030 USA
T 626/441-2767
F 626/441-8922
An old-fashioned toy store, chock full with the latest dinosaur toys and supplies. Recently voted Best Toy Store in the L.A. area!

Dinosaur Inn & Gifts
251 E. Main St.
Vernal, UT 84078 USA
T 435/789-2660

The Dinosaur Store
299 W. Cocoa Beach Cswy
Cocoa Beach, FL 32931 USA
T 407/783-7300
F 407/783-7440
info@dinosaur.com
www.dinosaurstore.com/start.html
A fabulously, well-stocked outlet!

The Dinosaur Store
1907 Sand Lake W.
Orlando, FL 32809 USA
T 407/851-7600
F 407/851-3500
Sister store to the above, a must see!

Dinosaur Store
26664 Seagull Way
Malibu, CA 90265 USA

T 310/589-5988
Dinosaur stuff in the heart of surfing country.

Dinosaur Nature Association
1291 E. Highway 40
Vernal, UT 84078-2830 USA
T 800/845-3466
dna@dinosaurnature.com
www.dinosaurnature.com
A fantastic source for videos, audiotapes, books, and posters.

Dinosaur World
Central Park Mall
622 NW Loop 410
San Antonio, TX 78216 USA
T 210/349-5566
george@dinosaurworld.com
www.dinosaurworld.com/main.html
Another fabulously equipped store.

Einstein's Emporium
Web-Shops Net
102 Old St.
Petersburg, VA 23803 USA
T 800/522-8281
F 800/732-8759
cust-serv@web-shops.net
www.einsteins-emporium.com
Without doubt, one of the biggest and most lavish sites on the web! A wonderful sources for toys, posters, books, and all other dino paraphernalia.

Everything Prehistoric
217 Main St.
Hill City, SD 57745 USA
T 605/574-3919
F 605/574-2518
dinomail1@everythingprehistoric.com
www.everythingprehistoric.com
Excellent source for fossils, home ware, books, and replicas.

Everything Prehistoric
607 Main St.
Rapid City, SD 57701 USA
T 605/399-2654
Sister store to the above.

Jurassic, Inc.
1519 Pacific Ave.
Venice Beach, CA 90291 USA
T 310/452-4100
F 310/452-5056
sales@jurassicstore.com
jurassicstore.com

Monstrosities
PO Box 1024
North Baldwin, NY 11510 USA
T 516/378-1338
monstrosities@mcimail.com
www.monstrosities.com
The ultimate source for kits, figurines, movies, posters, and fan-related materials.

National Dinosaur Museum
Gold Creek Village
Barton Highway
Gungahlin, ACT 2912 AUSTRALIA
T 61-2-6230-2655
F 61-2-6230-2357
natdino@contact.com.au
www.contact.com.au/dino-museum/
An amazing source for all kinds of dinosaur figures, toys, puzzles, accessories; check out their online catalog, mate!

Primordial Soup
Box 184
4736 Onondaga Blvd.
Syracuse, NY 13207 USA
T 888/880-1988
info@primordialsoup.com
www.primordialsoup.com/store/index.html
Tons of good stuff including T-shirts,

maps, cards, models, and mousepads.

Primeval Creations
7729 Knotty Pine Crt.
Woodridge, IL 60517 USA
T 630/985-6114
Rhedosaur@aol.com

The Saurusshoppe
Natural Science Center
4301 Lawndale Center
Greensboro, NC 27455 USA
T 336/288-3769
With a name like this, it MUST be good!

Wyoming Dinosaur Center
110 Carter Ranch Rd.
Thermopolis, WY 82443 USA
T 307/864-2997
F 307/864-5762
bones@wyodino.org
www.wyodino.org/giftshop.html
Many unusual gifts including a talking Tarbosaurus or Brachiosaurus activated by movement.

GLOBES

A Galaxy of Maps
5975 N. Federal Hwy
Fort Lauderdale, FL 33308 USA
T 800/388-6588
F 954/267-9007
sales@galaxymaps.com
www.galaxymaps.com/xinfdin.htm
Sells the Replogle 16" inflatable dinosaur globe, #16101.

GOLF

Dinosaur Golf
170 Parkway
Gatlinburg, TN 37738 USA
T 423/436-4449
The place to strut your putter-saurus!

Dinosaur Park
4946 Clifton Hill
Niagara Falls, Ontario
L2E 6S8 CANADA
T 905/358-3601
F 905/358-3818

dwquailgolf.net
2100 Roswell Rd., Ste. 200C
Marietta, GA 30062 USA
T 770/517-1505
quail@ix.net.com
www.dwquailgolf.net
    "Junior dinosaur decals" for putting.

HOLOGRAMS

AD 2000
780 State St.
New Haven, CT 06511 USA
T 203/624-6405
F 203/624-1780
information@ad2000.com
www.ad2000.com/

Armchair World
2240 Federal Ave.
Los Angeles, CA 90064 USA
T 310/477-8960
F 310/477-4910
orders@armchair.com
www.armchair.com/store/holo/holo1.html#dino

Fisher Price
636 Girard Ave.
East Aurora, NY 14052-1884 USA
T 716/687-3000
F 716/687-3636

Holograms & Lazers, International
PO Box 2159
Houston, TX 77242-2159 USA
T 281/498-0235

Holographic Dimensions, Inc.
16115 A Southwest 117th Ave. #21A
Miami, FL 33177 USA
T 305/255-4247
F 305/255-0339
www.shadow.net/~holodi/stock.htm

Holographic Studios
240 E. 26th St.
New York, NY 10010-2436 USA
T 212/686-9397
F 212/481-8645
drlaser@interport.net
www.holostudios.com

Holographics North
444 S. Union St.
Burlington, VT 05401 USA
T 802/658-2275
F 802/658-5471
jp@holonorth.com
www.holonorth.com
    This company offers a 30 x 40"
    Tyrannosaur that rises and swishes its
    tail.

Inquisitoy
W6037 Highway B
Peshtigo, WI 54157 USA
T 800/576-9569
linda@inquisitoy.com
inquisitoy.com

Royal Holographic Art Gallery
122 Market Square
560 Johnson St.
Victoria, British Columbia
V8W 3C6 CANADA
T/F 250/384-0123
office@holograms.bc.ca
www.holograms.bc.ca/

INFLATABLES

Big Events, Inc.
1801 Diamond St.
San Marcos, CA 92069 USA
T 760/761-0909
F 760/761-4290
Ctrim92020@aol.com
www.surfernet.com/big-events/

Cameron Balloons, Ltd.
St. John St.
Bedminster, Bristol
BS3 4NH ENGLAND
T 44-0-117-9637216
F 44-0-117-9661168
webmaster@cameronballoons.co.uk
wwco.uk/w.cameronballoons.co.uk/

Chaz Air Jazz
PO Box 20082
Carterville, GA 30102 USA
T 770/336-5261
F 770/336-5907
selrahc@bellsouth.net
www.chazairjazz.com/
A large selection of somewhat scale dinos offered.

Cutting Edge Creations
801 E. Cliff Rd.
Burnsville, MN 55337 USA
T 612/882-8651
www.cutting-edge-creations.com
A 25-foot tall Tyrannosaur.

Dynamic Displays
7243 Pearblossom Hwy, Bldg 11
Little Rock, CA 93543 USA
T 877/411-6200
F 661/-944-6519
jael2@earthlink.net
A splendid 60 foot and very-scale Tyrannosaurus balloon. Check this out!

Full Mall Industrial Co.
3F, No. 136 Chun Jih Rd.
Taoyuan, TAIWAN
T 886/-3-335-2583
F 886-3-335-2971
fullmall@ms23hinet.net
www.fullmall.com/dinos.html
Source for several pet-sized inflatable dinos.

Total Rebound
6610 Goodyear Rd.
Benicia, CA 94510 USA
T 707/748-0117
F 707/748-0116
info@totalrebound.com
www.totalrebound.com/

JEWELRY

Fossil Image
PO Box 398
Pleasant View, TN 37146 USA
T 615/746-4182
digsbymail@aol.com
members.aol.com/digsbymail/
A pewter dinosaur tack pin.

Frausto Fabrications
4314 Navajo Dr.
Laramie, WY 82072 USA
T 307/742-7721
pfrau@aol.com
members.aol.com/pfrau/jewelry.htm
Very nice T-rex bolo tie.

Golden Wonders
4419 Valley Forge Rd.
Durham, NC 27705 USA
T 919/382-0164
F 919/384-9126
gwbf@aol.com
www.goldenwonders.com/catalog/page?dino
A wonderful series of tiny sculptures of Velociraptor, Tyrannosaurus,

Triceratops, Brachiosaurus, and Parasaurolophus, available as pins or pendants.

House of Onyx, Inc.
120 N. Main St.
Greenville, KY 42345-1504 USA
T 270/-338-2363
F 270/338-9605
onyx@muhlon.com
www.houseofonyx.com
An 18 kt set of dino bone earrings.

Jewelry by Janine
PO Box 8474
Port St. Lucie, FL 34985 USA
janine@metrolink.net
Silver Apatosaurus earrings.

Kenneth Kolb
2180 Fisher Lane
Salt lake City, UT 84109 USA
T 801/485-7663
www.qcontinuum.com/~dinosaur/
Specializing in agatized dinosaur bone eggs, spheres, and earrings.

Nature's Jewelry
222 Mill Rd.
Chelmsford, MA 01824-3692 USA
T 800/-333-3235

#1 Fashions in Jewelry
805 S. Orlando Ave., Ste. J
Winter Park, FL 32789 USA
T 800/379-1048
home@1fashionsinjewelry.com
www.1fashionsinjewelry.com

Pelham-Grayson, Inc.
PO Box 310
North Stonington, CT 06359 USA
www.uconect.net/~ruschpgi/index.html
Several cast pendants and a "Brontosaurus ring."

PM Creations
2648 E. Workman Ave., Ste. 424
West Covina, CA 91791 USA
T 800/392-9240

Victor Porter
PO Box 555
Windfall, IN 46076 USA

Raun Harman Exports, Ltd.
D-262, Ashok Vihar-I
Delhi-110052 INDIA
T 91-11-7216673
F 91-11-7441130
raunharman@indiaenterprise.com
punn.com/bodydots/dino.htm
Dino castings set with real jewelry.

Stone Pony Designs
PO Box 15022
Baton Rouge, LA 70895 USA
caguillot@msn.com
surfandshoppe.com/merchants/gem/dino.htm
Dinosaur bone pendant.

Stoneage Jewelry
89 N. Main St.
Moab, UT 84532 USA
T 435/259-1981
Offers four dinosaur bone bolo ties.

Sunwest Silver
324 Lomas Blvd. NW
Albuquerque, NM 87102 USA
T 505/243-3781
F 505/843-6183
A small selection of dinosaur charms.

JUMPERS

Aerobounce Manufacturing, Inc.
9215 Thomasville Dr.
Houston, TX 77064 USA
T 281/890-0570
F 281/955-6451

aerobounce@webtv.net
www.aimsintl.org/aerobounce.htm

Astrojump
more-info@astrojump.com
www.astrojump.com/
  Offices in 14 states, start bouncin'.

Dino Jump International
619 S. Cleveland St.
Oceanside, CA 92054 USA
T 760/754-5186
F 760/754-5181
info@dinojump.com
www.dinojump.com/

D & L Inflatables
1101 Bjork Dr.
New Lenox, IL 60451-1063 USA
T 815/485-2266
F 815/485-2277
sales@800jumping.com
www.800jumping.com/default.htm

Era Import-Export Trading Company
275 S. Marengo Ave., Ste. 22
Pasadena, CA 91101 USA
T 626/792-1195
F 626/792-1729
era@eraimpex.com
www.eraimpex.com/jump/jump.html

Jumpers
PO Box 17309
San Diego, CA 92177 USA
T 619/272-2268
jumprz@aol.com
www.jumps.com

Kidz Jump
PO Box 67096
Albuquerque, NM 87193 USA
T 505/792-1946
www.kidzjump.com/subtric.htm

Space Walk Sales
PO Box 641479
Kenner, CA 70064-1479 USA
T 352/873-9255
jump4fun@bouncehouse.com
www.bouncehouse.com/

Starline Productions
1865 Parker Blvd.
Tonawanda, NY 14150 USA
T 716/832-6494
magician@webt.com

KIT BUILDING

Dave Acker
5 Palm Lane
Levittown, PA 19054 USA
T 215/943-1656

Amazing Figure Modeler
PO Box 30885
Columbus, OH 43230 USA
T 614/882-2125
  Occasionally contains good dinosaur articles.

Dinosaur Art and Modeling
www.indyrad.iupui.edu/public/jrafert/dinoart.html
  An essential site with sections on "Sources," artists, kits, reader art, books, and galleries. Maintained by John Rafert.

Tommy Ellis
2293 N. Ranch Road
Murfreesboro, TN 37129 USA
T 615/890-9415
paleoart@ccast.com
www.ccast.com/paleo

Tom Henson
6317 Sommerset Rd.
Lansing, MI 48911 USA

T 517/394-0752

Kalmbach Publishing
PO Box 1612
Waukeshaw, WI 53187-1612 USA
T 800/533-6644
F 414/796-1615
www.kalmbach.com
> *Where to buy Ray Rimell's book*
> *Building and Painting Model*
> *Dinosaurs, #12167, $15.95.*

Kit Builders
Box 210
Sharon Center, OH 44274-0201USA
T 330/239-1657
F 330/239-2991
> *Another good modeling source with*
> *some dinosaur coverage.*

Ray Lawson
7776 Bostic Rd.
Raeford, NC 28376 USA
T 910/848-3535
MODLBLDR2@aol.com
> *Varied interests, dinosaurs are his*
> *specialty.*

Darren McDonald
119 Bishop Lane
Somerset, PA 15501 USA
T 814/443-4495
mesozoicera@hotmail.com

Megalania Dinosaur Modeling Pages
megalania@hotmail.com
members.tripod.com/~megalania/
> *An informative model site maintained*
> *by Larry Dunn, featuring many releases*
> *in a variety of mediums.*

Modeling Times
439 Chestnutland Rd.
New Milford, CT 06776 USA
> *Another useful magazine of note.*

Modeler's Resource
4120 Douglas Blvd. #306-292
Granite Bay, CA 95746-5936 USA
T 916/784-9517
F 209/322-9053
www.modelersresource.com
> *Frequently includes articles about*
> *dinosaur products.*

Mysterium Gallery
23641 San Fernando Rd. #102
Santa Clarita, CA 91321 USA
T 805/259-8118
angelfire.com/ca3/mysteriumgallery

Orbit Graphics
PO Box 2008
Madison, TN 37116-2008 USA
> *Sells Model Mania, a VHS tape.*

Michael Rusher
2005 Palo Verde Ave. #171
Long Beach, CA 90815 USA
Dinotreker@earthlink.net
home.earthlink.net/~dinotreker/index.html

Marc J. Tassone
3700 Rose Circle
Rio Rancho, NM 87124 USA
T 508/896-4593
jat@nmia.com

LECTURES

Fossil Records
2805 N. Keystone St.
Burbank, CA 91504 USA
T 818/848-2646
F 818/353-0170
> *Sells taped lectured by the "Grand Old*
> *Men of Paleontology," Edwin H.*
> *Colbert and Elmer S. Riggs.*

LIFE-SIZED MODELS

Animal Makers, Inc.
12473 Gladstone Ave. Unit A
Sylmar, CA 91342 USA
T 818/838-3440
F 818/838-3441
www.animalmakers.com/index.html

Chiodo Brothers Productions
110 W. Providencia Ave.
Burbank, CA 91502 USA
T 818/842-5656
klowns@chiodobros.com
www.chiodobros.com

CM Studios
600 N. Adams St.
Gillespie, IL 62033 USA
T 217/839-2593
F 217/839-2558
mail@cmstudio.com
www.cmstudio.com

Creations E. T.
261-E Kennedy Blvd.
Beauceville, Beauce
Quebec G0S 1A0
CANADA
T/F 418/774-3188 (French)
T 514/875-1910 (English)
creations@creationset.com
www.creationset.com

Cycad Productions
63 Woodbine Ave.
East Hampton, NY 11937 USA
T 516/769-3951
Cycadproductions@yahoo.com

Stephen and Sylvia Czerka
6350 S. Hwy 191
Monticello, UT 84535 USA
T 435/587-2074
F 801/587-2054

www.dinosaur-museum.org

Dreams to Reality Studios
56 Buttonwood
Norristown, PA 19401 USA
T/F 610/313-1821
dtr@icdc.com
www.icdc.com/~dtr/dinos.html

Dreamstar Productions
18111 FM 762
Needville, TX 77461 USA
T 409/553-3675
www.global-expos.com/dreamstar/default.htm

Enchanted Castle Studios
4942 South Lee Hwy
Natural Bridge, VA 24578 USA
T 540/291-2353
F 540/291-2684

George Florides
11 Korinthiakov P/SSA
1048 Nicosia CYPRUS
T 357-2-337911
gflo@spidernet.com.cy
www.geocities.com/SoHo/Museum/4314/

Gondwana Studios
Queen Victoria Museum and Art Gallery
Wellington St.
Lauceston, Tasmania 7250
AUSTRALIA
T 03-63-951437
F 03-63-233770
gondwana@microtech.com.au
www.microtech.com.au/gondwana

House of FX
4405 Belvidere St.
Orlando, FL 32809 USA
T 402/352-7950
Houseoffx@aol.com
members.aol.com/houseoffx
     Bruce Miller provides marvelous, life-

size dinosaur sculptures.

Louis Paul Jonas Studios
304 Miller Rd.
Hudson, NY 12534 USA
T 518/851-2211
F 518/851-2284
demerritt@jonasstudios.com
www.jonasstudios.com

Joshua Knuth
294 E. Johnson
Fond Du lac, WI 54935 USA
T 920/923-3363
Knuth@aecom.yu.edu
bulky.aecom.yu.edu/users/kknuth/josh/josh/ht
m

Payne Studios
140 Roberts St. #C
Asheville, NC 28801 USA
T 828/281-3050
sculpsteel@circle.net
www.circle.net/~sculpsteel/
    A source for sculpted steel skeletons.

Rodolfo Salas Gismondi
Labrotorio de Paleontologia de Vertebrados
Casa Honorio Delgado-UPCH
AV. Armendaris 445 Miraflores
Lima PERU
F 0051-1-4450164
paleovert@hotmail.com

Sierra Sculpture
PO Box 7197
Auburn, CA 95604 USA
T 530/885-1756
F 530/823-1323
www.douglasvanhowd.com

Skulls Unlimited
PO Box 6741
Moore, OK 73153 USA
T 800/659-659-skul

F 405/794-6985
info@skullsunlimited.com
www.skullsunlimited.com

Staab Studios
154 Pine Rd.
Golden, CO 80401 USA
T 303/526-5369
F 303/526-2514
garyandlissi@www.staabstudios.com
www.staabstudios.com

Swede Creations
Box 230 66
Stockholm SWEDEN
T 46-8-297161
F 46-8-313141
swede-creations@the-lair.com
www.swedecreations.com/index.htm

Taylor Studios, Inc.
1320 Harmon Dr.
Rantoul, IL 61866 USA
T 217/893-4874
F 217/893-1998
taylor@shout.net
www.taylorstudios.com/

Trcic Studio
245 Roca Roja Rd.
Sedona, AZ 86351 USA
T/F 520/284-0619
trcicstudio@sedona.net

Watson Sculpture and Studio
3500 Fallowfield Rd.
Nepean, Ontario
K2J 4A9 CANADA
watsondn@magma.ca
www.magma.ca/~watsondn/

Larry Williams Studio
1495 W. 9th St, Ste. 502
Upland, CA 91786 USA
T 909/931-7122

larry@citylimits.com
www.citylimits.com/artist/larryw
      Larry specializes in steel skeletons.

LIGHT SWITCHES

Sunshine Creations, L. L. C.
1832 14th St SW
Minot, SD 58701 USA
T/F 701/852-7076
sunshine@minot.com
www.minot.com/~sunshine/dinosaur.html
      A colorful Tyrannosaurus switch plate!

MAGNETS

Evergreen Classics
3946 Park Lane
Traverse City, MI 49686 USA
T 231/938-2582
www.evergreenclassic.com/Page14.html
      A large selection of very attractive
      designs.

Fridgefun! Inc.
3345 Industrial Dr. #16
Santa Rosa, CA 95403-2061 USA
T 707/527-9891
F 707/527-9892
office@fridgefun.com
www4.viaweb.com/fridgefun
      48 little scale magnets for only $5.00!

A Head of Their Time
338 Divisadero St.
San Francisco, CA 94117 USA
T 415/431-9724

Kayty's Magnets
PO Box 4679
Dublin, CA 31040 USA
T 800/853-1985
F 815/853-0706
sales@kaysmagnets.com
kaysmagnets.com/

MEDALS

Dinosaur Medallions
PO Box 32
Westbury, NY 11989 USA

Medallic Art Company, Ltd.
VIP Image
100 Old Saybrook Rd.
Charleston, SC 29418 USA
T 843/760-1000
corpoffice@vipimage.com
www.vipimage.com/mac/dinosaur_1.htm
      Six large and very impressive bronze
      castings sculpted by Don Everhart.

MOBILES

Artisangifts.com
555 Stanford Ave.
Palo Alto, CA 94306 USA
T 650/855-9560
F 650/855-9590
feedback@artisangifts.com
www.artisangifts.com/artisangifts/dewa-04.html
      Colorful dino mobile by Dewa
      Suardana of Bali.

Skyflight Models
PO Box 974, Dept. E
Woodinville, WA 98072 USA
T 800/766-8005

MODELS AND SCULPTURE

Action Hobbies
720 Rummage Rd.
Cox's Creek, TN 40013 USA
T 502/543-9282

Alchemy Works
PO Box 773
Cleburne, TX 76033 USA
T 817/6517-5968

F 817/556-2641
a0001979@airmail.net

Ants
PO Box 9208
Albuquerque, NM 87119 USA
T 800/642-9267
F 505/842-9195
www.ants-inc.com

Bone Clones
21416 Chase St. #1
Canoga Park, CA 91304 USA
T 818/709-7991
F 818/709-7993
kronen@boneclones.com
www.boneclones.com

Bowman Arts Studio
2111 NE 23rd #2
Portland, OR 97212 USA
bbow@teleport.com
www.teleport.com/~bbow/

Michael Burnett Productions
9948 Glenoaks Blvd.
Sun Valley, CA 91352 USA
T 818/768-6103
F 818/768-6136
www2.mbpfx.com/mbpfx/catalog/resinkits.htm
l

CM Studio
600 N. Adams St
Gillespie, IL 62033 USA
T 217/839-2593
F 217/839-2558
mail@cmstudio.com
www.cmstudio.com

Continental Creatures
492 E. 200 S #2
Provo, UT 84606 USA
T 801/375-2146

Creation Science Evangelism
29 Cummings Rd.
Pensacola, FL 32503 USA
T 850/479-3466
F 850/479-8562
dino@drdino.com
www.drdino.com/products/fossils.htm

Cretaceous Creations (Cdn)
265 Dubois St.
Breckenridge, Quebec
J0X 2G0 CANADA
marty0069@hotmail.com
www.microplus.ca/dino/default.htm

Cretaceous Creations
8420 Craig Hill St.
St. Louis, MO 63123 USA
T 314/849-9754

Cycad Productions
63 Woodbine Ave.
East Hampton, NY 11937 USA
T 516/769-3951
Cycadproductions@Yahoo.com

Alan C. Davis
3532 Beverly Dr.
Toledo, OH 43613 USA
T 419/385-2373
AlancD@aol.com
members.aol.com/AlancD/index.html

Dino Art
11 Riggs Rd.
Glouchester, MA 01930 USA
T 978/283-7186
dinoart@jimedia.com
www.jimedia.com/dinoart/

Dinosaur Studios
116 Bowdoin St.
Medford, MA 02155 USA
T 617/386-8066
F 617/396-8177

webmaster@dinosaurstudio.com
www.dinosaurstudio.com

Dragon, Inc.
15 Sandalwood Dr.
Smithtown, NY 11787 USA
T 516/724-6583

Dragon Attack!
320 W. Johnson St.
Colton, CA 92324 USA
T 909/824-5928
drgnatk1@aol.com

Dreams to Reality Studios
56 Buttonwood
Norristown, PA 19401 USA
T/F 610/313-1821
dtr@icdc.com
www.icdc.com/~dtr/dinos.html

Dreamstar Productions
18111 F. M. 762
Needville, TX 77461 USA
T 409/553-3675
77461fischner@fbtc.net
www.global-expos.com/dreamstar/default.htm

Michael Eddy
Haleot, Porkellis
Helston, Cornwall
TR13 0LB ENGLAND
T 01144-1326-340849
F 01144-1209-313029

ESPI Productions
11 Jena Ave.
Loundonville, NY 12211-0232 USA
T 518/438-0454

Fantasy Creations
2010 S. Batson Ave. #203
Rowland Heights, CA 91748 USA
T 818/913-6328

Jerry Finney
12419 E. 212 St.
Lakewood, CA 90715-2309 USA
T 562/809-3235

Mike Fredericks
145 Bayline Circle
Folsom, CA 95630-8077 USA
T 916/985-7986
PreTimes@aol.com
members.aol.com/pretimes/horizon.html

Mike Furuya
2736 Dew St.
Honolulu, HI 96817 USA
T 808/595-0046
F 808/247-6343
Mike@ohia.com

Dana Geraths
2431 C. Coral Ave. NE
Salem, OR 97305 USA
T 503/581-3216

Hell Creek Creations
1208 Nashua Lane
Bartlett, IL 60103 USA
T 630/289-7018
Hellcreek@aol.com
members.aol.com/hellcreek/index.html

Horizon Models
PO Box 5187
Hacienda Heights, CA 91745 USA
T 626/333-0230
F 626/337-2370
horizon@horizonoriginal.com
horizonoriginal.com/home/index.htm

Hunt Studios
2780 Chaparral Lane
Paso Robles, CA 93446 USA
T 800/761-1039
F 805/237-0956
bhunt@fix.net

www.fix.net/~bhunt/index.htm

Integrity Productions
7320 Hawthorne Ave., Ste 301
Los Angeles, CA 90046 USA
T/F 310/410-0720
dickens@spimageworks.com

J & S Fossils
17 Jeff Rd.
Largo, FL 33774 USA
T 813/595-2661
F 813/595-8544
fossil@gte.net
home1.gte.net/fossils/

Louis Paul Jonas Studios
304 Miller Rd.
Hudson, NY 12534 USA
T 518/851-2211
F 518/851-2284
dmerritt@jonasstudios.com
www.jonasstudios.com

Mike Jones
2034 Brighton, Apt. D
Burbank, CA 91504 USA
T 818/845-3379

Kaiyodo
6-10 Tonoshima-cho
Kadoma City, Osaka Pref. 571 JAPAN
www.kaiyodo.co.jp/

Kit Kraft
12109 Ventum Place
Studio City, CA 91604 USA
T 818/984-0780

Joshua Knuth
294 E. Johnson
Fond du Lac, WI 54935 USA
T 920/923-3363
Knuth@aecom.yu.edu
www.bulky.aecom.yu.edu/users/kknuth/josh/jo

sh.html

David Krentz
25853 Anzio Way
Valencia, CA 91355 USA
T 818/526-3792
dkrentz@earthlink.net

Jary Lesser
5702 Rutherglenn
Houston, TX 77096-4806 USA
T 713/721-9397

Staffan Linder
Vanadisvagen 18
S-113 46 Stockholm SWEDEN
staffan.linder@mailbox.swipnet.se

Link and Pin Hobbies
7868 S. Magnolia Way
Englewood, CO 80112 USA
T 303/741-4712
F 303/843-6367
nanorex@ix.netcom.com
www.linkandpinhobbies.com/Dino.htm

Living Resin Productions
117 W. Indiana Ave.
Goshen, IN 46526 USA
T 219/534-6546
JCPlane@aol.com

Lost Art Sculpture
72 Timberland
Aliso Viejo, CA 92656-2143 USA
T 949/448-7153
F 949/448-7154
bill@studiomonteleone.com
www.studiomonteleone.com

Lunar Models
1835 Thunderbolt Dr. #C
Porterville, CA 93257 USA
T 209/784-7121
F 209/784-7889

lublin@lightspeed.net
www.lunarmodels.com

Maxilla & Mandible, Ltd.
451-5 Columbus Ave.
New York, NY 10024 USA
T 212/724-6173
F 212/721-1073

Menagerie Productions
535 Alabama St.
San Francisco, CA 94110 USA
T 415/861-2570
F 415/861-8259
info@menagerieproductions.com
www.menagerieproductions.com/fig/paleo.htm
l

Mental Mischief
PO Box 2638
Clackmas, OR 97015-2638 USA
T 503/658-7460
mmischief@earthlink.net

Merrithew, Tony
PO Box 66435
Portland, OR 97236 USA
T 503/775-5270

Monsters in Motion
330 E. Orangethorpe, Unit H
Placentia, CA 92670 USA
T 714/577-8863
F 714/577-8865
www.monstersinmotion.com/dino

Monstrosities
PO Box 1024
North Baldwin, NY 11510 USA
T 516/378-1338
monstrosities@mcimail.com
www.monstrosities.com

Musashi Enterprises
PO Box 340765

Milwaukee, WI 53234-0765 USA
T/F 414/383-7791
Honshudino@aol.com
members.aol.com/honshudino

Mark Musy
PO Box 1143
Hayesville, NC 28904 USA
T 828/389-3491

Jonathan Neill
3854 N. Orchard Lane, Apt. A
Calabasas, CA 91302 USA
Neilopolis@aol.com
www.neillfineart.com

Paleocraft
RRT 3, Box 512
Wagoner, OK 74467 USA
T 918/488-8264
Area53@IBM.net

Prehistoric Presentations
PO Box 9080
Denver, CO 80209 USA
T 800/875-8886

Primeval Creations
7729 Knotty Pine Ct.
Woodridge, IL 60517 USA
T/F 603/985-6044
Rhedosaur@aol.com

Hugh Rose Studios
5320 N. Camino Sumo
Tucson, AZ 85718 USA
T 520/299-4251

Maximo Salas
10a Avenida #122
Col. Cumbres 1er Sector
Monterrey, N. L. 64610 MEXICO
T 011-528-346-0698
F 011-528-348-1652
maxsalas@nl1.telmex.net.mx

Studio Sculpture
25885 Trabuco Rd., Ste. 134
Lake Forest, CA 92630 USA
T 714/855-4350

Skulls of Antiquity
PO Box 227
Calistoga, CA 94515 USA
T 707/942-5292
ycomis@earthlink.com

Joseph Tippmann Studios
4409 E. Prospect Rd.
Fort Collins, CO 80525 USA
T 970/221-0809
josepht@ezlink.com
www.ezlink.com/~josepht

Time Travel Trophies
3205 Alcazar NE
Albuquerque, NM 87110 USA
T 505/883-8061

Hirokazu Tokugawa
A-fragi@po.teleway.ne.jp
www.teleway.ne.jp/~A-fragi/index.in.E.htm

Trcic Studio
245 Roca Roja Rd.
Sedona, AZ 86351 USA
T/F 520/284-0619
trcicstudio@sedona.net

Ignacio Vallejo
Obregon Sur #914-3
2500 Saltillo Coahuila
MEXICO
T 011-52-84-122264

Tim Vittetoe Originals
22542 NE 18th St.
Redmond, WA 98053 USA
T 425/836-1973
tvo@oz.net
www.oz.net/tvo/products.htm

Watson Sculpture and Models
3500 Fallowfield Rd.
PO Box 29022
Nepean, Ontario
K2J 4A9 CANADA
watsondn@magma.ca
www.magma.ca/~watsondn/

Wiccart
420 St. Augustine Dr.
Oakville, Ontario
L6K 3E9 CANADA
www1.centtel.com/wiccart/index.htm

Mick Wood
527 S. Mariposa St.
Burbank, CA 91506 USA
mickwood@hotmail.com

X-0 Facto
PO Box 341368
Los Angeles, CA 90034 USA
T 310/559-8512
F 310/838-9146
Facto2@aol.com
hallucinet.com/xofacto/

MOUSE PADS

Computer Fun
8250 Valdosta Ave.
San Diego, CA 92126-2130 USA
garyo@computerfun.com
www.computerfun.com/animal.html
Item #766 is a dinosaur mouse pad.

MUGS

Dennisaurs!
PO Box 74
Sallisaw, OK 74955 USA
members.tripod.com/~Dennisaurs
*A series of mugs imprinted with
humorous designs.*

MUSEUM DISPLAYS

David Dann Studios
PO Box 396
4 East Hill Rd.
White Sulphur Springs, NY 12787 USA
T 914/292-1679
davidann@catskill.net
www.fastwww.com/daviddannstudio/museum.
htm

Jan Spoerri & Co.
134 Cedar St.
East Hampton, NY 11937 USA
T 516/329-3289
spoerri@panix.com

MUSIC

Electronic Courseware Systems, Inc.
1713 South State St.
Champaign, IL 61820-7242 USA
T 217/359-7099
F 217/359-6578
    The KIDS CD-Rom features Dinosaur's
    Lunch, *meant to impart placement of
    musical notes.*

Fossil Records
2805 N. Keystone St.
Burbank, CA 91504 USA
T 818/848-2646
F 818/353-0170
    The source for the tapes Dinosaur
    Tracks, More Dinosaur Tracks, *and*
    Dinosaur Tracks Again, *as recorded by
    The Iridium Band!*

Hejira Music
PO Box 95465
University Station
Seattle, WA 98145 USA
T 877/472-3036
dinotunes@aol.com
members.aol.com/jh99/bergman.htm

*Sells a nine-song musical dinosaur CD
by Bergman Broome.*

Bonnie Phelps
PO Box 9656
Denver, CO 80209 USA
T 800/395-6791
F 303/749-8742
bphipps@indra.com
www.abmall.com/cmc/choir.html
    The tape and CD recording of Dinosaur
    Choir.

Glenn Tunes
4357 Sunfield Ave.
Long Beach, CA 90808 USA
glenntunes@aol.com
simplifun.com/glenntunes/
    Glenn hawks his Rockin' Dinosaurs
    tape.

Mesolithic Music
banamba.com/cave/music.html
    *Dr. Demento's hideously schlocky
    discography of dinosaur/caveman songs
    through the ages. Remember Alley
    Oop?*

Mother's Heartland Music
PO Box 33494
Granada Hills, CA 91394 USA
F 818/360-8796
Pelican@aol.com
members.aol.com/Pelicaneen/DMD.htm
    The family oriented Dinosaur's Musical
    Day *cassette.*

Musicware, Inc.
8654 154th Ave. NE
Redmond, WA 98052 USA
T 425/881-9797
F 425/881-9664
musicware@musicwareinc.com
www.musicwareinc.com/
    The 12-CD set MiDiSaurus *is a*

complete, animated music learning system for young children.

Random Factors
3754 W. 170th St.
Torrance, CA 90504-1204 USA
T 310/329-6772
F 310/538-9208
creasy@worldnet.att.net
www.random-factors.com/midlife.htm
Tape or CD recordings of Fossil Fever and Dr. Jane's Remains.

Rock N' Learn
PO Box 3595
Conroe, TX 77305 USA
T 800/348-8445
F 409/539-2659
info@rocknlearn.com
www.rocknlearn.com
Makers of the Dinosaur Rap cassette, where science meets street jive!

Sonic Images
PO Box 691626
West Hollywood, CA 90069 USA
T 323/650-1016
F 323/650-1000
sonicimages@sonicimages.com
sonicimages.com/
The source for the fantastic Lost World: Jurassic Park Game soundtrack on CD. Really compelling dino music here.

NEWS

Dino Data
www.dinodata.net
Nice site maintained by Fred Bervoet; partly in Dutch with extensive coverage of events.

Dino-Source Newsletter
dinotreker@earthlink.net
home.earthlink.net/~dinotreker/Dinonews.html

#NEWS
A monthly, online newsletter hosted by Michael Rusher; free, but readers must subscribe.

Dinoland Dinosaur Gazette
www.geocities.com/CapeCanaveral/Galaxy/8152/dinoland.html
Bi-monthly round up of news and events, including the far-ranging activities of sponsor Steve Brusette.

Dinosaur Interplanetary Gazette
www.dinosaur.org/frontpage.html
Shamelessly cheesy, tacky, and maudlin about dinosaurs; indisputably, my favorite spot on the web! Indispensable for keeping up with events.

In Recent Fossil News
www.extinctions.com/fossilnews/
Excellent, well-stocked site.

PaleoNet
listproc@ucmpl1.berkeley.edu
A professional forum for the exchange of ideas, commentary, etc. Free, but users must subscribe online.

Paleontology Newsgroup
news:sci.bio.paleontology
A usenet newsgroup that must be subscribed to online. Extensive discussion of a wide variety of issues!

Prehistorics Illustrated
members.xoom.com/prehistorics/Newspg_1.htm
Colorful site with an extensive archives of news clippings and releases.

ORGANIZATIONS

Alberta Paleontological Society
PO Box 35111

Sarcee Postal Outlet
Calgary, Alberta
T3E 7C7 CANADA
www.geocities.com/SoHo/9094/aps.html

Austin Paleontological Society
105 E. Victory
Temple, TX 76501-1709 USA
WallaceTX@aol.com
www.utexas.edu/research

Dallas Paleontological Society
PO Box 223846
Dallas, TX 75222-3846 USA
T 972/640-4492
www.dallaspaleo.org

Delaware Valley Paleontological Society
PO Box 686
Plymouth Meeting, PA 19462-0686 USA

Dinamation International Society
Paleontology Foundation
PO Box 1362
Glenrock, WY 82637 USA
T 877/WYO-DINO
connely@coffey.com

Dinofriends: An Interactive Dinosaur Club
301 Breesport
San Antonio, TX 78216 USA
scent@dcci.com
www.scentchips.com/dino.html

Dino-Trekking Club
1042 15th Ave.
Longmont, CO 80501 USA

Dinosaur Club
Department of Earth and Planetary Science
Western Australian Museum
Francis St.
Perth, Western Australia 6000
AUSTRALIA

Dinosaur Natural History Association
PO Box 33
Brooks, Alberta
T1R 1B2 CANADA
T 403/793-8065

Dinosaur Nature Association
1291 E. Highway 40
Vernal, UT 84078-2830 USA
T 800/845-3466
dna@dinosaurnature.com

Dinosaur Society
1900 Benjamin Franklin Parkway
Philadelphia, PA 19103-1101 USA
T 516/277-7855
F 516/277-1479
dsociety@aol.com
www.dinosociety.org
*Still dearly-departed, but we eagerly
await its resurrection.*

Dinosaur Society, UK
PO Box 329
Canterbury, Kent
CT4 5GB ENGLAND
T 011-44-1277
F 011-44-1277-700473
Funny, THEIRS is doing just fine!

The Dry Dredgers
Department of Geology
PO Box 210013
University of Cincinnati
Cincinnati, OH 45221 USA
jackk@corecomm.net

Friends of Dinosaur Dreaming
Monash Science Center
Monash University
Wellington Rd.
Clayton, Victoria 3168
AUSTRALIA

Friends of the Dinosaurs
Big Horn Basin Foundation
PO Box 31
Thermopolis, WY 82443 USA
T 307/864-2259
F 307/864-5762
bhbf@thermopwy.net
www.thermopwy.net/bhbf/trends.html

Geological Society of America
3300 Penrose Place
PO Box 9140
Boulder, CO 80301-9140 USA
T 303/447-2020
F 303/447-1133

International Paleontological Association
Paleontogisk Museum
Sars Gate 1
N-0562 Oslo NORWAY
F 22 47221810

Kentucky Paleontological Society
365 Cromwell Way
Lexington, KY 40503 USA
T 606/277-3148

Mid-America Paleontology Society
4800 Sunset Dr, SW
Cedar Rapids, IA 52404 USA

New Mexico Friends of Paleontology
PO Box 26145
Albuquerque, NM 87101 USA

Paleontological Association
Institute of Earth Studies
University of Wales
Aberystwyth, Dyfed SY23 3DB
UNITED KINGDOM

Paleontological Division
Geological Association of Canada
Memorial University of Newfoundland
St. Johns, Newfoundland

A1B 3X5 CANADA
T 709/737-7660
F 709/737-2532
gac@sparky2.esd.mun.ca

Paleontological Fund
6809 Crossman St.
Annandale, VA 22003 USA
cpaleo@aol.com
www.paleofund.org

Paleontological Institute
121 Lindley Hall
University of Kansas
Lawrence, KS 66045 USA
T 785/864-3338
F 785/-864-5276

Paleontological Research Institution
1259 Trumansburg Rd.
Ithaca, NY 14850 USA
T 607/273-6623
F 607/273-6620
WDA1@cornell.edu
www.englib.cornell.edu/pri/pri1.html

Paleontological Society
Box 28200-16
Lakewood, CO 80228-3108 USA
T 303/236-9228
F 303/236-5690
twhenry@usgs.gov
www.uic.edu/orgs/paleo/homepage.html

Rockwatch: The Club For Young People
The Kiln, Waterside
Mather Road, Newark
NG24 1NT ENGLAND
rockwatch@wildlife-trusts.cix.co.uk
www.earthlines.com/rockwatch/

Society of Vertebrate Paleontology
PO Box 1276
Bedford Park, IL 60499 USA
T 847/480-9095

F 847/480-9080
svp@sherwood-group.com
www.museum.state.il.us/svp/

South African Society for Amateur Paleontology
PO Box 671
Silverton 0127
SOUTH AFRICA
T 082-301-4085
www.icon.co.za/~cryptic/

Southern California Paleontological Society
2608 El Dorado St.
Torrance, CA 90503 USA
scpaleo@aol.com

Western Interior Paleontological Society
Denver Museum of Natural History
PO Box 200011
Denver, CO 80220 USA
aam421@ecentral.com
www.wipsppc.com/

PAINTING

Balitono, Inc.
26 Pleasant Valley Way
Princeton Junction, NJ 08512 USA
T 609/936-8807
F 609/936-8869
> *Paint the Wild: Dinosaurs contains a hand-carved, wooden Allosaur and Brachiosaur for prehistoric Picassos.*

PALEONTOLOGY COURSES

Baylor University
PO Box 97388
Waco, TX 76798-7388 USA
T 817/755-2911
F 817/755-2969

Brigham Young University
Department of Geology

Provo, UT 84602 USA
T 801/378-3918
F 801/378-8143

Brown University
Department of Ecology and Evolutionary Biology
Box G-B2
Providence, RI 02912 USA
T 401/863-2515
F 401/863-7544

Cambridge University
Department of Zoology
Downing St.
Cambridge, CB2 3EJ ENGLAND
T 44-1223-336600
F 44-1223-336676

Fort Hays State University
Department of Geosciences
Hays, KS 67606-4099 USA
T 913/628-4041
F 913/628-4096

George Washington University
Department of Biological Sciences
2023 G St. NW
Washington, DC 20052 USA
T 202/994-7144
F 202/994-6100

Idaho State University
Department of Geology
Pocatello, ID 83209 USA
T 208/236-4151
www.isu.edu

Johns Hopkins University
Department of Cell Biology and Anatomy
725 N. Wolfe St.
Baltimore, MD 21205 USA
T 410/955-1697
F 410/955-4129

Montana State University
Department of Earth Sciences
Museum of the Rockies
408 Traphagen
Bozeman, MT 59717 USA
T 406/994-5178
F 406/994-5122
www.montana.edu

Murray State University
Department of Biological Sciences
Murray, KY 42701 USA
T 502/762-3934
F 502/762-4887

North Carolina State University
Department of Marine, Earth, & Atmospheric
Sciences
1125 Jordan Hall
Raleigh, NC 27695-8208 USA
T 919/515-7648
F 919/515-7802

Ohio University
Department of Biological Sciences
Athens, OH 45701 USA
T 614/593-9489
F 614/593-0300

**South Dakota School of Mines and
Technology**
Department of Geology
501 East St. Joseph St.
Rapid City, SD 57701-3995 USA
T 605/394-2467
F 605/394-6131

Southern Methodist University
Department of Geological Sciences
Dallas, TX 75275 USA
T 214/768-2750
F 214/768-2701
www.geology.smu.edu

University of Alberta
Laboratory for Vertebrate Paleontology
Department of Biological Sciences
Edmonton, Alberta
T6G 2E9 CANADA
T 403/492-5408
F 403/492-9234

University of Birmingham
School of Earth Sciences
Edgbaston, Birmingham
B15 2TT ENGLAND
T 44-121-414-4173
F 44-121-414-3971
www.birmingham.ac.uk/EarthScinces/

University of Bristol
Department of Geology
Bristol BS8 1RJ ENGLAND
T 44-117-925-8202
F 44-117-925-3385

University of California, Los Angeles
Department of Biology
Los Angeles, CA 90095-1606 USA
T 310/825-9110
F 310/206-3987
www.lifesci.ucla.edu/bio/

University of California, Riverside
Department of Earth Sciences
Riverside, CA 92521 USA
T 909/787-5028
F 909/787-4324

University of Chicago
Department of Geophysical Sciences
Haskell Hall, Rm 119
1126 East 59th St.
Chicago, IL 60637 USA
T 312/702-8551
F 213/702-4503

University of Cincinnati
Department of Geology

Geology/Physics Bldg.
Cincinnati, OH 45221-0013 USA
T 513/345-8507
F 513/345-8501
www.uc.edu/~storrsgw/

University of Colorado at Boulder
Campus Box 250
Boulder, CO 80309-0250 USA
T 303/492-5211
F 303/492-2606

University of Florida
Florida Museum of Natural History
PO Box 117800
Gainesville, FL 32611-7800 USA
T 352/392-1721
F 352/846-0287
www.flmnh.ufl.edu/

University of Illinois at Chicago
Department of Biological Sciences
845 West Taylor (m/c 066)
Chicago, IL 60607-7060 USA
T 312/413-2643
F 312/413-2435

University of Kansas
Department of Systematics and Biology
Natural History Museum
Lawrence, KS 66045-2454 USA
T 913/864-5639
F 913/864-5335

University of London
Department of Anatomy and Developmental
Biology
Rockefeller Bldg., Gower St.
London WC1E 6BT ENGLAND
T 44-171-209-6156
F 44-171-380-7349
ucgasue@ucl.ac.uk

University of Otago
Department of Geology

Box 56, Dunedin NEW ZEALAND
www.otago.ac.nz/

University of Saskatchewan
Saskatoon, Saskatchewan
S7N 5E2 CANADA
T 306/966-5687
F 306/966-8593

University of Texas at Austin
Department of Geological Sciences
Austin, TX 78712 USA
T 512/471-5171
F 512/471-9425

University of Texas at El Paso
Department of Biological Services
El Paso, TX 79968-0519 USA
T 915/747-6985
F 915/747-5808
www.utep.edu/~leb/home.html

University of Victoria
School of Earth and Ocean Sciences
PO Box 3055
Victoria, British Columbia
V8W 3P6 CANADA
T 604/721-6102
F 604/721-6200
ceor.seos.uvic.ca

University of Wyoming
Department of Geology and Geophysics
Laramie, WY 82071 USA
T 307/766-5178
F 307/766-6679

PAPER DINOSAURS

Card Models
9910 SW Bonnie Brae Dr.
Beavertown, OR 87008-6045 USA
T 503/646-4289
F 506/646-4289
cc_cardmodels@catalogcity.com

st7.yahoo.com/cc1785
Sells a very scale set of dinosaur
models by Usborne.

Dinosaur Lady
3575 Hwy 11
Hazel Green, WI 53811 USA
T 608/748-4530
johnrich@pcii.net
The source for several large dino paper
kits and plans for a life-sized paper
Velociraptor!

Download A Dinosaur
philfear@rain.org
www.rain.org/~philfear/download-a-
dinosaur.html
Several simple origami designs for free.

Fascinating Folds
PO Box 10070
Glendale, CA 85318 USA
T 800/968-2418
F 888/433-6537
www.fascinating-folds.com/
Advanced origami designs.

L. D. D.
2518 A Etiwan Ave.
Charleston, SC 29414 USA
T 803/556-9337
Nice paper Triceratops skeleton.

Paper Paradise
PO Box 64189
Tucson, AZ 85728 USA
T 520/622-2700
F 520/627-3700
welcome@paperparadise.com
www.paperparadise.com
A good source for many paper dinosaur
books published by Dover.

David Peters Studio
12812 Wood Valley Crt.

St. Louis, MO 63131-2051 USA
T/F 314/646-0541
Dpters@stlnet.com
home.stlnet.com/~azero
For $1.32, you have own plans to cut
out a very scale, 20" Pteranodon
hanging model!

Rainbow Symphony Store
6860 Canby Ave., Ste. 120
Reseda, CA 91335 USA
T 818/708-8400
F 818/708-8470
feedback@rainbowsymphony.com
st7.yahoo.net/rainbowsymphony/dinheadcarmo
.html
Exact scale skulls of Tyrannosaurus
and Triceratops!

Sasuga Japanese Bookstore
7 Upland Rd.
Cambridge, MA 02140 USA
T 617/497-5460
F 617/497-5362
sasuga@sasugabooks.com
www.sasugabooks.com
The source for dinosaur origami books
in both English and Japanese.

PARKS

Crystal Palace Museum
84 Anerly Rd.
London SE19 2DA ENGLAND
T 0181-778-2173

Dino Park
Conny Land
Bodensee Freizeitpark
CH-8564 Lipperswil
SWITZERLAND
www.connyland.ch/

Dinoland
Astorp, SWEDEN

T 042-26-20-39
dinoparken@telia.com
www.dinoparken.se/valkommen.htm

Dinosaur Gardens
11160 US 23 South
Ossineke, MI 49766 USA
T 517/471-5477

Dinosaur Gardens
Utah Field House of Natural History
235 E. Main St.
Vernal, UT 84078 USA
T 435/789-3799

Dinosaur Land
Coombe St.
Lyme Regis, Dorset
ENGLAND
T 01297-443541

Dinosaur Land
Rt. 1
White Post, VA 22663 USA
T 540/869-0951
info@dinoaurland.com
www.dinosaurland.com/

Dinosaur Park
4946 Clifton Hill
Niagara Falls, Ontario
L2E 6S8 CANADA
T 905/358-3601
F 905/358-3818

Dinosaur Provincial Park
PO Box 60
Patricia, Alberta
CANADA
T 403/378-4342

Dinosaur Valley State Park
Box 396
Glenrose, TX 76043 USA
T 254-897-4588

Dinosaur World
RR 2, Box 408
Eureka Springs, AR 72632 USA
T 501/253-8113

Dinosaurier Park
Alte Zollstr. 5
31547 Rehburg Loccum
GERMANY
T 05037/20-73
F 05037/57-39
Dino-park@t-online.de
www.dino-park.de/

Dinosaur World
5145 Harvey Tew Rd.
Plant City, FL 33565 USA
T 813/717-9865
F 813/707-9776

George S. Eccles Dinosaur Park
1544 East Park Blvd.
Ogden, UT 84401 USA
T 801/393-3466

International Petrified Forest
1001 Forest Dr.
PO Box 8
Holbrook, AZ 86025 USA
T 520/524-9178

Island of Adventure: Jurassic Park
1000 Universal Studio Plaza
Orlando, FL 32819-7610 USA
T 407/363-8000
www.usf.com

Jurassic Park
Universal Studios
100 Universal City Plaza
Universal City, CA 91608 USA
T 818/777-1000

Luray Dinosaur Park
1087 US Hwy 211 West

Luray, VA 22835 USA
T 540/743-4113

Nakasato Dinosaur Center
51-2, Kagahara
Nakasato-mura
Tano-gen, Gunma 370-1602 JAPAN
T 0274-58-2829
F 0274-58-2088
webmaster@nakasato.org
www.dino-nakasato.org

Nash Dinosaur Land
Amherst Rd, Rte. 116
South Hadley, MA 01075 USA
T 413/467-9566

Petrified Creatures Museum of Natural History
PO Box 751
Richfield Springs, NY 13439 USA
T 315/858-2868

Prehistoric Gardens
36848 Hwy 101 South
Port Orford, OR 97465 USA
T 541/322-4463

Prehistoric Park
Calgary Zoo
PO Box 3036, Box B
Calgary, Alberta
T2M 4R8 CANADA
T 403/232-9372

Prehistoric World
Upper Canada Road
Exit 758 from Hwy 401
Morrisburg, Ontario
K0C 1X0 CANADA
T 613/543-2503

Valley of Dinosaurs
Chorzow, POLAND

Wildlife-Dinosaur Park
Coombe Martin, North Devon
EX34 0NG ENGLAND
T 44-0-1271-883374
F 44-0-1271-882486
Stay at the nearby Jurassic Hotel!

PARTY SUPPLIES

All the Right Stuff
4472 White Oak Circle
Kissimmee, FL 34746 USA
T 407/397-4037
F 407/397-4217
info@alltherightstuff.com
alltherightstuff.com
One of the most best-stocked party suppliers on the web.

Amon Party Collections
PO Box 94
Williamston, MI 48895 USA
samon349@aol.com
Sells the birthday party dinosaur game "Tyro Lost a Tooth."

Birthday in a Box
18609 Willow Oak Dr.
Rockville, MD 20855-1463 USA
T 301/924-2224
F 301/947-1466
boxbday@aol.com
www.birthdayinabox.com/partyprice.asp?id=16
A basic dinosaur birthday kit with an extensive list of add-on party favors.

Birthday USA
200 Veirs Mill Rd.
Rockville, MD 20851 USA
T 800/390-2509
F 240/453-0911
lisa@birthdayusa.com
www.birthdayusa.com
A Good source for theme-decorated dinosaur party supplies.

Business Builders, Ltd.
Sandbeck Way, Wetherby
W. Yorkshire LS22 7DN
ENGLAND
T 01937-588885
F 01937-587785
mail@bblnet.co.uk
www.bblnet.co.uk

Dinosaur-Us
301 E. Alosta Ave.
Glendora, CA 91740 USA
T 626/852-0920
www.dinosaur-us.com
A one-stop dinosaur birthday shop!

Let's Pretend Parties
1000 Arbor Rd. #2
Menlo Park, CA 94025 USA
T 650/327-8446

Lisa's Toys
Rt. 3, Box 11816
Tool, TX 75143 USA
orders@lisastoys.com
www3.geocities.com/Enchantedforest/Palace/4
626/index.html

Party and Paper Worldwide
PO Box 677
500 Park Ave., Ste. 110
Lake Villa, IL 60046 USA
T 847/631-3310
F 847/265-9799
orders@partypro.com
partypro.com/html/nonlicensed.htm
Item #1112326 is the "Dinosaur Birthday in a Box."

Party, Etc.
1818 West Thomas St.
Hammond, CA 70401 USA
T 877/387-2789
F 504/345-9600
party@partyetc.com

www.partyetc.com

Party Outfitters
PO Box 8373
Lacey, WA 98509 USA
T 360/438-2211
F 360/438-3614
generalinfo@partyoutfitters.com
www.partyoutfitters.com
The source for an 60-foot inflatable dino-slide.

Party Works
2221 Heine Rd.
Chewelah, WA 99109 USA
T 509/935-8880
orders@thepartyworks.com
thepartyworks.com

Partyshop
13300 US 98
Sebring, FL 33870 USA
T 941/655-5454
F 941/655-3240
sales@1800partyshop.com
www.1800partyshop.com/index.html
"Party-O-saurus" theme packs.

Alvin Peters Company
Empire State Plaza
PO Box 2400
Albany, NY 12220-0400 USA
T 518/477-6064
F 518/477-5538
apcom@wizvax.net
www.wizvax.net/apcomp/dinosaur.html
A huge assortment of dino goods; check this out!

A Piece of Cake
2089 Linden Lane
Palatine, IL 60067 USA
T 847/303-0636
info@piece-of-cake.com
www.piece-of-cake.com/dinoland.htm

The *"Dino-land Party package" for eight children.*

Simplifun Studios
2070 Stratford Dr.
Milpitas, CA 95035 USA
T 408/946-8632
F 408/946-8552
simplifun@simplifun.com
www.simplifun.com
The "Dino Blast Party Kit."

PET SUPPLIES

T. F. H. Publications
1 TFH Plaza
3rd and Union Avenues
Neptune City, NJ 07743 USA
T 732/988-8400
F 732/988-5466
info@tfh.com
www.tfh.com
Sells Nylabone rubber dinosaur bones for removing doggie tartar.

Worldwide Pet Supply
727 Rubber Ave.
Naugatuck, CT 06770 USA
T 888/800-PETS
F 203/723-7529
customer_service@worldwidepetsupply.com
www.mailorderpetsupply.com
Item B0010403 is a dinosaur chomp toy that flosses Fido's teeth while he chews!

PEWTER DINOSAURS

Albuquerque's 505 Wholesale Jewelry
3131 Candelaria NE #119
Albuquerque, NM 87107 USA
T 505/889-3785
F 505/889-8027
info@frescos.com
frescos.com
A good selection of Tyrannosaur,

Stegosaur, and Apatosaur figures.

Dandl Creations
PO Box 55313
Hayward, CA 94545 USA
DSTEFA4621@aol.com
www.dandlcreations.com

Franklin Mint
Franklin Center, PA 19091-0001 USA
T 610/459-6000
Offers a small but expensive line of very scale dinosaurs for collecting.

Stuart Hill Pewter Shop
PO Box 10812
McLean, VA 22103-9812 USA
sjhhill@aol.com
www.delta1.org/~pewter
Six nice designs, including Garudimimus, Stegosaurus, Pteranodon, Triceratops, Spinosaurs, and Tyrannosaurus.

Michael Holland Productions
825 South Grand Ave.
Bozeman, MT 59715 USA
T 406/587-1815
An impressive line of 18 miniature skull profiles.

Maksim Krivelev
2445 W. Bancroft #4
Toledo, OH 43607 USA
T 419/531-0807
F 419/474-0603
www.geocities.com/WallStreet/Floor/4515/dinos/
Offers a 9 inch Tarbosaurus, elaborately decorated.

R. Luther Company
11900 Elena Dr NE
Albuquerque, NM 87122 USA
T 505/822-1187

F 505/823-668
wholesale@rluther.com
www.rluther.com
> Sells the "Extinctions Collection" of 12
> very scale figures. Buy the set and get a
> free dino belt buckle.

Madhouse
PO Box 882
Thorndale, PA 19372 USA
jfasano@vocienet.com
www.digitalmadhouse.com/dinosaur.htm
> Makers of "Tyrant Prince," a six-inch
> Tyrannosaurus sculpture for $99.95.

C. B. C. Mignot
Les Loges
49390 La Breille-Les-Pins
FRANCE
T 02-41-38-79-77
F 02-41-38-79-78
cbg-mignot@saumur.net
> A large Diplodocus and other metal
> beasts.

Miller Enterprises
2871 Indian Hills Dr.
Provo, UT 84604 USA
T 801/375-5058
F 801/375-2151
PFHM@aol.com
> An exquisite series of pewter designs
> including Allosaurus, Torvosaurus,
> Ceratosaurus, Stegosaurus,
> Ultrasaurus, Triceratops,
> Tyrannosaurus, and Utahraptor.

National Dinosaur Museum
Gold Creek Village
Barton Hwy
Gungahlin, ACT 2912
AUSTRALIA
T 61-2-6230-2655
F 61-2-6230-2357
natdino@contact.com.au

www.contact.com.au/dino-museum/
> Sells a series of Australian-based
> dinosaurs including Leallynasaura,
> Allosaurus, Muttaburrasaurus, Minmi,
> and Timimus.

Parker's Pewters
PO Box 885
Bryan, OH 43506 USA
www.parkerspewters.com/616.html
> Nice silver Struthiomimus

Ral Partha
5938 Carthage Crt.
Cincinnati, OH 45212-1197 USA
T 513/631-7335
F 513/631-0028
rpartha19@mail.idt.net
www.fasa.com/ralpartha/catalog/SubSubline13
34.html
> Impressive Tyrannosaurus, Triceratops,
> Pteranodon, Velociraptor,
> Parasaurolophus, and Stegosaurus.

Pewter Image
2341 Porter Lake Dr. #205
Sarasota, FL 34240 USA
T 877/941-2160
info@pewterimage.com
www.pewterimage.com
> A nice, six piece set, including
> Tyrannosaurus, painted or unpainted.

Rawcliffe Pewter
155 Public St.
Providence, RI 02903-4991 USA
T 401/331-1645

Michael Ricker Pewter, Inc.
2050 Big Thompson
Estes Park, CO 80517-2570 USA
T 800/373-9837
F 970/586-4609
www.ricker.com
> Includes a metal Apatosaurus,

Spinosaurus, Tyrannosaurus, and Pteranodon, with a similar series of juvenile figures.

Silverstreak, Inc.
2001 W. 10th Place
Tempe, AZ 85281 USA
T 480/894-9528
info@silverstreakinc.com
www.silverstreakinc.com
A source for silver Tyrannosaurus, Apatosaurus, Triceratops, and Dimetrodon.

Sunwest Silver
324 Lomas Blvd. NW
Albuquerque, NM 87102 USA
T 505/243-3781
Sells a small assortment of silver dinosaur charms.

PICTURE FRAMES

Woodswork
779 Skyridge Lane #317
Agoura Hills, CA 91377 USA
T 800/584-4395
st5.yahoo.com/woodsworksart/dinosaurframe.html
Item DF-1001 is a dinosaur picture frame with glow in the dark eyes!

PINATAS

Mexican Pinatas.com
1201 Airway Blvd., Ste. C2
El Paso, TX 79925 USA
T 915/781-2225
F 915/772-0376
info@mexicanpinatas.com
www.mexicanpinatas.com
Smash this neat Triceratops!

Paper & Paper Worldwide
PO Box 677

500 Park Ave., Ste. 110
Lek Villa, IL 60046 USA
T 847/631-3310
F 847/265-9799
orders@partypro.com
partypro.com/html/nonlicensed.htm

Pinata Design
298 Lemon Grove
Irvine, CA 92620 USA
T 800/975-5597
gatirado@pacbell.net
www.pinatadesign.com
A big red dinosaur!

Unique Party Supplies
2400 S. Weccacoe Ave.
Philadelphia, PA 19046-4298 USA
T 215/336-4300
F 800/888-1490
unique@favors.com
www.favors.com

PLACE MATS

The Straight Edge, Inc.
296 Court St.
Brooklyn, NY 11231 USA
T 718/643-2794
F 718/403-9582
straedge@aol.com
www.straightedgeinc.com
A small assortment of colorful, education place mats for young students.

PLAQUES

Action Hobbies
720 Rummage Rd.
Cox's Creek, KY 40013 USA
T 502/543-9282

Cretaceous Creations
265 Dubois St.

Breckinridge, Quebec
J0X 2G0 CANADA
marty0069@hotmail.com
www.microplus.ca/dino/

The Dinosaur Foundry
559 Sperling Rd.
Nanaimo, British Columbia
V9R 5T6 CANADA
T/F 250/753-2402
dino@nanaimo.ark.com
www.dinosaurfoundry.com

Dinosaur Productions
9520 Owensworth Ave., Unit 5
Chatsworth, CA 91311 USA
T 877/346-6366
Dinodon@aol.com
www.dinodon.com

Michael Eddy
Halcot, Porkellis
Helston, Cornwall
TR13 0LB ENGLAND
T 01144-1326-340849
F 01144-1209-313029

Fossilnet, Inc.
1517 Greentree Lane
Garland, TX 75042 USA
ccampbell@spindle.net
www.fossilnet.com/Cast/cast.htm

GEOU
Department of Earth Sciences
The Open University, Walton Hall
Milton Keynes MK7 6AA
ENGLAND
T/F 44-0-1908-654871
geou@open.ac.uk
geou.open.ac.uk/Fossils/fossilmain.html

S. G. Hoffman
42 Gabreil Rd.
Cochecton, NY 12726 USA

T 800/716-2548
sghoffman@juno.com
www.catskill.net/statue/other.html

Horizon
15910 Maracaibo Place
Hacienda Heights, CA 91745 USA
T 626/333-0230
F 626/333-2370
horizon@horizonoriginal.com
www.horizonoriginal.com

Scott Howard
RR 1, Box 499C
Old Town, ME 04468 USA
wshoward@aol.com
hometown.aol.com/wshoward/page/fossils.htm

Ron Jordan
4456 Old River St.
Oceanside, CA 92057 USA
T 760/754-0257
members.home.net/rjaj58/dinofossil/

Mentis Group
2316 Delaware Ave. #310
Buffalo, NY 14216 USA
www.paleocast.com

Mt. Blanco Fossil Company
PO Box 559
Crosbyton, TX 79322 USA
T 806/675-2421
F 806/675-7777
entrophy9@hotmail.com
www.mtblanco.com

North Eastern Geologic
291 Sheppler St.
Rochester, NY 14612 USA
F 716/663-0005
gartland@frintiernet.net
www.frontiernet.ner/~gartland

Prehistoric Products
Box 1151
205 Indian Creek Rd.
Happy Camp, CA 96039 USA
T 530/493-5170
www.finishingfirst.com/Dino/

Taylor Studios
1320 Harmon Dr.
Rantoul, IL 61866 USA
T 217/893-4879
F 217/893-1998
taylor@shout.net
www.taylorstudios.com/

Valley Anatomical Preparations
9520 Owensmouth Ave., Unit 5
Chatsworth, CA 91311 USA
T 818/700-8020
F 818/998-6218
VAPrep@worldnet.att.net

PLASTIC FIGURES

Maison Joseph Battat
8430 Darnley Rd.
Montreal, Quebec
H4T 1M4 CANADA
T 514/341-6000
F 514/735-3408

Bullyland
Bullystr. 1
73565 Spraitbach GERMANY
T 07176-303-0
F 07176-303-12
bully@bullyland.de

Bullyland
65 West 55th St.
New York, NY 10019-4951 USA
T 212/974-9815
F 212/974-9814
bully@ix.netcom.com

Lewis Galoob Toys
500 Forbes Blvd.
S. San Francisco, CA 94080 USA
T 415/952-1678
F 415/583-4996
info-galoob@galoon.com
www.galoob.com
> *Distributors of the very scale, six-set
> National Geographic dinosaur line.*

Glencoe Models
Box 846
Northboro, MA 01532 USA
T 508/869-6877
F 508/869-2482
sales@studiofx.com
> *Reproduces three plastic skeleton kits
> from the 1950s.*

John F. Green, Inc.
Box 55787
Riverside, CA 92517 USA
T 909/684-5300
F 909/684-8819
info@greenmodels.com
www.greenmodels.com
> *An excellent source for old and out of
> print dinosaur kits, including Horizon.*

K & M International
1955 Midway Dr.
Twinsburg, OH 44087 USA
T 330/425-2550
F 330/425-3777
staff@kmtoys.com
www.kmtoys.com

Play Visions
19180 144th Ave. NE
Woodinville, WA 98072 USA
T 425/482-2836
F 425/482-2842

Re Saurus
240 Outerbelt St., Ste. C

Columbus, OH 43213 USA
T 614/751-9352
F 614/751-9939
toybox@resaurus.com
www.resaurus.com
*Makers of the wonderful Carnage line
of dinosaurs, with 12 moveable joints!*

Safari Limited
PO Box 630685
Miami, FL 33163 USA
T 305/621-1000
F 305/624-9433
sales@safariltd.com
www.safariltd.com

Schleich Produktions
Postfach 1805
73508 Schwabisch Gmund GERMANY
T 07171-800-0
F 07171-800156
schleich@schleich-s.de
A small but nice line of dino products.

Starlux, Inc.
16 rue de 5eme Chasseurs
24000 Periquex FRANCE
A huge line of plastic products.

Tamiya America, Ltd.
2 Orion
Aliso Viejo, CA 92656-4200 USA
T 714/362-2240
*A small line of highly accurate plastic
kits.*

ToyWay
PO Box 55
Letchworth, Hertfordshire
SG6 1SG ENGLAND
T 01462-672509
F 01462-672132
*Distributes many different lines of
plastic figures, including the new
"Walking with Dinosaurs" set.*

Tsukuda Hobby
Taito-ku, Hashib 1-36-10
Tokyo 111-0023 JAPAN
T 03-3871-3210
F 03-3871-3200
*A small line of highly colorful dinosaur
models.*

Waiphoon, Ltd.
Flat A, 12/F
Cheong Tai Ind. Bldg.
50-56 Fui Yiu Kok St.
Tsuen Wan, NT Honk Kong CHINA
waiphoon@netvigator.com
www.waiphoon.com.hk
*Another small line of colorful
dinosaurs.*

POSTERS

Allwall.com
1321-101 Kirkland Rd.
Raleigh, NC 27603 USA
questions@allwall.com
www.allwall.com
*The most complete assortment of dino
posters on the web!*

Antiquarian Fossils
3217 Patton Way
Bakersfield, CA 93308 USA
T 800/249-5512
feedback@fossils.com
www.fossils.com

Art.com
13820 Polo Trail Dr.
Lake Forest, IL 60045 USA
T 888/287-3701
F 888/287-3702
lgrelier@alexanderogilvy.com
www.art.com/
*A good source for hard-to-find, art-
oriented dino posters.*

Cinewonders
PO Box 67492
Los Angeles, CA 90067 USA
Catalog: $5.00
A good source for film posters.

Sharon S. Cox
656 Honey Locust Way
Lexington, KY 40503 USA
T 606/277-9237
ssc@bestcreaturefeatures.com
www.bestcreaturefeatures.com
Several neat designs based upon her original artwork.

Fossils as Art
Box 980069
Houston, TX 77098 USA
T 281/250-2574
F 713/529-2447
fossils@fossils-as-art.com
www.fossils-as-art.com
A very large selection of educationally-based posters.

Monstrosities
PO Box 1024
North Baldwin, NY 11510 USA
T 516/378-1338
monstrosities@mcimail.com
www.monstrosities.com/products/Posters1.asp
A good choice of posters not found elsewhere.

Natural Tracks
49 Forest Ave.
Paramus, NJ 07652 USA
T 201/712-0209
sales@naturaltracks.com
www.naturaltracks.com

Nature Source
423 Ridge Rd.
Queensbury, NY 18804 USA
T 518/761-6702
F 518/798-9107
Mammoth357@aol.com
nature-source.com/

Novagraphics
PO Box 37197
Tucson, AZ 85740 USA
T 800/727-NOVA
F 520/292-9852
staff@novaspace.com
www.novaspace.com

Jerry Ohlinger's Movie Store
242 West 14th St.
New York, NY 10011 USA
T 212/989-0869
Another useful stop for film stuff.

Omni Resources
1004 S. Mebane St.
Burlington, NC 27218-2096 USA
T 800/742-2677
F 336/227-3748
custserve@omnimap.com
www.omnimap.com

Pan Terra, Inc.
PO Box 392
Afton, MN 55001 USA
T 800/-216-8130
F 612/436-7244
www.wmnh.com
Eye-catching, informative earth history chart.

Peabody Museum of Natural History
170 Whitney Ave.
New Haven, CT 06511 USA
T 203/432-3740
www.peabody.yale.edu/mural
The gift shop sells six and nine foot versions of the famous Zallinger ancient life mural.

Richard Penny
1212 Lujan St.
Santa Fe, NM 87505 USA
T 505/471-0705
talktous@dinosaur-man.com
www.dinosaur-man.com/
    *The 'Dinosaur Man' offers a small
    selection based upon his colorful
    artwork.*

Prehistoric World Images
PO Box 1151
Yorba Linda, CA 92887-1151 USA
T 800/970-1128
F 714/970-2780
contact@prehistory.com
www.prehistory.com
    *A large selection based on the artwork
    of Josef Moravec. Love those baby T.
    rexes!*

Rick's Movie Graphics
PO Box 23709
Gainesville, FL 32602-3209 USA
T 800/252-0425

John Sibbick
6 Bloomfield Ave.
Bath BA2 3AB ENGLAND
T/F 44-0-1225-422011

Smith Studios
34294 E. Frontage Rd.
Bozeman, MT 59715 USA
T/F 406/586-4296
exhibithall@mcn.net
lwl.ycsi.net/museum/dino2

Texas Parks and Wildlife
4200 Smith School Rd.
Austin, TX 78744 USA
T 888/336-9967
    Some Texas-sized dino posters.

PUBLICATIONS

Archosaurian Articulations
George Olshevsky
3305 Adams Ave. #221
San Diego, CA 92116 USA
dinogeorge@aol.com

Bones
Wyoming Dinosaur Center
Big Horn Foundation
PO Box 71
Thermopolis, WY 82443 USA

Digs By Mail
Fossil Image
PO Box 60684
Nashville, TN 37206 USA
T 612/262-8078
Fosimage@aol.com

Dinosaur Report
Dinosaur Society
1900 Benjamin Franklin Parkway
Philadelphia, PA 19103-1101 USA
T 516/277-7855
F 516/277-1479
dsociety@aol.com
www.dinosociety.org
    Still extinct, but let's hope for the best!

Dinosaur Times
Dinosaur Natural History Association
PO Box 33
Brooks, Alberta
T1R 1B2 CANADA
T 403/793-8065

Dinosaur World
Hell Creek Creations
1208 Nashua Lane
Bartlett, IL 60103 USA
T 630/289-7018
Hellcreek@aol.com
    Edited by dinosaur maven Allen Debus.

$16.60 for three issues a year; loads of interviews, modeling reports, and dino facts. Expect the unexpected here!

Dinosaurs
Dinosaur Club
Western Australian Museum
Francis St.
Perth, Western Australia 6000
AUSTRALIA

Dry Dredgers
Department of Geology
University of Cincinnati
Cincinnati, OH 45221 USA
homepages.uc.edu/~handgl/dredgers.htm

Earth Sciences History
History Department
Texas Tech University
Lubbock, TX 79409-1013 USA

Fossil News
1185 Claremont Dr.
Boulder, CO 80303 USA
T 303/499-5337
lynne@fossilnews.com
www.fossilnews.com
Edited by Lynne M. Clos; $28.00 a year for 12 issues. Despite its title, this is a slick, professional publication covering a wide variety of topics.

Fossils and Strata
Department of Paleozoology
Swedish Museum of Natural History
50007 S-104 05 Stockholm
SWEDEN
T 46-8-666-42-20
F 46-8-666-41-84
stefan.bengtson@nrm.se

Earth Science History
History of Earth Sciences Society
Northeastern Science Foundation, Inc.

PO Box 747
Troy, NY 12181 USA

Earth Science News
Earth Science Club of Northern Illinois
623 E. Highland
Villa Park, IL 60181 USA

Journal of Paleontology
Department of Geology
University of Iowa
121 Trowbridge Hall
Iowa City, IA 52242 USA
T 319/353-2598
F 319/335-1821
fossils@uiowa.edu
www.uic.edu/orgs/paleo/homepage.html

Journal of Vertebrate Paleontology
Society of Vertebrate Paleontology
60 North Revere Dr., Ste. 500
Northbrook, IL 60062 USA
T 847-480-9095
F 847/480-9282
svp@sherwood-group.com
www.museum.state.il.us/svp/
The most important journal of its kind.

Lethaia
Department of Paleozoology
Swedish Museum of Natural History, 5007
S-104 05 Stockholm SWEDEN
Christina.Franzen@nrm.se

MAPS Digest
Mid-America Paleontology Society
4800 Sunset Dr. SW
Cedar Rapids, IA 52404 USA

The Mosasaur
Academy of Natural Sciences
1900 Benjamin Franklin Pkwy
Philadelphia, PA 19103-1195 USA

NPS: Paleontological Research
PO Box 592
Kemmerer, WY 83101 USA
www2.nature.nps.gov/grd/geology/paleo/index.htm
A publication of the National Park Service.

Nature
Box 1733
Riverton, NJ 08077-7333 USA

Palaios
Department of Geology
Colby College
5820 Mayflower Hill
Waterville, ME 04901-8858 USA
palaios@colby.edu

Paleo Bios
Museum of Paleontology
1101 Valley Life Sciences Bldg.
University of California
Berkeley, CA 94720-4780 USA

Paleopelagos
Dipartimento di scienze della Terra
Universita La Sapienza
P. le Aldo Moro 5
00185 Roma ITALY

Paleobiology
Department of Paleobiology, NHB 21
Smithsonian Institution
Washington, DC 20560 USA

Palaeontographica Italica
Natural History Museum
Universita di Pisa
Via S. Maria 53
56126 Pisa ITALY
T 050-847268
F 050-500932
tong@dst.unipi.it

Paleontologica Electronica
www.erdw.ethz.ch/~pe/toc_fm.htm
An impressive online magazine run by the Coquina Press.

Paleontologia Africana
Bernard Price Institute for Paleontological Research
University of the Witwatersrand
Private Bag 3
2050 Wits, SOUTH AFRICA
106sjr@cosmos.wits.ac.za

Palaeontologia Polonica
Instytut Paleobiologii
ul. Twarda 51/55
00-818 Warzawa POLAND
paleo@twarda.pan.pl

Paleontological Journal
Russian Academy of Sciences
MAIK Nauka-Interperiodica
Mezhdunarodnyl Otdel, Profsoyuznava ul., 90
117864 Moscow RUSSIA
T 7-095-3361600
F 7-095-3360666
compmg@mail.rssi.ru
www.maik.rssi.ru/journals/paleng.htm

Paleontology
Blackwell Publishers
108 Cowley Rd.
Oxford OX4 1JF
ENGLAND
jninfo@blackwellpublishers.co.uk
www.blackwellpublishers.co.uk

Park Paleontology
Fossil Butte National Monument
PO Box 592
Kemmerer, WY 83101 USA
Vincent_santucci@aps.gov

Prehistoric Times
145 Bayline Circle

Folsom, CA 95630-8077 USA
T 916/985-7986
members.aol.com/pretimes
> *Edited by Mike Fredericks; $24.00 a year for six issues. Ostensibly the best dino mag ever; chock full of interviews, science facts, and product reviews. The ads alone made this an invaluable source!*

Quarterly Magazine
Dinosaur Society, UK
PO Box 329
Canterbury, Kent
CT4 5GB ENGLAND

Trackways
Royal Tyrrell Museum Cooperating Society
Box 7500
Drumheller, Alberta
T0J 0Y0 CANADA
T 800/440-4240

Trilobite Tales
Western Interior Paleontological Society
PO Box 200011
Denver, CO 80220 USA
aam421@ecentral.com
www.wipsppc.com

Zinj Education Project
300 Rio Grande
Salt Lake City, UT 84101 USA
T 801/533-3565
F 801/533-3503
cehistory.zinjster@state.ut.us

PUPPETS

Acorn Naturalists
17821 E 17th St. #103
Tustin, CA 92780 USA
Emailacorn@aol.com
www.acorngroup.com
> *A nice Tyrannosaur, Velociraptor, and*

Pterodactyl

Club Earth
147 Martin St.
Cumberland, RI 02864 USA
T 401/333-3090
sales@clubearth.com
> *Offers "Fingerines," a small line of wonderfully scale finger puppets.*

Folkmanis, Inc.
1219 Park Ave.
Emeryville, CA 94608 USA
sales@folkmanis.com
www.folkmanis.com
> *The source for many wonderful animal puppets.*

Perspective Visuals
6804 Rhode Island Ave.
College Park, MD 20740 USA
T 301/927-3340
F 301/927-3341
dinosaur@idt.net
www.pvisuals.com/dinosaur_museum/puppets/puppet/_order.html
> *An impressive lineup of head puppets.*

Prehistoric World
1040 Henpeck Rd.
Utica, OH 43080 USA

PUZZLES

Access Quality Toys
T 805/987-2530
Aqt@jetlink.net
www.accessqualitytoys.com
> *An online source for dinosaur pegs puzzles.*

Bepuzzled, Inc.
22 East Newbury Rd.
Bloomfield, CT 06002 USA
T 800/471-0641

F 650/692-2791
orders@areyougame.com
www.bepuzzled.com/
They sell the 1,000 piece Buried
Blueprints: Puzzles from the Past.

Compoza-puzzle
1 Robert Lane
Glen Head, NY 11545 USA
T 516/759-0057
F 516/759-1102
mrpieces@compozapuzzle.com
www.compozapuzzle.com
Five different 5 x 8" puzzles for very
young children.

Peter Chapman
Box 45
Bent Mountain, VA 24059 USA
T 540/929-4358
peter@rev.net
216.71.5.213/puzzles/index.html
Sells a solid wood sculpture puzzle
sauropod.

Edu Sallent
Osona 1
08192 St. Quirze del Valles
Barcelona SPAIN
Source of big, colorful floor puzzles.

Gen Hwa Publishing Company
2550 Lapiniere Blvd., Ste. 106
Brossard, Quebec
J4Z 2M2 CANADA
T 514/672-4356
F 514/923-8359
cbinfo@china-biz.com
Sells many colorful dinosaur puzzles.

Great American Puzzle Factory
16 S. Main St. #1
South Norfolk, CT 06854 USA
T 203/838-4240
Several small dino puzzles for young

children with a new floor puzzle coming
soon.

Harco
675 The Parkway
Petersborough, Ontario
K9J 7K2 CANADA
T 705/743-5361
F 705/743-4312
tharris@harco.on.ca
www.harco.on.ca

Jigsaw Jungle
2529 Guenette St.
St. Laurent, Quebec
H4R 2E9 CANADA
T/F 877/758-6453
www.jigsawjungle.com

Joslin Photopuzzle Co.
PO Box 914
Southampton, PA 18966 USA
T 215/357-8346
F 215/357-0307
joslin@jigsawpuzzle.com
www.jigsawpuzzle.com
Offers your child's photo cut into
pieces shaped like dinosaurs.

Kid's Ketch Educational Toys
132 Second St.
Lewes, DE 19958 USA
T 302/645-8448
kids@dca.net
www.kidsketch.com

Learning Curve, International
314 W. Superior St., 6th Floor
Chicago, IL 60610 USA
T 312/654-5960
F 312/654-8227
sande@learningtoys.com
www.learningtoys.com
The source of several dinosaur puzzles
for young children.

Learning Resources
380 N. Fairway Dr.
Vernon Hills, IL 60061 USA
T 847/573-8400
F 847/573-8425
info@learningresources.com
www.learningresources.com/shop/lasso
*See the giant, 24-piece floor puzzle
"Dinosaurs on Display, LER1251.*

Lights, Camera, Interaction, Inc.
PO Box 590
Westport, CT 06881 USA
F 203/227-4499
*Offers a large selection of puzzles
including Dinosaurs in a Box.*

Mamasoes Puzzles and Games
6651 NW 23rd Ave.
Gainesville, FL 32606 USA
T 352/376-1649
F 352/335-9140
mamasoes@gnv.fdt.net

Marco Novelty Company
Main St., Box 705-P
Ashburn, GA 31714 USA
T 912/567-3185
boyce@planttel.net
planttel.net/~boyce/spare.htm
Sells small, 3 x 4" puzzles for children.

Ravensburger Spieleverlag GmbH
1 Robert-Boschstr.
Ravensburg, D-88214 GERMANY
T 49-751-860
F 49-751-86698
*Makers of several large, high-quality
dinosaur puzzles.*

Ravensburger F. S. Schmid
11 Puzzle Lane
Newton, NH 03858 USA
T 603/382-3377
American distributor for the above.

Frank Schaffer
23740 Hawthorne Blvd.
Torrance, CA 90509-2853 USA
T 800/421-5565
F 800/837-7260
fspinfo@aol.com
www.frankschaffer.com
*Manufactures many, colorful, high
quality dinosaur puzzles.*

Timbertown
633 Hope St.
Stamford, CT 66907 USA
T 203/353-1222
Timber@tiac.net
www.timbert.com
*Sells a 48-piece dinosaur puzzle plus a
four-set "Dinosaurs in a Box."*

The Toy Box
108 South Market St.
Ligonier, PA 15658-1205 USA
T 724/238-6233
F 724/238-3169
st3.yahoo.com/tbx
*Sells the circular "World of Dinosaurs"
puzzle.*

Wintergreen Learning Materials
14 Connie Circle, Unit 10
Concord, Ontario
L4K 2W8 CANADA
T 905/669-2815
F 800/567-8054
info@wintergreenlearning.com
www.wintergreenlearning.ca

RECIPES

Crunch-a-saurus Crispies
www.wilton.com/ri/crispies.html

Dinosaur Burger
soar.berkeley.EDU/recipies/burgers/dinosaur1.rec

Dino Cake
www.geocities.com/Heartland/Hills/9654dinoc
ake.html

Dinosaur Claws
www.geocities.com/Heartland/Ranch/3413/pag
e7.html

Dinosaur Cookies
aace.Virginia.edu/curry/class/Museums/Teache
r_Guide/Science/A.Unit.on.Dinosaurs.html

Dinosaur Dip
cookbook.herald-
mail.com/snacks/dino_dip_snac.html

Dinosaur Punch
members.tripod.com/~Angiecooks/kids/dinopu
nch

Dinosaur Roar
www.wilton.com/ri/bday/dinoroar.htm

Fossil Soup
aace.Virginia.edu/curry/class/Museums/Teache
r_Guide/Science/A.Unit.on.Dinosaurs.html

REFERENCE

Academic Press
525 B. Street, Ste. 1900
San Diego, CA 92101-4495 USA
T 619/231-6616
ap@acad.com
    The source for Phil Currie's book,
    Encyclopedia of Dinosaurs for $99.95.

American MPC Research, Inc.
9816 Alburtis Ave.
Santa Fe Springs, IA 90670 USA
T 562/801-0108
F 502/801-0138
ampc@Vividnet.com
www.americanmpc.com
    CD-ROM #10523 is Fossil Worlds.

APA Multimedia, Ltd.
8 Henley Bus Park, Trident Close
Medway City Estate, Rochester, Kent
ME2 4ER ENGLAND
T 44-1634-295222
F 44-1634-710193
    They sell the Dinosaurs! CD-ROM.

Byron Press Multimedia
24 W. 25th St.
New York, NY 10010 USA
T 212/645-9870
F 212/645-9874
    Makers of the Ultimate Dinosaur CD-
    ROM.

Creative Multimedia Corporation
PO Box 780
Pleasant Grove, UT 84062-0780 USA
T 800/262-7668
    In Dinosaur Safari, you can visit 310
    dig sites around the globe.

Dataworks
34 Henderson Rd.
Rowville 3178 AUSTRALIA
T 61-03-9764-8344
F 61-03-9763-2089
support@dataworks.com.au
www.dataworks.com.au/showroom/dinosaurs.h
tml
    The CD-ROM Tales From the
    Kangaroos' Crypt features several
    animated dinosaurs in their natural
    settings. Check out the 'Fangaroo'!

Dinobase
palaeo.gly.bris.ac.uk/dinobase/dinomenu.html
    A wonderful, terribly proper British site
    with complete species lists, cladistics,
    references, and much more!

Dinosaur Reference Center Home Page
sarima@ix.net.com
www.crl.com/~sarima/dinosaurs/

A useful reference site hosted by Stanley Friesen, featuring a complete listing of all known species and frequent updates.

EduArt Multimedia, Pty.
PO Box 263
Launceston, Tasmania 7250
AUSTRALIA
F 61-3-6334-0042
eduart@eduart.com.au
www.eduart.com.au
> *This firm offers the informative CD-ROM Ghosts of the Great Russian Dinosaur Tour.*

Encyclopedia Britannica
310 S. Michigan Ave., 8th Floor
Chicago, IL 60604-4293 USA
T 800/747-8503
www.dinosaurs.eb.com
> *Buy the wonderful CD-ROM Discovering Dinosaurs here; it is packed with illustrations and data!*

Hary & Company
5-4-8 Shimotakaido
Suginami-ku, Tokyo 168
JAPAN
T 81-3-3290-6104
F 81-3-3290-6107
> *Makers of The World of Dinosaurs CD-ROM.*

Hyperworks Reference Software
25 Clifton St.
Scarborough, Western Australia 6019
AUSTRALIA
hyperworks@hotmail.com
> *Offers The Dinosaur Encyclopedia, the most complete species listing available, is on four 3.5" discs.*

Illustrissimus Productions
Cesta 9 Avgusta 8d
1410 Zagorje ob Savi

SLOVENIA
T/F 38660161569
veselink.stanisavac@siolnet
www.geocities.com/CapeCanaveral/Lab/1638/index.html
> *Noted artist Berislav Krzic markets and illustrates his own Concise Illustrated Dinosaur Encyclopedia (still under development at the time of this writing).*

Indiana University Press
601 N. Morton St.
Bloomington, IN 47404-3797 USA
T 812/855-6804
F 812/855-7931
iuporder@indiana.edu
> *Publishes James O. Farlow and M. K. Brett-Surman's excellent The Complete Dinosaur for $59.95.*

The Learning Company
6493 Kaiser Dr.
Freemont, CA 94555 USA
T 510/713-6081
F 510/713-6072
www.learningco.com
> *The Dinosaur Museum CD-ROM was designed in cooperation with the Smithsonian Institution and includes movie clips!*

McFarland Company
Box 611
Jefferson, NC 28640 USA
T 336/246-4460
F 336/246-5018
www.mcfarlandpub.com
> *Here is Donald F. Glut's massive Dinosaurs: The Encyclopedia at $145.00, and Supplement 1, for $60.00.*

MacroMedia
600 Townsend St., Ste. 310W
San Francisco, CA 94103 USA
T 415/252-2000

F 415/626-0554
Makers of Prehistoria: A Multimedia Who's Who of Preshistoric Life.

Mathematical.com
www.mathematical.com/dinocdcatalog.html
Distributes the Russian Dinosaur Exposition CD-ROM, containing 1,000 images for only $15.00!

Media Design Interactive, Ltd.
The Old Hop Kiln
1 Long Garden Walk
Farnham, Surrey GU9 7HP
ENGLAND
T 44-252-737630
F 44-252-710948
Sells the jolly old Dinosaurs! The Multimedia Encyclopedia CD-ROM.

National Geographic
Educational Media Division
1145 17th St NW
Washington, DC 20036 USA
T 800/368-2728
F 515/362-3366
www.nationalgeographic.com
A very lavish CD-ROM, The Age of Dinosaurs.

Perspective Visuals
6804 Rhode Island Ave.
College Park, MD 20740 USA
T 301/927-3340
F 301/927-3341
dinosaur@idt.net
www.pvisuals.com/dinosaur_museum/dinosaur_museum.html
Makers of the Smithsonian Institution's Dinosaur Museum CD-ROM in 3D!

REMedia
13525 Midland Rd., Ste. I
Poway, CA 92064 USA
T 619/486-5030

F 619/486-0679
helpdesk@remedia.com
www.remedia.com
A useful CD-ROM, Z00Guides, Vol. 9: Prehistoric Animals, documents evolutionary advances in major animal groups.

ROM Tech, Inc.
2000 Cabot Blvd., Ste. 110
Langhorne, PA 19047 USA
T 215/750-6606
F 215/750-3722
Another useful disc, Dinosaur Discovery.

Westwind Media
Box 27578
Panama City, FL 32411 USA
T 904/235-3579
F 904/235-7971
An impressive CD-ROM, Dino-Source.

RESEARCH

Jurassic Foundation
1201 Second Ave. West
Drumheller, Alberta T0J 0Y2 CANADA
pcurrie@mcd.gov.ab.ca
This is a private foundation which awards research grants of up to $5000 to students and scholars undertaking original research in paleontology.

RESTAURANTS

Dinosaur Bar-B-Que
246 W. Willow St.
Syracuse, NY 13303 USA
T 315/476-4937
For the best ribs and the best blues north of Dixie!

Dinosaur Bar-B-Que
99 Court St.

Rochester, NY 14604 USA
T 716/325-7090
> *Sister store to the above; check out the food and the music!*

Dinosaur Barbeque
511 NE 4th St.
Bryington Beach, FL 33435 USA
T 561/731-0155

Dinosaur Pizza & Restaurant
1275 M 1/4 Rd.
Loma, CO 81524 USA
T 970/858-1117

Flying Dinosaur Gourmet Foods
11220 Amaranth Lane
Austin, TX 78754 USA
T 512/272-9240

Dinosaur-Us
301 E. Alosta Ave.
Glendora, CA 91740 USA
T 626/852-0920
> *A family entertainment center with food, games, gifts and parties.*

ROCKERS

Concepts in Wood
12424 E. Britton Rd.
Jones, OK 73049 USA
T 405/399-2249
www.craftmark.com/concept/crafts.htm
> *A 36" wooden rocking Tyrannosaur!*

Wood Works and More
7905 Glen Rose Hwy
Granbury, TX 76048 USA
T 817/573-0006
woodcrafter@iname.com
> *Sells a wooden bronto-rocker!*

RUBBER STAMPS

American Science Surplus
3605 W. Howard St.
Skokie, IL 60077 USA
T 847/982-0874
F 800/934-0722
help@sciplus.com
sciplus.com/
> *A set of five pre-inked designs.*

Creative Gifts
PO Box 25185
Rochester, NY 14625 USA
T 888/222-4470
stamps@frontiernet.net
www.frontiernet.net/~stamps/fant.htm
> *Really nice Triceratops, Stegosaurus, Tyrannosaurus, Apatosaurus, and Plateosaurus.*

Hodges & Reed Services, Inc.
PO Box 23504
Stanley, KS 66223 USA
T 913/681-0443
sales@hrweb.com
www.ierc.com/index.html
> *Two giant-sized stamps!*

Oliver's Treasures
410 E. Houghton Ave.
W. Branch, MI 48661 USA
T 517/345-3200
sales@michstar.com
www.michstar.com
> *A very large selection of dinosaurs with names.*

Rubber Stamp Store
1537 Pineview Ave.
Rathdrum, ID 83858 USA
T 208/687-5255
info@rubberstampstore.com
www.rubberstampstore.com/stamps/pid_047.html

Rubber Stamp Zone
Ghiradelli Square
900 North Point St. #122
San Francisco, CA 94109 USA
T 800/993-9119
F 415/929-1539
order@stampzone.com
www.stampzone.com

Stamp of Excellence
1105 Main St., PO Box 46
Canon City, CO 81215-0046 USA
T 719/275-8422
F 719/-275-7950
stampsox@stampofexcellence.com
www.stampofexellence.com

Stampa Barbara
19 W. Ortega St.
Santa Barbara, CA 93101 USA
T 805/462-4077
F 805/568-0330
shop@stampabarbara.com
www.stampabarbara.com

Stamparoo
263 Beacon St.
Andover, MA 01810 USA
sales@stamparoo.com
www.stamparoo.com
    *Item #1278J is a complimentary "Nice
    Work" Apatosaurus.*

The Stampin' Place
PO Box 43
Big Lake, MN 55309 USA
T 612/263-6646
F 800/634-3718
info@stampin.com
www.stampin.com/online/designs/93.htm

SAND BOXES

Rubbermaid Sales
1147 Akron Rd.

Dept. K
Wooster, OH 44691-6000 USA
T 330/264-7592
F 330/264-3312
www.rubbermaid.com:80/productdata/ltikes/t4
303.html
    *Item # 4303, a very large, flattened out
    purple dinosaur sandbox, complete with
    cover.*

SCREEN SAVERS

Ocean of America
333 W. Santa Clara St., Ste. 820
San Jose, CA 95113 USA
T 408/289-1200
F 408/289-1889
ocean@aimnet.com
www.oceanltd.com
    *Makers of Jurassic Park: The Screen
    Saver.*

Galt Technology
PMB 237
100 Powdermill Rd.
Acton, MA 01720 USA
T 978/436-3520
info@galtech.com
galttech.simplenet.com/ssheaven/00241.html
    *Offers Dinoshred: a raptor runs across
    your screen, clawing it to pieces!*

Moon Valley Software
1880 Santa Barbara St., Ste. D
San Luis Obispo, CA 93401 USA
T 805/781-3890
F 805/781-3898
info@moonvalley.com
www.moonvalley.com/themes/dinosaur/
    *A complete graphics systems for screen
    icons; the system also growls over
    program errors!*

Prehistory
5650 Westfield St.

Yorba Linda, CA 92887 USA
T 714/970-1128
F 714/970-2780
www.prehistory.com
> Sells a beautiful screen savers based on
> the artwork of Josef Moravec.

Sound Source Interactive
26115 Mureau Rd.
Calabasas, CA 91302-3126 USA
T 800/877-4778
F 818/878-0007
soundsource@ssiimail.com
www.soundsourceinteractive.com
> Sells the magnificent and must have
> _Lost World: Jurassic Park_
> _Entertainment Utility_ CD-ROM. This is
> packed with 25 video clips, 75 still
> images, sound bites, screen savers,
> music and icons. A limited edition item,
> so buy now for only $19.99!

Websites Plus
23191 La Cadena, Ste. 101
Laguna Hills, CA 92653 USA
T 949/951-2836
F 413/228-6217
infor@screensaver.com
www.screensaver.com
> The _Wayne Barlow Dinosaur Art_
> _Screen Saver_ features 20 beautiful
> illustrations for only $9.95.

SCULPTING

Hell Creek Creations
1208 Nashua Lane
Bartlett, IL 60103 USA
T 630/289-7018
> A source for the impressive booklet
> _Dinosaur Sculpting: A Complete_
> _Beginner's Guide_, by Allen and Diane
> Debus and Bob Morales; only $19.95.

United Sculptors of America
12 Ashwood Dr.
Scottsville, NY 14546 USA USA
T 716/889-4231
F 716/889-5059
usa1@sandsculpture.com
www.sandsculpture.com/dino1.htm
> Really cool photos of unbelievable sand
> sculpture!

SILHOUETTES

Red Rock Design Studio
Kingston, WA 98346-0129 USA
T 360/-638-2987
F 360/638-2909
www.tagonline.com/Ads/RedRock/
> Sells five very large skull designs; most
> impressive!

Wildnet Africa
PO Box 73528
Lynnwood Ridge
0040 SOUTH AFRICA
F 27-12-991-3851
basecamp@wildnetafrica.com
www.wildnetafrica.co.za/font.html
> Offers dinosaur images on a 3.5"
> diskette for R60.00.

SIGNS

Gridmark Signs
442 W. Sinto Ave.
Spokane, WA 99201 USA
T 509/327-2385
cgridley@gridmark.com
gridmark.com/graphics.htm
> Three simple line designs.

C & C Out of the Woods
2200 45th St.
Rock Island, IL 61201 USA
T 309/793-1606
SignMakers@signsofwood.com

www.signsofwood.com/gifts/animals.htm
A Triceratops door sign.

P. C. S. Pet Pro
16324 Swartz Canyon Rd.
Ramona, CA 92065 USA
T 760/788-3805
petpro@perpro.com
www.petpro.com/rubberstamps/dinosaur.html
Quaint "Dinosaur Crossing" signs.

SLEEPING BAGS

All the Right Stuff
4472 White Oak Circle
Kissimmee, FL 34746 USA
T 407/397-4037
F 407/397-4217
info@alltherightstuff.com
www.alltherightstuff.com/dinosau2.html
*A large 30 x 64" Stegosaurus sleeping
bag; matching pillow also available!*

SOAP

Chelsee Soap Company
119 Columbia St.
Brooklyn, NY 11251 USA
T 718/488-0789
F 718/488-5926
info@soaprize.com
endpointsecure.com/soaprize/
A Spinosaur encased in a clear gel bar!

North County Mercantile Online
Box 5368
West Lebanon, NH 03784 USA
T 603/795-2843
northcountry@northcountymercantile.com
www.northcountrymercantile.com/
Several nice dinosaur soap molds.

Sunrise Herb Company
4808 Dreams End Dr.
Louisville, KY 40241 USA

T 502/493-7132
F 502/493-3886
information@sunrise.com
www.sunriz.com
*Features green dino soap imported
from Germany.*

SOUNDS

Jonkey Enterprises
663 W. California Ave.
Glendale, CA 91203-1505 USA
T 818/247-6219
F 818/241-1333
chuck@jonkey.com
www.jonkey.com/music/Dinosaur
*A CD or cassette compilation of
simulated dinosaur noises by musician
Chuck Jonkey.*

SPECIAL EFFECTS

Wizard Studios International
14483 62nd St N.
Clearwater, FL 33760 USA
T 813/531-1231
F 813/535-4322
sales@wizardstudios.com
www.wizardstudios.com
*Offer a 14 x 40 foot painted backdrop,
replete with Brachiosaurs!*

SPORTS

Toronto Raptors
www.nba.com/raptors/
*Official online site of our favorite
hoopsters. Also includes information on
how to rent their mascot for special
occasions!*

STAMPS

Charlestown Stamps
PO Box 357

Charlestown, NSW 2290
AUSTRALIA
T/F 061-02-4943-8739
Charlsta@hunterlink.net.au
users.hunterlink.net.au/chasta/dinos.html
> *Maintains a large listing of stamps from down under and neighboring Asia.*

The Completely Philatelic Tyrannosaurus
members.aol.com/Tyrantrex/tyrant.html
> *Fran Adams provides a 16-page history of dinosaurs on stamps!*

Dino Fossil Club
geocities.com/Heartland/5997/dinofol.html
> *A club dedicated to dino stamps run by Jose Gregorio Contreras of Caracas, Venezuela.*

Dinosaurs on Stamps
RMarguls@cybercomm.net
www.cybercomm.net/~rmarguls/d-stamps.html
> *An exhaustive reference site maintained by stamp maven Robert Margulski.*

DOMFIL Catalogs Tematicos Internacionales
33 Doctor Puig St.
PO Box 271
E-08202 Sabadell, Barcelona SPAIN
T 00-34-93-725-12-11
F 00-34-93-715-51-98
Domfil@afinsa.com
www.domfil.com/reptiles.htm
> *Markets a 160 guide to dinosaur stamps available around the world.*

GEOU
Department of Earth Sciences
The Open University, Walton Hall
Milton Keyes MK7 6AA ENGLAND
T/F 44-0-1908-654871
geou@open.ac.uk
> *Sells the book Dinosaur Stamps of the World by S. Baldwin and B. Halstead.*

Greg Caron Stamps
PO Box 5125
Vacaville, CA 95696-5125 USA
T 707/448-1111
coolstamps@cool-stamps.com
www.coolstamps.com/dino.html
> *An absolutely huge web site with many foreign selections to choose from.*

Hans Tropicals
PO Box 32315
Baltimore, MD 21208 USA
> *Offers stamps from Guyana.*

Ilan's Tropicals
PO Box 371
Arnold, MD 21012 USA
T 800/-245-7597
F 410/573-0025
abirman@evols.com
www.stampcenter.comn/dino.html

Judaica Sales Registered
PO Box 55, St. martin
Laval Quebec
H7V 3P4 CANADA
T 514/687-0632
> *Isidore Baum has a wide variety of dinosaur and other prehistoric animals to choose from.*

Keimar Stamps
PO Box 2677
Garden Grove, CA 92842-2677 USA
T 714/539-4862
F 714/539-2515
Keimar1@ix.netcom.com
www.keimarstamps.com/

R. D. Miner
Box 865
Cochrane, Alberta
T0L 0W0 CANADA
T 403/932-2947
> *Sells an extensive assortment of stamps,*

souvenir sheets and covers.

Modlow-Arvai Stamps
RR 1, Box 138-G
Mt. Vision, NY 13810 USA
mastamps@aol.com
www.modlow-arvai.com/dinosaurs.htm
Impressive site hosted by William M.
Arvai; many foreign selections.

Mount Dana Stamp Company
21822 Third Ave.
Mount Dana, FL 32757-9620 USA
mdsc@mail.cde.com
www.cde.com
A huge variety of stamps from around
the world.

National Philatelic Centre
75 St. Ninian St.
Antigonish, Nova Scotia
B2G 2R8 CANADA
T 902/863-6550
F 902/863-6796
www.stampquest.com
Item #341128 is the "International
Dinosaur Collection."

New Zealand Post Stamps Centre
Private Bag 3001
Wanganui, NEW ZEALAND
enquiry@wgmsc.nzpost.co.nz
www.nzpost.co.nz/nzstamps

Paleontology on Stamps
35 Avenida Norte y calle las Orquideas No. 1C
Reparto Santa Fe, 001164 San Salvador
EL SALVADOR
mgalan@wenet.net
www.hooked.net/users/galan/paleo02.htm
A nice site run by Mario Galan.

Shades Stamp Shop, Ltd.
54 Shades Arcade, Cashel St.
Christchurch, NEW ZEALAND

T 64-3-3666390
F 64-3-3746001
steve@phonecards.co.nz
www.newzeal.com/steve/
Markets a 1993 Dinosaur souvenir
sheet.

Topic Stamps, Registered
1221 Fleury Est., CP 35046
Montreal, Quebec
H2C 3K4 CANADA
T 514/388-0157
Janice Dugas sells stamps and other
postal items relating to dinosaurs and
prehistoric life.

Western Mountain
51 E. Main St.
PO Box 323
Warner, NH 03278 USA
T 603/456-2141
wmsc@conknet.com
www.conknet.com/~wmsc/packets.htm
Item TP-2 is a world-wide dinosaur
stamp packet.

World of Dinosaur Stamps
Postmaster
241 N. 4th St.
Grand Junction, CO 81501-9991 USA
The source for the James Gurney
dinosaur set.

STATIONARY

Fossil Dust Greeting Cards
1042 15th Ave.
Longmont, CO 80501 USA

Party Invitations
2794 Stoney Creek Lane
Montrose, CO 8140 USA
T 970/240-0303
F 970/240-9646
www.party-invitations.com

Colorful invitation cards for
"dinosaurs" over 50!

STENCILS

Craft Industries
410 Wentworth St. N
Hamilton, Ontario
L8L 5W3 CANADA
T 800/661-0010
F 905/572-1164
www.craftco.com
A large selection, many designs.

Golden Creative Designs
PO Box 12
Timonium, MD 21094-0012 USA
Emilyandshelia@goddessdesign.com
goddessdesigns.com

Raun Harman Exports, Ltd.
D-262, Ashok Vihar-I
New Dehli 110 052 INDIA
T 91-11-7716673
F 91-11-7441130
raunharman@indiaenterprise.com
www.indiaenterprise.com/henna/dinasaur.htm
A large assortment of designs.

Tam Cam Creations
751 Main St. #204
Omaha, NE 68127 USA
T 402/593-8534
F 402/593-2622
tamcam@novia.net
promotionalproducts.com

Visio Solutions Library
211 Elliott Ave.
Seattle, WA 98121 USA
www.visio.com/solutions/index.html

STICKERS

DK Multimedia
95 Madison Ave.
New York, NY 10016 USA
T 212/213-4800
F 212/213-5202
www.dk.com
Where you can buy one of the biggest
and best-looking assortment of stickers
in the world!

Gen Hwa Publishing Company
2550 Lapiniere Blvd., Ste. 106
Broussard, Quebec
J4Z 2M2 CANADA
T 514/672-4356
F 514/923-8359
cbininfo@china-biz.com
www.china-biz.com
A large, colorful assortment.

California Pacific Designs
PO Box 2660
Alameda, CA 94501 USA
T 510/521-7914
F 510/865-0851
Four different and colorful sets,
including glow-in-the-dark!

Freely Creative
PO Box 1363
Stowe, VT 05672 USA
T 802/253-2011
F 802/253-8752
freelyc@websticker.com
www.websticker.com

Gentle Creations
1140 NW Lester Ave.
Corvallis, OR 97330 USA
T 800/682-3712
F 888/999-4568
stickers@peak.org
www.stickervilleUSA.com

Holograms & Lasers, International
PO Box 42159
Houston, TX 77242-2159 USA
T 281/498-0235
F 281/498-6337
shop@holoshop
www.holoshop.com
A large assortment of colorful designs.

King Shimmer Industry Co., Ltd.
6F, No. 3, 163 Lane Hsin Yi Road
Panchiao, Taipei TAIWAN
T 886-2-29646370
F 886-2-29511224
sticker@ms25.hinet.net
www.stickers.com/tw/

Palladium Interactive
899 Northgate, 4th Floor
San Rafael, CA 94903 USA
T 415/446-1700
F 415/446-1730
webstar@palladium.net
Sells the Dino Sticker Time CD-ROM.

U. S. Toy
Constructive Playthings
13201 Arrington Rd.
Grandview, MO 64030-2886 USA
T 800/255-6124
F 816/761-9295
ustoy@ustoyco.com
ustmagic.com/stickers.html
Offers several different puffy designs.

STUFFED DINOSAURS

A & A Plush
311 W. Artesia Bvd.
Compton, CA 90220 USA
T 800/227-5874
F 310/631-0965
A wonderful assortment of near-scale dinosaurs–cute, too!

Binkley Toys Gift Shop
163 Beach Rd.
Hamilton, Ontario
L8L 4A5 CANADA
T 800/304-6642
F 905/547-4245
info@binkley-toys.com
www.binkley-toys.com/custom.shtml
Featuring "Gobi," a custom-made, plush green dinosaur to be bought in quantity.

Nature Company
PO Box 6432
Florence, KY 41022-6432 USA
T 800/477-8828
F 606/342-5630
DCOL_Customer_service@discobery.com
www.natureco.com
Four excellent plush designs, very cute and yet very scale. That Struthiomimus is to die for!

U. S. Toys
Constructive Playthings
13201 Arrington Rd.
Grandview, MO 64030-2886 USA
T 800/255-6124
F 816/761-9295
ustoy@ustoyco.com
www.ustmagic.com
Numerous 12" plush toys, assorted colors and designs.

SWINGS

Kootenay Wood Specialties
PO Box 699
Fruitvale, British Columbia
V0G 1L0 CANADA
T 250/367-0065
F 250/367-0066
woodcrafters@netidea
www.netidea.com/woodcrafters/rob.htm
A Protoceratops-head swing design.

T-SHIRTS

Animation Shirts
PO Box 2536
Santa Cruz, CA 95063-2536 USA
ashirts@cruzio.com
www.3dshirts.com
Six stunning airbrush designs!

Sharon S. Cox
656 Honey Locust Way
Lexington, KY 40503 USA
T 606/277-9237
ssc@bestcreaturefeatures.com
www.bestcreaturefeatures.com
*Featuring several nice designs based
upon her original artwork.*

Davis Liquid Crystals, Inc.
15021 Wicks Blvd.
San Leandro, CA 94577 USA
T 510/351-2295
F 510/351-2328
*Maker of Solarzone Dino T-shirts that
change color when exposed to sunlight!*

Dennisaurs!
PO Box 74
Sallisaw, OK 74955 USA
members.tripod.com/~Dennisaurs
*Several humorous designs with dinos
surfing, rocking out, skating, etc.*

Dinamos
PO Box 80057
Appleby Postal Outlet
Burlington, Ontario
L7L 6B1 CANADA
T/F 905/681-9268
dinamos@netcom.ca
www.dinamos.com
Various shorts, caps, embroidery.

Dolphin Shirt Company
757 Buckley Rd.
San Luis Obispo, CA 93401 USA
T 800/377-3256, Ex 26
dolphin@dolphinshort.com
www.dolphinshirt.com/sotw.htm
*Three wonderful designs by Molly
Eckler; Tyrannosaurus, Triceratops,
Stegosaurus babies.*

Dream and Fantasy Creations
PO Box 10481
Costa Mesa, CA 92627 USA
T 714/641-3028
www.dreamandfantasy.com/pocpetdino.html
*A glow in the dark Coelophysis skelton
shirt!*

Fossil Films
PO Box 1123
Vista, CA 92085 USA

Fossils as Art
Box 980069
Houston, TX 77098 USA
T 281/250-2574
F 713/529-2447
fossils@fossils-as-art.com
www.fossils-as-art.com
*Several colorful designs, including
"Rock-a-saurus."*

G. C. Design
PO Box 2680
Coppell, TX 75019 USA
T 817/329-8250
F 817/840-5017
gcdesigns@cmpu.net
www.gcdesigns.com
*Markets the "Prehistoric Passions" line
of shirts to promote good behavior in
children.*

Geographics
7 Commerce Dr.
Eureka Springs, AK 72632 USA
T 501/253-6830

F 800/243-6830
geograph@ipa.net
www.estc.net/t-shirt/
*Excellent assortment of pen and ink
drawings, including my favorite,
"Adios, Amoeba!"*

Harborside Graphics
PO Box 346
4 Airport Rd.
Belfast, ME 04915 USA
info@harborsidegraphics.com
www.harborsidegraphics.com
Some dinosaur sportswear.

Darcy Howard
16001 Vimey Woods Road
Mablevale, AR 72103-4012 USA
dhoward954@aol.com
members.aol.com/dhoward954/arkdino.gif

Ink Mark Exotic Birds
PO Box 278
Cary, IL 60013 USA
T 847/854-1172
inkmark@owc.net
www.inkmarkbirds.net/dinosaur.htm
*Four wonderfully colorful designs,
including a great-looking Velociraptor!*

Marc 'et Novel-Tees
37570 Colorado Ave.
Avon, OH 44011 USA
T 440/934-6132
marcet@marcet.com
www.marcet.com/cgi-bin/T-shirts.pl
A colorful stock of species and scenes.

Mesozoic World
PO Box 412
Annapolis, MD 21402-2142 USA
T 410/721-7772
F 410/643-9496

Paleoartisans
255 Harper Farm Lane
Rocky Mount, SC 27801 USA
T 252/985-2877
paleoartisans@hotmail.com
browser.to/paleoartisans
*Several black and white dinosaur,
pterosaur, and marine reptile skeleton
designs; highly accurate.*

Paleo Park
ronbuckley@fuse.net
home.fuse.net/paleopark/
*Ron Buckley sells a colorful
Gorgosaurus design T-shirt.*

Pocket Pets
700 Haverhill Crt.
Raleigh, NC 27609 USA
T 919/981-5816
F 919/878-6193
pocketpets@worldnet.att.net
www.pocket-pets.com/shadows.htm
*A handful of wonderful color head
studies and species scenes.*

The Shirt People
313 N 95th, Ste. 137
Milwaukee, WI 53226 USA
T 414/454-0109
fantasy@execpc.com
www.execpc.com/~fantasy/dinosaurs.html
*Several excellent designs by Todd
Anthony; learn the other reason why
dinosaurs became extinct!*

Solar Magic
5417 Aurora Ave., Ste. 144
Des Moines, IA 50310 USA
T 515/276-5105
ray@solarmagic.com
www.solarmagic.com/t-shirt_kids_1.htm
*Charming black and white dino scene
explodes into color once exposes to
sunlight!*

Strawberry Mountain
PO Box 54
Canyon City, OR 97820 USA
T 541/575-0012
F 541/575-1068
smg@orednet.org
www.orednet.org/~smg/
Dino skeleton T-shirts.

Texas Memorial Museum Store
University of Texas
2400 Trinity St.
Austin, TX 78705 USA
T 512/232-4278
tmmshop@uts.ccu-texas.edu
web3.cc.utexas.edu/depts/tmm/store/kids.html
Item #YTTR is an awesome
Tyrannosaurus T-shirt!

Tour Merchandise
PO Box 210893
Nashville, TN 37221 USA
donna@tourmerchandise.com
www.tourmerchandise.com/
A colorful series of dino shirts.

United Design Corporation
PO Box 1200
Noble, OK 73068 USA
T 800/727-4883

Wilderness Furnishings
5420 Manor Dr.
Sugarland, TX 77479 USA
T 281/403-9013
F 281/261-9184
www.wildfur.com/T-shirts/liberty.html
"Dinosauria" design for children.

Wyoming Dinosaur Center Store
110 Carter Ranch Rd.
Thermopolis, WY 82443 USA
orders@wyodino.org
www.wyodino.org/giftshop.html
An extensive and humorous "Bad to the

Bone" series of dino T-shirts!

TATTOOS

J. Rousek Toy Company
PO Box 1759
Bishop, CA 93515 USA
T 800/423-5198
F 800/873-1758
jrousek@jrousek.com
www.jrousek.com
Item #173 is a removable tattoo set.

THREE-DIMENSIONAL

Almost Human
8445 Warner Dr.
Culver City, CA 90232 USA
T 310/838-6993
almosthuman@earthlink.net
almosthuman.net/double3dstuff.html
A good source for 3D digital effects
modeled in Lightwave.

3-D Dinosaur
www.3dviewmax.com/page61.htm
A plug for #-D Viewmax, which can
examine a set of 16 different color
stereographs.

TOPIARY

Hammacher & Schlemmer
9180 Le Saint Dr.
Fairfield, OH 45014-5475 USA
T 212/421-9000
www.hammacher.com
A 49" Brachiosaur or Tyrannosaur
frame.

Tavenier Topiary
Rt. 2, Box 22
Davis, CA 95616 USA
tavenier@mother.com
A sixteen-foot high Velociraptor frame!

Topiary, Inc.
4520 Watrous Ave.
Tampa, FL 33629 USA
T 813/286-8626
F 813/282-9345
mbgreiwe@topiaryinc.com
topiaryinc.com
A source for two 12" Triceratops and Apatosaurus frames.

Topiary Joe
PO Box 321
Hobe Sound, FL 33455-0321 USA
T 561/230-0586
F 561/287-8750
topiaryj@hotmail.com
www.topiaryjoe.com
The source of really HUGE topiary frames, made to order!

Yardzoo.com
2549 E. Cameron Ave.
W. Covina, CA 91791 USA
Large Apatosaurus and Tyrannosaurus frames.

TOYS

Abacus Toys, Inc.
PO Box 28479
Remuera, Auckland NEW ZEALAND

Accents Plus
4302 13th Ave.
Brooklyn, NY 11219 USA
T/F 718/438-6244

Akita International
1205 College Ave.
Alameda, CA 94501 USA
www.greatmallofchina.com/import/akita/game.htm

All the Right Stuff
4472 White Oak Circle

Kissimmee, FL 34746 USA
T 407/397-4037
F 407/397-4217
info@alltherightstuff.com
www.alltherightstuff.com
A wide assortment of toys for all occasions: dino backpacks, sleeping bags, puzzles, canned dinosaurs, coins, mugs, wood kits, and stuffed dinosaurs.

Allenby's Wonderful World of Myth
4185 W. Lake Mary Blvd., Ste. 186
Lake Mary, FL 32746 USA
help@legendsandmyths.com
www.legendsandmyths.com/alby1/kidstuff.htm
Another well-stocked source.

AMC Sales
3241 Winpark Dr.
Minneapolis, MN 55427 USA
T 800/262-0332
F 612/545-0480
amcsaleinc@aol.com
members.aol.com/amcsaleinc/dino.htm
Big variety of dino toys, magnets, stickers, slates, tatoos, pencils, erasers, etc.

Baly Joy Toys
24811 Clover Rd.
Willits, CA 95490 USA
T 707/459-5006
joy@pacific.net
www.pacific.net/~joy/bjt/dinosaur.html
Home of "Dot Dot Dinosaur", the stuffed Stegosaurus.

Brainstorms
8221 Kimball
Skokie, IL 60076 USA
T 800/231-6000

Cadaco, Inc.
4300 W. 47 th St.
Chicago, IL 60632 USA

T 773/927-1500
F 773/927-3937
cadacos@aol.com
www.cadaco.com
> Makers of "Dinosaur Chalk eggs" with
> a tiny dino inside!

Child Dreams
13340 Ventura Blvd.
Sherman Oaks, CA 91423 USA
T 888/869-4438
F 818/995-4484
child@childdreams.com
www.childdreams.com
> The "Dino Fun Kids-Krate," stuffed
> with neat puppets, toys, and other stuff.

Chloe's Cottage
PO Box 6548-109
Orange, CA 92863-6548 USA
T/F 714/771-4135
omschloe@gowebway.com
www.chloescottage.com/dinosaur.htm
> A very nice Dino Theme Gift Basket"
> for very young children.

Creative Imaginations, Inc.
10879-B Porta Dr.
Los Alamitos, CA 90720 USA
T 714/995-2266

Dinamos
Box 80057
Burlington, Ontario
L7L 3V2 CANADA
T 905/681-9268
> Roger Deslauriers sells a complete line
> of quality dinosaur toys plus less
> expensive items.

Dr. Bug's Adventure Club
PO Box 1661
Battle Creek, MI 49016-1661 USA
T 616/963-3336
drbug@drbug.com

www.drbug.com
> A nice "Dinosaur Dig-Up" kit for
> teaching young children the principles
> of paleontology!

Dragons Are Too Seldom, Inc.
1501 Pine Heights
Rapid City, SD 57709-8046 USA
T 605/343-8200
F 605/343-8226
> Really colorful "Dinosaur Tub
> Buddies" to wash with!

Dragonfly Toys
291 Yale Ave.
Winnipeg, Manitoba
R3M 0L4 CANADA
T 203/453-2222
F 204/453-2320
sales@dftoys.com
www.dragonflytoys.com
> Home of "Krinkles Dinosaur Land Set"
> of plastic blocks and dinos.

Educational Insights
Hodges & Reed Services
PO Box 23504
Stanley, KS 66283 USA
T 887/888-1604
webmaster@hrweb.com
www.ierc.com
> The search function reveals a huge
> variety of toys and games for students,
> K-12.

Educational Toys, Inc.
PO Box 630685
Miami, FL 33163 USA
T 800/554-5414, Ex. 109

Elements of Nature
45 Forks Market Rd.
Winnipeg, Manitoba
R3C 4T6 CANADA
T 204/957-0636

bongo@elementsofnature.com
www.elementsofnature.com

Enchanted Learning.com
2 Alpha
PO Box 1807
Bellvue, WA 98009-1807 USA
T 425/746-4140
F 425/746-4252
info@2alpha.com
https://www.2alpha.com/store/
*A good source for a wide selection of
puppets, games, and other toys.*

Lewis Galoob Toys
500 Forbes Blvd.
S. San Francisco, CA 94080 USA
T 415/952-1678
F 415/583-4996
info-galoob@galoob.com
www.galoob.com
*An impressive collection of dinosaur
toys and figures.*

Gift Basket Express
1055 W. College Ave. #162
Santa Rosa, CA 95401 USA
T 800/649-7181
F 717/581-1779
basketeers@giftbasketexpress.com
www.giftbasketexpress.com/dinosaurs.html
*Item W28 is "Dinosaur Attack!, a big
gift basket full of figures, puzzles,
stickers, and puppets.*

How to Get A Head Without Hunting
15151 Old Ranch Road
Los Gatos, CA 95033 USA
T 408/357-2501
F 408/357-2502
merikay@animalhead.com
www.animalhead.com/dinosaur.html
*Sells two surrealistic Triceratops head
designs made from fabric!*

International Playthings
120 Riverside Rd.
Riverside, NJ 07437 USA

Just A Lil' Toy Store
17031 Cedar Ave.
Sonoma, CA 95476 USA
nature@microwles.com
www.microweb.com/nature/vendor.html
A good source for Safari figures.

Lifestyle Fascination
1935 Swarthmore Ave.
Lakewood, NJ 08701-8123 USA
T 800/669-0987
F 732/364-4448
sales@lifestylefascination.com
www.lifestylefascination.com
*Sells a small motion-detection dinosaur
that growls when activated.*

Magic Crystal Dino
7251 Garden Grove Blvd., Ste E
Garden Grove, CA 92841 USA
T 800/792-3373
F 714/892-3373
info@magic-garden.com
magic-garden.com
*Maker of Magic Crystal Dinos, which
grow for several months.*

National Wildlife Federation
1400 16th St NW
Washington, DC 20036-2266 USA
T 800/432-6564

Natural Curiosity
2595 W 9545 South
South Jordan, UT 84095 USA
questions@naturalcuriosity.com
www.naturalcuriosity.com/index.html
*A big selection of dinosaur models,
toys.*

Natural Tracks
49 Forest Ave.
Paramus, NJ 07652 USA
T 201/712-0209
sales@naturaltracks.com
www.naturaltracks.com
Many toys, puzzles, posters, and kits.

Novar Cottage
PO Box 3009
Dryden, Ontario
P8N 2Y9 CANADA
T 897/223-2381
F 807/-223-2907
service@novarcottage.com
www.novarcottage.com

One Small Step
5501 SE Beach Blvd.
Jacksonville, FL 32207 USA
T 904/396-1784
F 909/396-2455
cooltoys@onesmallstep.com
www.onesmallstep.com

Oriental Trading Company
PO Box 2308
Omaha, NE 68103-2308 USA
T 800/228-2269
www.oriental.com
A large assortment of plastic toys, stickers, finger puppets, and erasers.

Peacock Feather
1096 Great Plain Ave.
Needham, MA 12492 USA
T 877/751-4879
PeacockF@aol.com
childrensgiftguru.com/dino%20demons.htm
Excellent source for kites, pencils, soap, transfers, clocks, and puppets.

Rockville Creative Learning
785 F Rockville Pike, Ste. 515
Rockville, MD 20852 USA

T 301/294-9729
info@sciencekits.com
www.books4kids.com

Salix
60 E. 600 South
Salt Lake City, UT 84111 USA
T 801/531-800
Very fine dinosaur play sand.

Shanghai Aviation Import & Export
Corporation, Division 5
Rm 103, No. 18
Free Apartment, No. 166 Qixin Rd.
Shanghai, CHINA
T 86-21-647-88821
F 86-21-64790371
ma@sonicnet.cn
www.sd-info.com/
Sells cute and colorful dinosaur bricks!

Full Moon Imports
2311 Chand Rd.
Joppa, MD 21085 USA
T 301/676-3207
Many imported dinosaur toys.

SMT-Logic
970 Greybrooke Dr.
Woodstock, GA 30189 USA
The "Dino-lite" for toddlers.

Someday Isle
58 Wakelee Rd.
East Dover, VT 05341 USA
T 802/254-6201
F 802/254-9568
sales@somedayisle.com
www.somedayisle.com
Nice selection of figurines and "Feltkids" dino cutouts.

Spree.Com Corporation
1155 Phoenix Pike, Ste. 103
West Chester, PA 19380 USA

T 888/887-7733
www.spree.com/gifts
*Sell the "Dinosaur Garden" indoor
activity kit.*

Teachers Treasure Trove
914 E. Gail Dr.
Gilbert, AZ 85296 USA
T 877/-TT-TROVE
F 602/857-8435
thetrove@inficad.com
www.teachingsupplies.com/main_site.html
*A huge selection of diverse items-I
mean huge--check this out!*

Terry's Gift World
PO Box 1113
Youngstown, OH 44511 USA
catalog@terrysgiftworld.com
www.terrysgiftworld.com

Toy Connection
312 Bayview Ave.
Inwood, NY 11096 USA
T 516/371-9206
F 888/562-TOYS
sales@toyconnection.com
www.toyconnection.com/index.htm
*Good for finger puppets, glow in the
dark dinos, and dino head rings.*

Transonics
3209 W 9th St.
Lawrence, KS 66049 USA
T 785/841-3089
F 785/841-0434
kits@xtronics.com
www.xtronics.com/kits/
*A plastic, walking Apatosaurus kit,
#MK-103.*

Whyte's Web Ware
15 Capella Ct., Unit 124
Nepean, Ontario
K2E 7K1 CANADA

T 613/723-5687
sales@jgwhyte.com
www.jgwhyte.com/children.htm
*Various dinosaur toys for young
children.*

TRACKS

Dino Trax, Inc.
107 Ranch Road, 620 South #36D
Austin, TX 78734 USA
T 800/214/7271
F 512/266-8007
Dinotrax@compuserve.com

Dinocast
PO Box 120067
East Haven, CT 06512 USA

Gaston Design
1943 K Road
Fruita, CO 81521 USA
T 970/858-4785
gastondesign@compuserve.com

Jurassic Casts
337 N. Green
Wichita, KS 67212 USA
T 316/264-4991
jurisict@southwind.net
www.dinosaurtracks.com

Taylor Studios
1320 Harmon Dr.
Rantoul, IL 61866 USA
T 217/893-4874
F 217/893-1998
taylor@shout.net
www.taylorstudios.com

TRAVEL BAGS

J. P. Productions
RR 2, Box 426
New Martinsville, WV 26155-9453 USA

T 304/337-9019
F 304/337-8713
www.jpproductions.com/html/travelbags.html
*Item #TBDL DinoLand travelbag
ensures a fun trip for your child!*

TRAVELING ACTS

Debbie's Dancing Dinosaur
21196 Valle San Juan
Salinas, CA 93907 USA
T 831/442-3002
*More proof you can walk softly and
carry a big schtick...*

Dino Discovery
Stone Enterprises
1024 Country Rd. #368
Taylor, MO 63471 USA
T 800/723-9571
www.dinodiscovery.com/dinodis.html

Dinoman!
Ice Fire Performance Troop
PO Box 13
Warren, VT 05674 USA
T 800/392-8061
icefire@madriver.com
www.icefire.net
*A national touring company with
educational overtones.*

Dinosaur Simulator
511 King St. W, Ste. 300
Toronto, Ontario M5V 2Z4 CANADA
T 416/ 597-1585
F 416/597-0350
simex@simex.ca
www.simex.ca/dinosim/dinosim.htm
*A state of the art, full sensory traveling
exhibit with hyper-realistic dinosaurs!*

Dr. Fossil's Dinosaur Show
53480 Bridal Falls Road
Rosedale, British Columbia

V0X 1X0 CANADA
T 604/794-7410
F 604/794-3161
dino@uniserve.com

Jurassic Journey
Burning Tree Casting Company
4600 Ridgely Tract Rd.
Newark, OH 43056 USA
T 888/373-4667
F 740/522-5781
www.dinodiscovery.com
*A three-day extravaganza with over 50
dinosaurs!*

VIDEO

AIMS Multimedia
9710 De Soto Ave.
Chatsworth, CA 91311-4409 USA
T 818/773-4300
Here lurks Dinosaurs: Terrible Lizards
(10 min), and A Magical Field Trip to a
Dinosaur Museum *(15 min).*

AGC/United Learning
6633 W. Howard St.
Niles, IL 60714-0718 USA
T 847/647-0600
F 847/647-0918
They sell the juvenile Exploring
Dinosaurs *(18 min) and* Fossil Life: An
Introduction *(19 min).*

Agency for Instructional Technology
1800 N. Stonelake Dr., Box A
Bloomington, IN 47401-0120 USA
T 812/339-2203
F 812/333-4218
Featuring Dinosaurs *(14 min), a how-
to-draw instructional film, the career-
oriented* Paleontologist *(15 min), and*
Raptors *(5 min).*

T 812/339-2203
F 812/333-4218
  Featuring Dinosaurs (14 min), a how-to-draw instructional film, the career-oriented Paleontologist (15 min), and Raptors (5 min).

Ambrose Video Publishing, Inc.
28 W. 44th St., Ste. 2100
New York, NY 10036 USA
T 212/768-7373
F 212/768-9282
  Sells one of the biggest selections on the market: the multi-episode Paleo World series, (40 min ea).

American Portrait Films
Grace Communications
PO Box 19266
Cleveland, OH 44119-1545 USA
  Here you'll find the religious-inspired Dinosaurs & the Bible (120 min), and Fossil Evidence of Creation (27 min)

Arts & Entertainment Network
235 E 45th St.
New York, NY 10017 USA
T 212/210-1319
F 212/685-2625
  They market the lavish, four part series Dinosaurs!, hosted by Walter Cronkite; a striking visual encyclopedia.

Barr Media Group
100 Wilshire Blvd., Flr. 3
Santa Monica, CA 90401-1121 USA
T 626/338-7878
  Offers Fossils! Fossils! (18 min) For young students.

Bridgestone Multimedia Group
300 N. McKenny Ave.
Chandler, AZ 85226-2618 USA
T 602/940-5777

F 602/950-8924
  Offers the Creationist film Death of the Dinosaur (30 min).

CLEARVUE/eav, Inc.
6465 N. Avondale Ave.
Chicago, IL 60631-2788 USA
T 773/775-2788
F 773/775-9855
  Where to buy Digging Dinosaurs (12 min) and Dinosaurs & Other Prehistoric Animals (32 min) for children.

Cleval Films, Ltd.
2532 Lincoln Blvd., Ste. 155
Marina Del Rey, CA 90291 USA
T 310/821-9233
F 310/306-0079
  Distributors of America's Dinosaur Parks (30 min), a guided tour of sites around the country, Dinosaur Digs: A Fossil Finders Tour (30 min), and Dinosaurs, Next Exit (48 min).

Concord Video
7506 N. Broadway Extension, Ste. 505
Oklahoma City, OK 73116 USA
T 405/840-6031
F 405/848-3960
  Buy Dinosaurs & Strange Creatures (33 min) here.

Coronet, The Multimedia Company
2349 Chaffee Rd.
St. Louis, MO 63346 USA
  They market An Alphabet of Dinosaurs (13 minutes), describing each species, The Dinosaur Who Wondered Who He Was (13 min), Fossils: From Site to Museum (11 min), Prehistoric Times (10 min), What's the Biggest Living Thing (11 min) and How Big Were Dinosaurs? (11 min).

Creation Research Society
PO Box 8263
St. Joseph, MO 64508-8263 USA
CRSnetwork@aol.com
creationresearch.org/video_list.html
> *Where to buy Fossil Evidence of*
> *Creation: The Foot Steps of Leviathan.*

DeBeck Educational Video
Box 33738
Vancouver, British Columbia
V6J 4L6 CANADA
T 604/739-7696
F 604/739-7609
debeck@vanbc.com
> *Dinosaurs! is a VHS excursion into*
> *exhibits at the Tyrrell Museum.*

Discovery Channel Online Service
PO Box 6448
Florence, KY 41022-6448 USA
T 800/889-9950
DCOL_customer_service@discovery.com
www.discovery.com
> *Where to buy the lavishly-produced*
> *Ultimate Guide to T. rex, Beyond T. rex,*
> *and Bonehead Detectives of the*
> *Paleoworld; also When Dinosaurs*
> *Ruled & Creatures of the Skies (90 min)*
> *They may also soon market the fantastic*
> *British series Walking with Dinosaurs,*
> *soon.*

Disney Educational Production
105 Terry Dr., Ste. 120
Newtown, PA 18940 USA
T 800/295-5010
> *Buy the science-oriented Dinosaurs:*
> *Reptiles (52 min); Dinosaurs: Those*
> *Big Boneheads! (50 min) and*
> *Dinosaurs (26 min) with Bill Nye, The*
> *Mating Dance (45 min), Mighty*
> *Megalosaurus (45 min), Power Erupts:*
> *A New Leaf (45 min).*

DK Multimedia
95 Madison Ave.
New York, NY 10016 USA
T 212/213-4300
F 212/213-5202
www.dk.com/us/
> *Home of the Eyewitness Dinosaur video*
> *for young children (35 min), and*
> *Prehistoric Animals (30 min).*

Educational Record Ctr.
3233 Burnt Mill Dr., Ste. 100
Wilmington, NC 28403-1637 USA
T 800/438-1637
F 919/343-0311
> *A juvenile film, Dinosaurs (30 min)*
> *about an imaginative trip to*
> *dinosaurland, Dinosaurs (50 min), an*
> *educational film narrated by Dudley*
> *Moore, and How to Build a Dinosaur!*
> *(30 min) about skeletons.*

Encyclopaedia Britannica Educational Corp.
310 S. Michigan Ave.
Chicago, IL 60604-4293 USA
T 312/347-7000
F 312/347-7966
> *Sells the technically impressive*
> *Dinosaurs & Asteroids (14 min),*
> *Fossils: Exploring the Past (16 min),*
> *and The Great Dinosaur Discovery (23*
> *min).*

Family Entertainment
6100 Colwell Blvd.
Irving, TX 75039 USA
T 972/402-7100
> *Sells the Golden Books inspired film*
> *Dinosaurs!*

Film Ideas, Inc.
308 N. Wolf Rd.
Wheeling, IL 60090 USA
T 847/419-0255
F 847/480-7496

Here you'll find Fossils: Uncovering Clues to the Past (15 min), More About Dinosaurs (9 min), and Story of Dinosaurs (9 min)

Films for Christ
1044 N. Gilbert Rd.
Gilbert, AZ 85234-3304 USA
T 800/332-2261
Sells the religion-oriented The Fossil Record (32 min).

Films for the Humanities & Sciences
Box 2053
Princeton, NJ 98543-2053 USA
T 609/275-1400
F 609/275-3767
Here are the scientific films Fossils: Plants and Tetrapods (20 min) and Fossils: Reptiles and Mammals (20 min).

GoodTimes Video/Entertainment
16 E. 40th St.
New York, NY 10016 USA
T 212/951-3000
F 212/779-7885
Featuring the abbreviated Dinosaurs! (100 min), with Walter Cronkite, and The Great Dinosaur Bone Hunt (96 min).

GPN
PO Box 80669
Lincoln, NE 68501 USA
T 402/472-2007
F 402/472-4076
Where to buy the Reading Rainbow episode Digging Up Dinosaurs (30 min), Dinosaurs: From Toe Bone to Complete Skeleton (30 min), Dinosaurs (30 min), a science film for young children.

Image Entertainment
9333 Oso Ave.
Chatsworth, CA 91311 USA
T 818/407-9100
F 818/407-9111
Here is the tape Dinosaurs: Fantastic Creatures that Ruled the Earth (60 min).

Instructional Video
727 O St.
Lincoln, NE 68508-1323 USA
T 402/475-6570
F 402/475-6500
Here you'll find the instructional video Dinosaurs, with visits to Dinosaur National Monument and the Dinosaur Museum in Vernal, Utah.

Jack Van Impe Ministries
PO Box 7004
Troy, MI 48007-7004 USA
T 248/852-5225
jvimi@jvim.com
www.jvim.com/catalog/idotdv.html
Offers The Death of the Dinosaur, another Creationist perspective.

Kimbo Educational
PO Box 477
Long Branch, NJ 07740 USA
T 732/229-4949
F 732/870-3340
Home of The Busassaurus (30 min), a part of the magic School Bus Series, and Prehistoric Animals and Reptiles (30 min).

Library Video Co.
PO Box 850
Wynnewood, PA 19096 USA
T 610/645-400
F 610/645-4050
A large assortment including Beyond Jurassic (55 min), Buried in Ash (60

min), _Digging for Dinosaurs: A Musical Adventure_ (35 min), _Dinosaurs of the Gobi_ (60 min), _Dinosaur!_ (60 min) hosted by Christopher Reeve, _Dinosaur_ narrated by Martin Sheen, _Dinosaur Hunters_ (60 min), The 5-volume _Dinosaur Series_ hosted by Gary own (150 min), _Dinosaurs_ (67 min), produced by the Smithsonian, the Great Minds of Science episode _Dinosaurs_ (40 min), _Dinosaurs & Prehistoric Mammals_ (30 min), _EPIC: Days of the Dinosaurs_ (70 min) directed by John Huston, _Invasion of the Robot Dinosaurs_ with Gary Owens (30 min), the four volume _Learn About Dinosaurs_ (128 min), _Return of the Dinosaurs_ (20 min) with Jack Hanna, _Skeletons in the Sand_ (60 min) with Bill Kurtis, _T-Rex: "The Real World,"_ (35 min), and _What Ever happened to the Dinosaurs_ (30 min) with Gary Owens.

Live Home Video
PO Box 10124
Van Nuys, CA 91419-0124 USA
T 800/326-1977
F 818/908-0320
> Distributors of _The Infinite Voyage: The Great Dinosaur Hunt_ (60 min) with Stephen Jay Gould.

Lucerne Media
37 Ground Pine Rd.
Morris Plains, NJ 07950 USA
T 800/341-2293
F 973/538-0855
Lm@lucernemedia.com
www.lucernemedia.com
> Sells _Mass Extinctions: The Dinosaurs Disappear_, and _Dinosaur_ (60 min).

Master Books
PO Box 727
Green Forest, AR 72638-0727 USA

T 870/438-5288
F 870/438-5120
> Offers the religion-based _Fossils & The Flood_ and _What Really Happened to the Dinosaurs_ with Ken Ham.

Mazon Productions
PO Box 2427
Northbrook, IL 60065-2427 USA
> Distributes _I Dig Fossils_ for younger viewers.

Mazzarella Productions
88 Valley St., PO Box 1831
Bristol, CT 06011 USA
T 800/583-1988
> They sell the film _Digging for Dinosaurs_ (35 min), a children's show.

National Geographic Society
1145 17th St. NW
Washington, DC 20036-4688 USA
T 800/647-5463
www.ngstore.com
> Four excellent titles; _Dinosaurs and Other Creature Features_ (45 min), _Asteroids: Deadly Impact_ (59 min), _Fossils: Clues to the Past_ (23 min), and _Dinosaurs: Then and Now_ (25 min).

New Dimension Media, Inc.
611 E. State St.
Jacksonville, IL 62650 USA
T 217/243-4567
F 217/479-0060
> They sell _Dinosaur Discoveries_ (15 min).

PBS Video
1320 Braddock Place
Alexandria, VA 22314-1698 USA
T 703/739-5380
F 703/739-8938
www.pbs.org/
> Also sells many NOVA titles.

Paramount Home Video
5555 Melrose Ave.
Hollywood, CA 90038-3197 USA
T 213/956-8090
F 213/862-1100
> The source for _The Adventures of Corduroy: The Dinosaur Egg_ (25 min), about a field trip to a natural history museum.

Phoenix/BFA Films & Video
2349 Chaffee Dr.
St. Louis, MO 63146 USA
T 314/569-0211
F 314/569-2834
> Purchase _Dinosaurs: The Age of Reptiles_ (17 min) for young adults; an oldie but goodie, _The Dinosaur Age_ (15 min-1958!), _Dinosaurs: A First Film_ (10 min), _Fossils are Interesting_ (11 min), and Australian _Muttaburrasaurus: The Gondwana Dinosaur_ (26 min)

Public Media, Inc.
4411 N. Ravenswood Ave., 3rd Flr.
Chicago, IL 60640-5802 USA
T 773/878-2600
F 773/878-8648
> See Eleanor Kish sculpting in _Dinosaurs: Remains to Be Seen_ (22 min), and _The New Explorers: Skeletons in the Sand_ (60 min)

Pyramid Media
PO Box 1048
Santa Monica, CA 90406 USA
T 301/828-7577
F 301/453-9083
> The place for _Dinosaur_ (14 min), wherein a classroom report comes to life!

Rainbow Educational Media, Inc.
4540 Preslyn Dr.

Raleigh, NC 27616-3177 USA
T 919/954-7550
F 919/954-7554
> For young students there is _Fossils: Windows into the Past_ (26 min), and _Where Did They Go? A Dinosaur Update_ (15 min).

Rhino Home Video
10635 Santa Monica Blvd.
Los Angeles, CA 90025-4900 USA
T 310/474-6573
F 310/441-6573
> See Doug McClure in his latest bomb, the _Hollywood Dinosaur Chronicles_ (42 min).

R. E. D. Productions
PO Box 17253
Beverly Hills, CA 90209 USA
T 310/276-3964
redprods@earthlink.net
www.redprods.com/dtae.html
> Robert Dunlap sells the VHS tape _Dinosaur: The Arctic Expedition_.

SRA/McGraw-Hill
250 Old Wilson Bldg., Ste. 310
Worthington, OH 43085 USA
T 614/438-6600
F 614/428-6633
> The film _Dinosaurs to the Rescue_ (16 min) offers practical advice to environmental problems.

SVE & Churchill Media
6677 N. Northwest Hwy
Chicago, IL 60631-1304 USA
T 773/775-1900
F 773/775-5091
> Source for the juvenile _Box Investigates Dinosaurs_ (20 min).

Spoken Arts, Inc.
8 Lawn Ave.

New Rochelle, NY 10801-4206 USA
> *The juvenile films Plesiosaurus (10 min), and Prehistoric Beasts (46 min), Pteranodon (12 min).*

Stevens, Gareth, Inc.
River Ctr. Bldg.
1555 N. River Center Dr., Ste. 201
Milwaukee, WI 53213 USA
T 414/225-0333
F 414/225-0377
> *They offer Did Comets Kill the Dinosaurs?*

Superior Home Video
22159 N. Pepper Rd., No. 9
Barrington, IL 60010 USA
T 847/381-0909
F 847/381-1178
> *Offers the juvenile Dinosaurs (30 min) as part of the Polka-Dot Series.*

Twin Tower Enterprises
1888 Century Park E, No. 1500
Los Angeles, CA 90067-1719 USA
T 310/659-9644
> *Where to buy the three-part series Dinos! Dinos! Dinos!*

Universal Studios Video, Inc.
70 Universal City Plaza, No. 435
Universal City, CA 91608 USA
T 818/777-4300
F 818/733-0226
> *Distributes a film called The Real Jurassic Park.*

Wehman Video
2366 Eastlake Ave. E, Ste. 312
Seattle, WA 98102 USA
T 800/717-1158
F 206/726-0273
wehmanvid@aol.com
> *The source for Dino Digs and America's Dinosaur Parks.*

WGBH
PO Box 2284
South Burlington, VT 05407-2284 USA
T 800/255-9424
F 800/864-9846
www.wgbh.org
> *The excellent NOVA series episodes T. rex Exposed (60 min), The Curse of T. rex (60 min), and The Case of the Flying Dinosaur (60 min).*

Wishing Well Video Distributing Co.
PO Box 7040
Santa Rosa, CA 95407 USA
T 707/525-9355
F 707/ 542-3724
> *They distribute Dinosaurs: Flesh on the Bones (60 min).*

VITAMINS

T. Hartman
RD #3, Box 160 A-1
Shelocta, PA 15774-1155 USA
T 877/435-8296
F 847/598-9043
www.angelfire.com/biz2/tjhearts/happykids.html
> *Dino Kids offers a complete line of vitamins, Dinoshakes, bath and body lotions.*

Herbalife
22422 N. 100th St.
Westfield, IL 62474 USA
T 888/275-5259
F 209/882-8282
www.herbalife.com/products/nutritional/childrens_vitamins.html
> *Buy a bottle of Dinomins for the kiddies!*

Nature's Sunshine
PO Box 464
Altoona, IA 50009 USA

T 888/300-6242
www.naturessunshine.com/
Offers the complete Herbasaurs line of products.

WOODEN TOYS

Action Products
344 Cypress Rd.
Ocala, FL 34472 USA
T 352/687-2202
rkaplan@apii.com
www.apii.com
Offers a complete line of 11 small but highly detailed skeletons.

Artisangifts.com
555 Stanford Ave.
Palo Alto, CA 94306 USA
T 650/855-9560
F 650/855-9560
feedback@artisangifts.com
www.artisangifts.com/artisangifts/dewa-06.html
Colorful Stegosaurus book ends; cleft in half!

Awards Unlimited
615 Main St.
Niagara Falls, NY 14302-2568 USA
T 905/339-3848
F 905/339-3037
sales@aunlimited.com
www.aunlimit.com
Carries the complete line of Wood Craft dinosaur skeletons, Tyrannosaur, Apatosaur, Triceratops, Plesiosaur, and Stegosaur.

B. C. Bonz, Inc.
PO Box 361
Grayton, CA 95444-0361 USA
T 800/331-3252
F 800/696-9006
www.bcbones.com

Makers of an extremely large and varied series of wooden dinosaur skeletons.

Bella Arts
12 Meadow Acre Rd.
Laramie, WY 82070 USA
T 307/755-6449
www.bellaarts.com
Two sets of handcrafted wooden dinos with moveable parts.

Blue Goose Wooden Puzzles
PO Box 1554
Warsaw, IN 46581-1554 USA
T 219/269-5288
susie@woodfun.com
www.woodfun.com
Maker of three quaint animal puzzles, "Dashing Dino," "Armor Dino," and "Rhino Dino."

Children's Workshop
PO Box 321
Acton, ME 04001 USA
T 207/636-2762
sales@childwood.com
www.childwood.com
Two colorful wooden crayon holders for children.

Dino-Bonz
5191 Miller Trunk Hwy
Duluth, MN 55811 USA
T 218/729-5373
F 218/729-0321
Bonz5191@msn.com
www.dino-bonz.com
Big skeletons of Tyrannosaurus, Pteranodon, Apatosaurus, Triceratops, and Styracosaurus.

Dino Works
101 Maple St.
Lexington, MA 02420 USA

T 781/863-9571
debandben@aol.com
www.gurus.com/dinoworks
*Home of some of the largest wooden
skeletons available.*

Dinosaur Patterns Plus
PO Box 28035
Las Vegas, NV 89126 USA
www.xts.net/dinopatterns/index.html
*Wooden pattern skeletons for
Apatosaurus, Brachiosaurus,
Pteranodon, Spinosaurus, Stegosaurus,
Styracosaurus, Triceratops,
Tyrannosaurus, and Velociraptor.*

Handmade Homemade Toy Shop
249 Allen's Way
Kittnell, NC 27544 USA
T 252/492-1882
manager@craftoys.com
www.crafttoys.com
*Four wonderful designs with moveable
arms and legs on wheels.*

Made n' Wyoming
PO Box 6775
Sheridan, WY 82801 USA
T 307/672-5595
F 307/673-5034
info@made-n-wyoming.com
st14.yahoo.com/made-n-
wyoming/hancrafcherw.html
*An attractive cherrywood Tyrannosaur
that walks on wheels.*

Primary Simulation, Inc.
2863 Mozart Dr.
Silver Spring, MD 20904 USA
T 301/572-2168
F 301/572-2169
psi@tronlink.com
www.psism.com/woodkits.htm
*Battery-powered, wooden Tyrannosaur
and Triceratops that walk!*

Safari, Ltd.
Box 630685
Miami, FL 33163 USA
T 305/621-1000
F 305/621-6894
sales@safariltd.com
www.safariltd.com
*A large and varied collection of species
and sizes.*

Spencer Toys
HC 72, Box 87
Parthenon, AR 72666 USA
T 870/446-2795
c3rain@oztech.com
newtoncoark.com/spencertoys
*A wheeled Apatosaurus with bobbing
head and tail.*

Wild Apples
4487 Rabbit Run Rd.
Trumansburg, NY 14886 USA
T 607/387-6315
F 607/387-4835
toys@wildapples.com
www.wildapples.com
*An entire line of wonderful push toys,
mobiles, puzzles, banks, and book ends.
The "Bronto Habitat" holds a series of
little wooden dinos!*

Woodpile Products
2194 W. Rainfall St.
Meridian, ID 83642 USA
F 208/887-3479
woodpile@woodpileproducts.com
www.woodpileproducts.com
*Three dino designs with moveable arms
and legs.*

WRITING UTENSILS

Collector's Connection
PO Box 22332
Eugene, OR 97402 USA

T 530/706-9219
F 603/925-7372
jabrams@efn.org
www.efn.org/~jabrams/pen.htm
   Two small pencil sharpeners.

Constructive Playthings
13201 Arrington Rd.
Grandview, MO 64030-2886 USA
T 800/255-6124
F 816/761-9295
ustoy@ustoyco.com
ustoyco.com/
   *A big selection of dino pens, pencils,
   and erasers.*

Imports Unlimited
2 Virginia Ave.
Beverly, MA 01915 USA
T 800/593-7076
F 978/524-0365
admin@importsunltd.com
www.importsunltd.com
   Several designs of dinosaur pencils.

Exploratoy
16941 Keegan Ave.
Carson, CA 90746 USA
T 800/995-9290
scitoys@exploratoy.com
www.exploratoy.com/products/atomicnight.htm
   *The "Atomic Night Writer" glows in the
   dark, complete with dinosaur head.*

Floaty
Dept. 260
2219 W. Olive Ave.
Burbank, CA 91506 USA
T 800/883-3627
F 818/566-4420
floaty@floaty.com
www.floaty.com
   Pens with floating dinosaurs inside!

Fossilnet, Inc.
1517 Greentree Lane.
Garland, TX 75042 USA
T 972/494-3443
docpaleo@home.com
www.fossilnet.com
   Pens made from genuine dinosaur bone.

Frausto Fabrications
4314 Navajo Dr.
Laramie, WY 82072 USA
T 307/742-7721
pfrau@aol.com
members.aol.com/pfrau
   *A charming series of wooden pencil
   boxes.*

Luen Fat Plastic Fty.
Blk A-B, 14.F, Wai-cheong Ind. Cr.
No. 5 Shek Pai Tau Rd.
Tuen Mun, NT, Hong Kong CHINA
T 852/2465-6602
F 852/2455-9120
1plastic@netvigator.com
   *A wide variety of dinosaur pencil
   sharpeners.*

Sand Scripts
PO Box 1143
Point Pleasant, NJ 08742-1143 USA
T 732/892-3135
F 732/892-0309
webmaster@sandscripts.com
www.sandscripts.com/contact.html
   A source for dinosaur pencils.

WinCraft, Inc.
1124 W. Fifth St.
PO Box 888
Winona, MN 55987 USA
T 800/533-8100
F 507/453-0690
mwalters@wincraft.com
www.wincraftusa.com
   Really neat Erasers.

Would You Believe
1118 Fairoaks Ave.
South Pasadena, CA 91030 USA
T 626/799-3828
wyb@wyb.com
www.wyb.com
> *Even more erasers.*

BESTIARY

ABILOSAURUS

Fossil Replicas
Skull
9cm (Gravino) $90.00 VALLEY MG08

ACROCANTHOSAURUS

Fossil Replicas
Arm
36" - $1,500.00 GEOLOGICAL VR60
Claw
5.5" - $22.00 NORTH EASTERN RD-154 [manus, matched with below]
6.5" - $22.00 NORTH EASTERN RD-154 [pes, matched with above]
14cm - $8.00 VALLEY CL01 [manus]
16cm - $8.00 VALLEY CL01A [pes]
Skeleton
56" - $1,100.00 BLACK HILLS SR0101
40' - $160,000.00 GEOLOGICAL VR36
Skull
3" (Knuth) $75.00 KNUTH
[$200.00]
4" - $75.00 BLACK HILLS SR0100
56.5" - $9,500.00 GEOLOGICAL VR48
Teeth
3" - $20.00 BLACK HILLS R00561
4" - $25.00 BLACK HILLS R00563
Life-sized Models
43' (Braun) $43,000.00 CYCAD PRODUCTIONS
Models and Sculpture
13.5" (Finney) $68.00 FINNEY [$78.00 with base]
14" (Salas) $254.98 LINK AND PIN
18" (Green) $125.00 CONTINENTAL [eating Tenatosaurus]
Plastic Figures
7" (Bos. Mus.) $9.00 BATTAT

ALAMOSAURUS

Life-sized Models
69'   (Braun) $69,000.00   CYCAD PRODUCTIONS

ALAXASAURUS

Fossil Replicas
Claw
6"   - $24.00   GASTON DESIGN   [manus]

ALBERTOSAURUS

Fossil Replicas
Arm
110cm   L200.00   GEOU CRR 26.3
110cm - $260.00   VALLEY C24A
Claw
3"   - $6.95   CRETACEOUS (Cdn)   [manus]
3"   - $8.00   SECOND NATURE SN-10   [manus]
4"   - $6.85   CRETACEOUS (Cdn)   [pes]
5"   - $20.00   SECOND NATURE SN-11   [pes]
Feet
30"   - $274.00   ANTIQUARIAN
90cm   L200.00   GEOU CRR 26.4
90cm - $260.00   VALLEY C25
Jaw
29"   - $124.00   ANTIQUARIAN   [left side]
Maxilla
20"   - $124.00   ANTIQUARIAN   [left side]
Skeleton
2.4m - $25,000.00   GEOLOGICAL VR38
22'   - $49,000.00   TRIEBOLD
9m   - $70,000.00   GEOLOGICAL VR37
28'   - $15,000.00   CREATIONS E. T.
Skull
30"   - $1,050.00   ANTIQUARIAN DL01
36"   - $2,200.00   CREATIONS E. T.
Teeth
3"   - $8.00   WESTERN
3.5"   - $8.00   SECOND NATURE SN-09
Life-sized Models
26'   (Braun) $26,000.00   CYCAD PRODUCTIONS

| 28' | - | $6,800.00 | CREATIONS E. T. | |

Models and Sculpture

?	(Morales)	$99.95	LINK AND PIN DS30	
4"	(Auger)	$15.95	CRETACEOUS (Cdn)	[hatchling]
7"	(Krentz)	$75.00	KRENTZ	[juvenile]
8"	**(Tischler)**	**$1,250.00**	**HUGH ROSE**	**['Double Header']**
9"	(Wenzel)	$85.00	DINOSAUR STUDIO	[finished, $310.00]
[$4,800.00]				
18"	(McGrady)	$110.00	CM STUDIO	
19"	(Krentz)	$130.00	KRENTZ	

ALIORAMUS

Life-sized Models

| 20' | (Braun) | $20,000.00 | CYCAD PRODUCTIONS | |

Models and Sculpture

1/10	(Salas)	CALL	SALAS	
8"	(Tokugawa)	$20.00	MUSASHI	
18"	(Jones)	$129.98	LINK AND PIN	
48"	(Graham)	$502.98	LINK AND PIN	

ALLOSAURUS

Fossil Replicas

Claw

77mm	-	$6.00	VALLEY CL22	
4"	-	$12.00	GASTON DESIGN	[manus-pinky!]
4.5"	-	$7.95	ANTS 100502101	[manus]
5.5"	-	$7.00	ANTIQUARIAN EE06	
6"	-	$18.00	GASTON DESIGN	[pes]
6.5"	-	$60.00	TAYLOR STUDIOS F040	[manus]
7"	-	$36.00	SMITH STUDIOS	[manus]
9"	-	$18.00	ANTIQUARIAN CO1	[manus]
9"	-	$23.00	BONE ROOM	[manus]
240mm		L12.00	GEOU JR 9.1	
9.5"	-	$26.00	GASTON DESIGN	[manus]
10"	-	$30.00	SECOND NATURE SN-29	[manus]
28cm	-	$14.00	VALLEY CL39	
12"	-	$34.00	GASTON DESIGN	[manus]
14"	-	$46.00	GASTON DESIGN	[removable sheath]

Feet

| 15" | - | $336.00 | GASTON DESIGN | [with base] |

Hand

| 15.5" | - | $160.00 | GASTON DESIGN | [with base] |

Humerus

15"	-	$45.00	GASTON DESIGN	

Leg

7'	-	$1,200.00	GASTON DESIGN	[with armature]

Skeleton

9"	(Maniscalco)	$240.00	MAXILLA	[AMNH]
9"	(Maniscalco)	$260.00	MAXILLA	['Feasting,' one on carcass]
9"	(Maniscalco)	$375.00	MAXILLA	['Combat,' two fighting]
9"	(Maniscalco)	$495.00	MAXILLA	['Hunting Pack,' three run]
12"	(Galey)	$42.95	SKULLDUGGERY 0730	[in rock slab]
26"	(Wagner)	$289.00	ANTS	[finished, $380.00]
[$1995.00]				

Skull

1.5"	(Maniscalco)	$45.00	MAXILLA	
3.5"	(Tskhondin)	$19.95	ANTS r100701106	[fossil color available]
8"	(Gerath)	$150.00	GERATH	
22cm	-	$199.00	SKULLS UNLIMITED VA-06	
8.5"	(Hoeger)	$190.00	VALLEY SH14	
20"	(Smith)	$700.00	SMITH STUDIOS	[juvenile]
22"	-	$590.00	ANTIQUARIAN EE01	
22"	-	$175.00	PREHISTORIC	[profile]
810mm		L1050.00	GEOU JR 9.0	
33"	-	$1180.00	ANTIQUARIAN S37	
35"	(Smith)	$1,200.00	SMITH STUDIOS	
80cm	-	$1700.00	VALLEY S37	[Cleveland-Lloyd]
84cm	-	$1599.00	SKULLS UNLIMITED VA-19	

Teeth

2.5"	-	$16.00	GASTON DESIGN
4"	-	$10.00	SECOND NATURE SN-28
5"	-	$14.50	SMITH STUDIOS

Life-sized Models

6'	(Braun)	$6,00.00	CYCAD PRODUCTIONS	[juvenile]
21'	(Braun)	$26,000.00	CYCAD PRODUCTIONS	
30'	-	$6.800.00	CREATIONS E. T.	

Models and Sculpture

8"	-	$67.95	LUNAR MODELS OD21C	[after Zallinger]
10"	(Tischler)	$1,250.00	HUGH ROSE	['Confrontation']
10"	(Tokugawa)	Y3,500	TOKUGAWA	
10"	(Tokugawa)	$40.00	MUSASHI	
11"	(LoRusso)	$85.00	DINOSAUR STUDIO	[finished, $310.00]
12"	(Knuth)	CALL	KNUTH	[recling]
13"	-	$56.00	MONSTROSITIES	[Kaiyodo]
15"	(Delgado)	$50.00	LESSER	
15"	-	$40.00	MONSTROSITIES	[Kaiyodo]
16"	-	$112.95	LUNAR MODELS OS20C	[after Knight]
20"	(Moneleone)	$1650.00	LOST ART	['Lana,' reclining]

24"	(Holmes)	L1,950	HOLMES	
25"	(Fischner)	$650.00	DREAMSTAR	
27"	(McGrady)	$185.00	CM STUDIO	[base, $15.00]
32"	-	$2,250.00	JONAS STUDIOS	[1964 World's Fair]

Plaques

8x11"	(Johnson)	$39.00	ACTION HOBBIES	
9x12"	-	$69.99	DINOSAUR FOUNDRY	[skull]

Plastic Figures

6"	(Wild Safari)	$5.00	SAFARI 2780-29	
9.5"	(Carnegie)	$10.00	SAFARI 4007-01	
11"	-	L5.99	TOYWAY 205	[Walking with Dinosaurs]

Posters

12x36"-	$2.95	NATURE SOURCE W2100	
20x30"(Gurche)	$40.00	MONSTROSITIES	
23x35"	$10.00	SMITH STUDIOS	

Wooden Toys

21"	-	$8.00	SAFARI 7401-11	[skeleton]

AMARGASAURUS

Life-sized Models

12m	-	$6,500.00	SALAS GISMONDI

Models and Sculpture

?	(Strasser)	CALL	DRAGON, INC	
9"	-	$200.00	MONSTROSITIES	[Kaiyodo]
18"	(Alchemy)	$178.98	LUNAR MODELS DS35	
32"	(Fischner)	$675.00	DREAMSTAR	

Plastic Figures

7.5"	(Bos. Mus.)	$8.00	BATTAT

AMMOSAURUS

Fossil Replicas
Claw

42mm -	$6.00	VALLEY CL03	

ANATOSAURUS

Life-sized Models

33'	(Braun)	$33,000.00	CYCAD PRODUCTIONS

ANCHICERATOPS

Life-sized Models
20'	(Braun)	$20,000.00	CYCAD PRODUCTIONS	

Models and Sculpture
12"	-	$47.00	MONSTROSITIES	[Kaiyodo]
26"	(Jones)	$550.98	LINK AND PIN	

ANCHISAURUS

Life-sized Models
7'	(Braun)	$7,000.00	CYCAD PRODUCTIONS	

ANKLOSAURUS

Fossil Replicas
Club
8"	**(Monteleone)**	**$400.00**	**LOST ART**	**['Exclusive Club']**

Skull
10"	-	$224.00	ANTIQUARIAN CC01	[cranium]

Life-sized Models
16'	-	$32,500.00	JONAS STUDIOS	[1964 World's fair]
33'	(Braun)	$33,000.00	CYCAD PRODUCTIONS	

Models and Sculpture
4.5"	-	$95.00	JONAS STUDIOS	[1964 World's Fair]
6"	(Fischner)	$45.00	DREAMSTAR	[hatchling]
7"	-	$67.95	LUNAR MODELS OS15C	[after Zallinger]
8"	**(Tischler)**	**$1,250.00**	**HUGH ROSE**	**['Double Header']**
9"	(McGrady)	$85.00	CM STUDIO	
15"	-	$57.00	MONSTROSITIES	[Kaiyodo]
19"	-	$1,750.00	JONAS STUDIOS	[1964 World's Fair]
20"	(McGrady)	$150.00	CM STUDIO	[finished, $260.00]
30"	(Fischner)	$750.00	DREAMSTAR	

ANUROGNATHUS

Life-sized Models
12"	(Braun)	$1,200.00	CYCAD PRODUCTIONS	

Plaques
3"	(Hoeger)	$7.00	VALLEY SH11	[skull]

APATOSAURUS

Fossil Replicas
Claw

17"	-	$45.00	GASTON DESIGN	

Femur

1.7m	-	$600.00	VALLEY B10	[Brigham Young]

Life-sized Models

65'	-	$175,000.00	JONAS STUDIOS	
70'	(Braun)	$70,000.00	CYCAD RODUCTIONS	

Models and Sculpture

5"	(Fischner)	$45.00	DREAMSTAR D-16-Sm	[hatchling]
6"	(Johnson)	$49.00	ACTION HOBBIES	
7"	(Fischner)	$65.00	DREAMSTAR D-10-Lg	[hatchling]
10"	-	$89.95	LUNAR MODELS OS16C	[after Zallinger]
12"	-	$145.00	JONAS STUDIOS	[1964 World's Fair]
12"	(Salas)	$100.00	SALAS	[calf]
22"	(Salas)	$140.00	SALAS	[female]
24"	(Salas)	$150.00	SALAS	[male]
24"	-	$3,500.00	JONAS STUDIOS	[juvenile, lying]
27"	-	$29.95	HORIZON HOR060	
28"	-	$55.00	MONSTROSITIES	[Kaiyodo]
34"	(Fischner)	$600.00	DREAMSTAR	
34"	-	$3,500.00	JONAS STUDIOS	[juvenile, standing]
36"	(McVey)	$760.00	MENAGERIE	
54"	(McGrady)	$600.00	CM STUDIO	[finished, $1,050.00]
64"	-	$6,000.00	JONAS STUDIOS	[1964 World's Fair]
96"	-	$14,000.00	JONAS STUDIOS	[1964 World's Fair]

Plastic Figures

6.5"	(Carnegie)	$7.00	SAFARI 4004-01	[juvenile]
9"	(Wild Safari)	$7.00	SAFARI 2781-29	
22"	(Carnegie)	$23.00	SAFARI 4003-01	

Wooden Toys

20"	-	$8.00	SAFARI 7003-11	[skeleton]
21"	-	$5.00	ACTION 18142	[skeleton]
36"	-	$7.00	DINOSAUR PATTERNS	[skeleton]
43"	-	$29.95	DINO BONZ 40103	[skeleton]

ARAEOSCELIS

Life-sized Models

24"	(Braun)	$2,400.00	CYCAD PRODUCTIONS

ARCHAEOPTERYX

Fossil Replicas
Skull

2"	(Hoeger)	$40.00	VALLEY SH17	
5cm	-	$39.00	SKULLS UNLIMITED VA-25	

Life-sized Models

14"	(Braun)	$1,400.00	CYCAD PRODUCTIONS
24"	-	$3,200.00	JONAS STUDIOS

Models and Sculpture

18"	(Finney)	$199.98	LINK AND PIN

Plaques

2x3"	(Hoeger)	$7.00	VALLEY SH06	[skull]
9x8"	-	$39.95	HORIZON 11252	
9x9"	-	$39.95	HORIZON 11254	[with feather]
10x14"		$95.00	PREHISTORIC	[Eichstatt]
10x19"		$175.00	PREHISTORIC	[Eichstatt]
12x15"		$69.95	CRETACEOUS (Cdn)	
18x15"		$195.00	TAYLOR STUDIOS F022	
18x24"		$100.00	MT. BLANCO	
19x15"		$48.00	NORTH EASTERN RD-52	

Posters

19x34"(Gurche)	$25.00	MONSTROSITIES

ARCHAEORNITHOMIMUS

Fossil Replicas
Skeleton

3.2m	-	CALL	GONDWANA

ARCHAEOTHYRIS

Life-sized Models

20"	(Braun)	$2,000.00	CYCAD PRODUCTIONS

ARCHELON

Fossil Replicas
Skeleton

16'	-	$65,000.00	BLACK HILLS R00715

Life-sized Models

12'	(Braun)	$12,000.00	CYCAD PRODUCTIONS

Models and Sculpture
11"   - $199.98   LINK AND PIN R-12   [Kaiyodo]

ARDEOSAURUS

Life-sized Models
8"   (Braun) $800.00   CYCAD PRODUCTIONS

ARGENTINOSAURUS

Models and Sculpture
38"   (Salas) $231.98   LINK AND PIN

ARRHINOCERATOPS

Life-sized Models
20'   (Braun) $20,000.00   CYCAD PRODUCTIONS
Models and Sculpture
26"   (Jones) $449.98   LINK AND PIN

ARSTANOSAURUS

Fossil Replicas
Skull
15cm   - $117.00   GONDWANA

ASKEPTOSAURUS

Life-sized Models
72"   (Braun) $7,200.00   CYCAD PRODUCTIONS

ASTRODON

Models and Sculpture
18"   (Finney) $149.98   LINK AND PIN   [four Utahraptors available]

AVACERATOPS

Models and Sculpture
13"   (Jones) $139.98   LINK AND PIN

AVIMIMUS

Fossil Replicas
Skeleton
| 1.5m | - | $1,296.00 | GONDWANA |

Skull
| 7.5cm | - | $89.00 | SKULLS UNLIMITED VA-66 |
| 8cm | (Hoeger) | $90.00 | VALLEY SH18 |

Life-sized Models
| 48" | (McGrady) | CALL | CM STUDIO |

BACTROSAURUS

Fossil Replicas
Skeleton
| 1.5m | - | CALL | GONDWANA |
| 2.1m | - | $5,000.00 | SMITH STUDIOS |

Life-sized Models
| 13' | (Braun) | $13,000.00 | CYCAD PRODUCTIONS |

BAGACERATOPS

Fossil Replicas
Skull
| 35mm | - | $65.00 | GONDWANA |

Life-sized Models
| 36" | (Braun) | $3,600.00 | CYCAD PRODUCTIONS |

Models and Sculpture
| 5" | (Jones) | CALL | ALCHEMY |

BARAPARSAURUS

Life-sized Models
| 49' | (Braun) | $49,000.00 | CYCAD PRODUCTIONS |

BAROSAURUS

Fossil Replicas
Skeleton
| 12" | (Maniscalco) | $330.00 | MAXILLA | [AMNH] |

Models and Sculpture
| 12.5" | (Morales) | $156.95 | LUNAR MODELS OS06 | [diorama with juveniles] |
| 37" | - | $401.98 | LINK AND PIN R-00 | [Kaiyodo; calf, Allosaurus] |

Posters
26x36"(Gurche) $15.00   MONSTROSITIES

BATRACHOGNATHUS

Life-sized Models
20"   (Braun) $2,000.00   CYCAD PRODUCTIONS

BAURUSUCHUS

Life-sized Models
5m   - $3,500.00   SALAS GISMONDI

BARYONYX

Fossil Replicas
Claw
8.5"   - $70.00   TAYLOR STUDIOS F052
230mm   L13.00   GEOU CRR 22.0
Skeleton
30'   - $15,000.00   CREATIONS E. T.
Skull
36"   - $2,200.00   CREATIONS E. T.
Life-sized Models
20'   (Braun) $20,000.00   CYCAD PRODUCTIONS
30'   - $6,800.00   CREATIONS E. T.
Models and Sculpture
21"   (Foulkes) $95.00   CRETACEOUS   [finished, $200.00]
30"   (Dickens) $200.00   INTEGRITY
Plastic Figures
9"   (Carnegie) $9.00   SAFARI 4033-01

BELLUSAURUS

Fossil Replicas
Skeleton
3.4m   - $12,000.00   SMITH STUDIOS
5m   -   CALL   GONDWANA

BERNISSARTIA

Life-sized Models
24"	(Braun)	$2,400.00	CYCAD PRODUCTIONS

BIARMOSUCHUS

Fossil Replicas
.75m	-	$680.00	GONDWANA

BRACHIOSAURUS

Fossils Replicas
Skeleton
70'	-	$75,000.00	CREATIONS E. T.	

Skull
36"	-	$2,500.00	CREATIONS E. T.	

Life-sized Models
70'	-	$35,000.00	CREATIONS E. T.	
75'	(Braun)	$75,000.00	CYCAD PRODUCTIONS	

Models and Sculpture
1/35	-	$80.00	TAMIYA	
8"	-	$49.95	VITTETOE	[bust]
16"	**(Tischler)**	**$1,170.00**	**HUGH ROSE**	
28"	(Morales)	$240.00	DRAGON ATTACK!	[finished, $390.00]
34"	(Fischner)	$550.00	DREAMSTAR	
36"	-	$65.00	MONSTERS IN MOTION	[Jurassic Park]

Plaques
320x320mm		L45.00	EDDY DNSP005	[skeleton]

Plastic Figures
9"	(Wild Safari)	$7.00	SAFARI 2782-29	
22"	(Carnegie)	$27.00	SAFARI 4002-01	

Posters
18x24"	(Franczak)	$25.00	MONSTROSITIES	
33x55"		$12.95	OMNI 99-8310	[glow in the dark]

Wooden Toys
19"	-	$8.00	SAFARI 7010-11	[skeleton]
20"	-	$5.00	ACTION 18147	[skeleton]
32"	-	$15.00	B. C. BONZ B-SML	[skeleton]
34"	-	19.50	SAFARI 7310-10	[skeleton]
34"	-	$7.00	DINOSAUR PATTERNS	[skeleton]
48"	-	$25.00	B. C. BONZ B-MED	[skeleton]
84"	-	$40.00	B. C. BONZ B-LRG	[skeleton]

BRACHYCERATOPS

Models and Sculpture
13"   (Jones) $139.98   LINK AND PIN

CALLOVOSAURUS

Life-sized Models
11'   (Braun) $11,000.00   CYCAD PRODUCTIONS

CAMARASAURUS

Fossil Replicas
Claw
6"   - $29.50   SMITH STUDIOS
9"   - $14.00   ANTIQUARIAN CL08
22cm   -   L12.00   GEOU JR 12.0
27cm   - $14.00   VALLEY CL08
Skull
2.5"   (Tskhondin) $25.95   ANTS r100701207   [fossil color available]
6"   - $135.00   ANTIQUARIAN RM112
10"   (Mjos) $129.95   NATURAL CANVAS
12.5"   - $390.00   ANTIQUARIAN DL04
21"   - $980.00   ANTIQUARIAN DL03
22"   - $1,000.00   SMITH STUDIOS
26"   - $1,200.00   WESTERN
Teeth
4"   - $10.00   SECOND NATURE SN-30
5"   - $14.50   SMITH STUDIOS
5.5"   - $16.00   GASTON DESIGN
Life-sized Models
59'   (Braun) $59,000.00   CYCAD PRODUCTIONS
Models and Sculpture
7"   (Fischner) $34.98   LINK AND PIN   [hatchling]
16"   - $39.98   LINK AND PIN MK-03   [Kaiyodo]
18"   (Salas) $120.00   SALAS
30"   (Fischner) $575.00   DREAMSTAR
51"   (Trcic)   CALL   TRCIC STUDIO
[CALL]
Posters
23x25" $10.00   SMITH STUDIOS
23x29"(Fricken) $13.95   NATURE SOURCE W2035
23x35"(Dinolab) $5.25   NATURE SOURCE W2032

CAMPTOSAURUS

Fossil Replicas
Claw

2"	-	$9.00	SMITH STUDIOS	[manus]
3"	-	$15.00	SMITH STUDIOS	[pes]

Feet

7"	-	$37.50	ANTIQUARIAN C18	
225mm		L20.00	GEOU JR 13.0	
15"	-	$250.00	BONE CLONES KO-014	

Hand

18cm	-	$30.00	VALLEY C18	[Cleveland-Lloyd]

Maxilla

5"	-	$26.00	SMITH STUDIOS

Skull

14"	-	$278.00	ANTIQUARIAN SO5A
33cm	-	$300.00	VALLEY S05A

Teeth

5"	-	$6.50	ANTIQUARIAN

Life-sized Models

20'	(Braun)	$20,000.00	CYCAD PRODUCTIONS

Models and Sculpture

9"	-	$99.98	LINK AND PIN DS37	[after Zallinger]

Posters

12x36"-		$2.95	NATURE SOURCE W2140

CAMPYLOGNATHOIDES

Life-sized Models

60"	(Braun)	$6,000.00	CYCAD PRODUCTIONS

CAPTORHINUS

Fossil Replicas
Skull

3"	-	$75.00	ROBERT REID
[$125.00]			
10"	-	$10.00	FOSSILNET

CARCHARODONTOSAURUS

Fossil Replicas
Teeth
5"	-	$12.00	SECOND NATURE SN-22	
13cm	-	$8.00	VALLEY T30	

Models and Sculpture
14"	(Salas)	$120.00	SALAS	
20"	(Green)	$105.00	CONTINENTAL	[$200.00 finished]
[$1100.00]				

Plastic Figures
7.5"	(Wild Safari)	$5.00	SAFARI 2783-29

CARNOTAURUS

Fossil Replicas
9"	-	$214.00	ANTIQUARIAN MG02

Skull
4"	(Gravino)	$40.00	VALLEY MG02
12cm	-	$39.00	SKULLS UNLIMITED VA-05
9"	(Gravino)	$270.00	VALLEY MG03
23cm	-	$249.00	SKULLS UNLIMITED VA-08
.60m	-	$450.00	SALAS GISMONDI

Life-sized Models
7m	-	$5000.00	SALAS GISMONDI

Models and Sculpture
10"	(Morales)	$134.95	LUNAR MODELS OS03	[with Hypacrosaurus]
13"	(McVey)	$164.98	LINK AND PIN	
14"	(Salas)	$119.98	LINK AND PIN	
25"	(Braun)	$2,500.00	CYCAD PRODUCTIONS	[flayed]
29"	(McGrady)	$225.00	CM STUDIO	[finished, $395.00]

Plastic Figures
6"	(Carnegie)	$5.00	SAFARI 4028-01
7"	(Bos. Mus.)	$7.50	BATTAT

CASEA

Fossil Replicas
Skull
3.5"	-	$38.00	NORTH EASTERN RD RD-50

Life-sized Models
48"	(Braun)	$4,800.00	CYCAD PRODUCTIONS

CATOPSALIS

Fossil Replicas
Skull
45mm - $65.00   GONDWANA

CEARADACTYLUS

Life-sized Models
13'   (Braun) $13,000.00   CYCAD PRODUCTIONS

CENTENOCHASMA

Life-sized Models
9'   (Braun) $9,000.00   CYCAD PRODUCTIONS

CENTROSAURUS

Fossil Replicas
Skeleton
17'   - $12,500.00   CREATIONS E. T.
Skull
48"   - $1,800.00   CREATIONS E. T.
Life-sized Models
17'   - $6,500.00   CREATIONS E. T.
20'   (Braun) $20,000.00   CYCAD PRODUCTIONS
Models and Sculpture
10"   (Jones) $158.98   LINK AND PIN   [bust]
17.5" (Wenzel) $300.00   DINOSAUR STUDIOS   [finished, $850.00]
25"   (Fischner) $650.00   DREAMSTAR

CERATOSAURUS

Fossil Replicas
Maxilla
11"   - $70.00   GASTON DESIGN
Skeleton
15'   - $20,000.00   WESTERN   [mounted, $35,000]
Skull
5"   - $135.00   ANTIQUARIAN RM113
7"   (Mjos) $129.95   NATURAL CANVAS
14"   (Auger) $29.95   CRETACEOUS (Cdn)   [half]

Teeth

3"	-	$8.00	WESTERN	

Life-sized Models

6m	-	CALL	FLORIDES	
20'	(Braun)	$20,000.00	CYCAD PRODUCTIONS	

Models and Sculpture

5"	(Dickens)	$35.00	INTEGRITY	
6"	(Fischner)	$45.00	DREAMSTAR	[hatchling]
9"	(DeVito)	$140.00	MONSTROSITIES	[bust]
10"	(Morales)	$144.95	LUNAR OS08	[fighting Stegosaurus]
16"	(McGrady)	$115.00	CM STUDIO	[finished, $205.00]
17"	-	$195.98	LINK AND PIN R-17	[Kaiyodo]
18"	(McGrady)	$140.00	CM STUDIO	[finished, $225.00]
18"	(Finney)	$174.98	LINK AND PIN	[two juveniles, $98.98]
18"	(Dickens)	$200.00	INTEGRITY	
18"	**(Hunt)**	**$950.00**	**HUNT STUDIOS**	
22"	(Salas)	$400.00	SALAS	
[$1,300.00]				
25"	(Fischner)	$650.00	DREAMSTAR	

Plastic Figures

5.5"	(Wild Safari)	$4.00	SAFARI 2784-29
6"	(Bos. Mus.)	$9.00	BATTAT

Posters

12x36"-	$2.95	NATURE SOURCE W2100
24x26"(Sibbick)	$6.00	MONSTROSITIES

CERESIOSAURUS

Life-sized Models

13'	(Braun)	$13,000.00	CYCAD PRODUCTIONS

CETIOSAURUS

Life-sized Models

60'	(Braun)	$60,000.00	CYCAD PRODUCTIONS

Models and Sculpture

18"	(Salas)	$120.00	SALAS

CHAMPASAURUS

Life-sized Models

60"	(Braun)	$6,000.00	CYCAD PRODUCTIONS

CHAMPSOSAUR

Fossil Replicas
Skeleton
60"   - $4,900.00   TRIEBOLD

CHASMATOSAURUS

Life-sized Models
72"   (Braun) $7,200.00   CYCAD PRODUCTIONS

CHASMOSAURUS

Fossil Replicas
Skeleton
17'   - $21,300.00   ANTIQUARIAN A112
17'   -   CALL   VALLEY   [Royal Ontario Museum]
Skull
4"   - $8.99   DINOSAUR FOUNDRY
2.1m   - $2,250.00   VALLEY A102S   [Royal Ontario Museum]
84"   - $2,650.00   ANTIQUARIAN S102
Life-sized Models
17'   (Braun) $17,000.00   CYCAD PRODUCTIONS
Models and Sculpture
1/35   - $30.00   TAMIYA
7"   - $97.98   LINK AND PIN R-18   [Kaiyodo]
8"   - $$49.95   VITTOE   [bust]
9"   (Jones) $158.98   LINK AND PIN   [bust, female]
10"   (Jones) $158.98   LINK AND PIN   [bust, male]
10"   - $40.00   MONSTROSITIES   [Kaiyodo]
13.5"   - $194.95   LUNAR MODELS F676   [fights cave men]
17"   (LoRusso) $295.00   DINOSAUR STUDIO   [male, finished, $845.00]
17"   (LoRusso) $295.00   DINOSAUR STUDIO   [female, finished, $845.00]
25"   (Fischner) $650.00   DREAMSTAR

CHILANTAISAURUS

Fossil Replicas
Claw
51mm   - $6.00   VALLEY CL06

CHIROSTENOTES

Fossil Replicas
Claw

3"	-	$25.00	BLACK HILLS R00503	[pes]
4"	-	$10.00	FOSSILNET	[manus]
4"	-	$25.00	BLACK HILLS R0050	[manus]
4.5"	-	$6.50	ANTIQUARIAN CL07	[manus]
5"	-	$12.00	SECOND NATURE SN-05	[manus]
6"	-	$30.00	NORTH EASTERN RD-151	[manus, part of set]
13cm	-	$6.00	VALLEY CL07	

Feet

12"	-	$110.95	CRETACEOUS (Cdn)	
19"	-	$45.95	CRETACEOUS (Cdn)	[slab]

Skeleton

15'	-	$45,000.00	TREIBOLD

CISTECEPHALUS

Life-sized Models

13"	(Braun)	$1,300.00	CYCAD PRODUCTIONS

CLAUDIOSAURUS

Life-sized Models

24"	(Braun)	$2,400.00	CYCAD PRODUCTIONS

CLIDASTES

Fossil Replicas
Skeleton

11'	-	$12,500.00	TREIBOLD

Skull

14"	-	$1,100.00	TREIBOLD

COELOPHYSIS

Fossil Replicas
Skull

4"	(Tskhondin)	$21.95	ANTS r100701208	[fossil color available]
8"	-	$225.00	NORTH EASTERN RD-132	

Life-sized Models
8'	(Braun)	$8,000.00	CYCAD PRODUCTIONS	
8'	-	$12,000.00	JONAS STUDIOS	
8.5'	(McGrady)	$5,600.00	CM STUDIO	

Models and Sculpture
9"	-	$425.00	JONAS STUDIOS	
24"	(Fischner)	$650.00	DREAMSTAR	
36"	(McGrady)	$400.00	CM STUDIO	[finished, $650.00]

Plaques
18x8"	-	$49.95	HORIZON 11250
36x70"		$800.00	NORTH EASTERN RD-95

COELUROSAURUS

Models and Sculpture
28"	(Fischner)	$650.00	DREAMSTAR

COELURUS

Fossil Replicas
Claw
1.5"	-	$6.00	GASTON DESIGN	[pes]
1.5"	-	$6.00	GASTON DESIGN	[manus]
4"	-	$10.00	GASTON DESIGN	[manus]

Skeleton
12'	-	$22,000.00	WESTERN

Skull
10.5"	-	$5,500.00	WESTERN

Life-sized Models
6'	(Braun)	$6,000.00	CYCAD PRODUCTIONS

COMPSOGNATHUS

Fossil Replicas
Skull
3.5"	-	$24.95	EARTHLORE

Life-sized Models
24"	(Braun)	$2,400.00	CYCAD PRODUCTIONS
36"	(McGrady)	$800.00	CM STUDIO

Models and Sculpture
18"	(Finney)	$174.98	LINK AND PIN
27"	(Fischner)	$650.00	DREAMSTAR
34"	(Knuth)	$650.00	KNUTH

Plaques
4.5"	(Hoeger)	$8.00	VALLEY SH07	[skull]
600x600mm		L40.00	GEOU JR 8.0	
14x16"		$185.00	PREHISTORIC	[skeleton]

CORYTHOSAURUS

Fossil Replicas
Skull
| 14" | - | $150.00 | PREHISTORIC | [profile, juvenile] |

Life-sized Models
| 26' | - | $37,000.00 | JONAS STUDIOS | [1964 World's Fair] |
| 30' | (Braun) | $30,000.00 | CYCAD PRODUCTIONS | |

Models and Sculpture
5"	-	$95.00	JONAS STUDIOS	[1964 World's Fair]
26"	(Fischner)	$575.00	DREAMSTAR	
31.5"	-	$1,750.00	JONAS STUDIOS	[1964 World's Fair]

Plastic Figures
| 8" | (Carnegie) | $8.00 | SAFARI 4023-01 | |

COTYLORHYNCHUS

Fossil Replicas
Skull
| 7.5" | - | $189.00 | SMITH STUDIOS | |

CRIORHYNCHUS

Life-sized Models
| 16' | (Braun) | $16,000.00 | CYCAD PRODUCTIONS | |

CROCODILIS

Models and Sculpture
| 9" | - | $425.00 | JONAS STUDIOS | |

CRYOLOPOSAURUS

Fossil Replicas
Skull
| 11" | (Milbourne) | $375.00 | DINOSAUR STUDIO | |

Models and Sculpture
14"   (Salas) $249.98   LINK AND PIN   [pair over prey]

CRYPTOCLEDIUS

Life-sized Models
11'   (Holmes)   L7,650   HOLMES
13'   (Braun) $13,000.00   CYCAD PRODUCTIONS

CYMBOSPONDYLUS

Life-sized Models
33'   (Braun) $33,000.00   CYCAD PRODUCTIONS

CYNOGNATHUS

Life-sized Models
36"   (Braun) $3,600.00   CYCAD PRODUCTIONS
Models and Sculpture
10"   (Salas) $158.98   LINK AND PIN

DACENTRURUS

Models and Sculpture
30"   (Fischner) $650.00   DREAMSTAR

DASPLETOSAURUS

Fossil Replicas
Teeth
2"   - $6.00   SECOND NATURE SN-12
3.5"   - $12.00   SMITH STUDIOS
Life-sized Sculpture
28'   (Braun) $28,000.00   CYCAD PRODUCTIONS
28'   (McGrady) $46,000.00   CM STUDIO
30'   - $6,800.00   CREATIONS E. T.
Models and Sculpture
39"   (McGrady) $400.00   CM STUDIO
36"   (Manit)   CALL   LIVING RESIN
40"   (McGrady) $400.00   CM STUDIO   [finished, $750.00]
41"   (Trcic) $5,950.00   TRCIC STUDIO

Posters
| 13x17"(Henderson) | $25.00 | MONSTROSITIES |
| 20x20"(Gurche) | $25.00 | MONSTROSITIES |

DATUOSAURUS

Fossil Replicas
Skeleton
| 14m | - | $68,000.00 | SMITH STUDIOS |

DEINOCHEIRUS

Fossil Replicas
Forelimbs
| 2.6m | - | $5,190.00 | GONDWANNA |

DEINONYCHUS

Fossil Replicas
Arm
| ? | - | $34.95 | WICCART | [finished, $74.95] |

Claw
3"	-	$12.95	PREHISTORIC	[pes]
4"	-	$7.00	ANTIQUARIAN CL15	[pes]
4"	-	$7.00	BONE ROOM	[pes]
4.5"	-	$7.95	ANTS r100502100	
4.5"	-	$10.95	SKULLDUGGERY 0228	[pes, with stand, $13.95]
4.5"	-	$30.00	NORTH EASTERN RD-151	[pes, part of set]
120mm		$7.00	VALLEY SH16	

Feet
| 4" | (Harvey) | $39.95 | WICCART | [finished, $79.95] |

Skeleton
| 40" | (Harvey) | $349.00 | WICCART | |

Skull
?	-	L180.00	GEOU CRR 28.0	
1.5"	(Tskhondin)	$19.95	ANTS r100701209	[fossil color available]
12"	(Hoeger)	$250.00	VALLEY SH13	
12"	-	$2,499.00	SMITH STUDIOS	[Yale specimen]
12.5"	-	$194.00	ANTIQUARIAN	
33cm	-	$249.00	SKULLS UNLIMITED VA-24	

Life-sized Models
| 9' | (McGrady) | CALL | CM STUDIO | |
| 9.5' | - | $14,500.00 | JONAS STUDIOS | |

DEINOSUCHUS

12'	(Taylor)	$8,500.00	TAYLOR STUDIOS	
13'	(Braun)	$13,000.00	CYCAD STUDIOS	

Models and Sculpture

7"	(Tskhondin)	$49.95	ANTS	
[$800.00]				
10"	**(Monteleone)**	**$450.00**	**LOST ART**	
11"	-	$147.98	LINK AND PIN R-16	[Kaiyodo]
12"	-	$650.00	JONAS STUDIOS	
13"	(Manit)	$85.00	LIVING RESIN	
14"	**(Merrithew)**	**$950.00**	**MERRITHEW**	
22"	(Alderson)	$187.98	LINK AND PIN	
27"	(Fischner)	$750.00	DREAMSTAR	
39"	(Neill)	$950.00	NEILL	[finished, $2,500.00]
[$4,000.00]				
46"	**(Merrithew)**	**$7,000.00**	**MERRITHEW**	**[pack with Tyrannosaurus]**

Plaques

230x320mm	L40.00	EDDY DNDR002	[skeleton]

Posters

24x39"-	$6.00	MONSTROSITIES	[described as "very cool!"]

Wooden Toys

126" -	$400.00	DINO WORKS	[skeleton]

DEINOSUCHUS

Life-sized Models

40'	(Braun)	$40,000.00	CYCAD PRODUCTIONS

Models and Sculpture

17"	(McGrady)	$145.00	CM STUDIO	
36"	(McGrady)	$400.00	CM STUDIO	[finished, $650.00]

Plastic Figures

8.5"	(Carnegie)	$8.00	SAFARI 4026-01

DELTADROMEUS

Plastic Figures

5"	(Carnegie)	$9.00	SAFARI 4032-01

DELTAVJATIA

Fossil Replicas
Skull

10.5" -	$120.00	FOSSILNET	

DESMATOCHELYS

Life-sized Models
6'   (McGrady) $8,500.00   CM STUDIO

DESMATOSUCHUS

Life-sized Models
16'   (Braun) $16,000.00   CYCAD PRODUCTIONS
Models and Sculpture
15"   (Alchemy) $179.98   LINK AND PIN DS04   [with Postosuchus]

DICERATOPS

Models and Sculpture
· 7"   (Green) $50.00   CONTINENTAL

DICRAEOSAURUS

Life-sized Models
41'   (Braun) $41,000.00   CYCAD PRODUCTIONS
Models and Sculpture
15"   (Salas) $120.00   SALAS
Posters
24x36"(Hallett) $6.00   MONSTROSITIES

DICYNODONT

Fossil Replicas
Skull
25cm   - $400.00   GONDWANA
Life-sized Models
48"   (Braun) $800.00   CYCAD PRODUCTIONS
72"   (McGrady) $8,000.00   CM STUDIO
Models and Sculpture
12"   (Manit)   CALL   LIVING RESIN
12"   (McGrady) $100.00   CM STUDIO   [finished, $175.00]

DILOPHOSAURUS

Fossil Replicas
Skeletons

4.2m	-	$32,000.00	SMITH STUDIOS	
6m	-	CALL	GONDWANA	

Skull

14"	(Auger)	$29.95	CRETACEOUS (Cdn)	[halfskull]

Teeth

3"	-	$6.00	SECOND NATURE SN-26	

Life-sized Models

20'	-	$1,800.00	CREATIONS E. T.	
20'	(Braun)	$20,000.00	CYCAD PRODUCTIONS	
20'	(McGrady)	$21,000.00	CM STUDIOS	

Models and Sculpture

7.5"	(LoRusso)	$75.99	DINOSAUR STUDIO	
8"	-	$52.98	LINK AND PIN R-03	[Kaiyodo]
10"	(Tokugawa)	$50.00	MUSASHI	
20"	(Gerath)	$165.00	GERATH	[finished, $375.00]
24"	-	$65.00	MONSTERS IN MOTION	[Jurassic Park]

Plastic Figures

4"	(Carnegie)	$7.50	SAFARI 4024-01	[two per box]
4"	(Bos. Mus.)	$6.00	BATTAT MS160	

DIMETRODON

Fossil Replicas
Claw

25mm	-	$5.00	VALLEY CL10

Skeleton

98"	-	$18,250.00	ANTIQUARIAN A113
132"	-	CALL	VALLEY

Skull

3.5"	-	$8.99	DINOSAUR FOUNDRY
16.5"	-	$864.00	ANTIQUARIAN S113
33cm	-	$500.00	VALLEY S113
43cm	-	$899.00	SKULLS UNLIMITED VA-21

Life-sized Models

3m	-	CALL	FLORIDES
10'	(Braun)	$10,000.00	CYCAD PRODUCTIONS

Models and Sculpture

6"	-	$98.98	LUNAR MODELS DS40	[after Zallinger]
11"	**(Tischler)**	**1,250.00**	**HUGH ROSE**	**['Consummate Predator']**
13"	-	$850.00	JONAS STUDIOS	[1964 World's Fair]

15"	(Morales)	$112.95	LUNAR MODELS OS11	[eating Diplocalus]
15"	(Debus)	$54.00	HELL CREEK	[includes base]
21"	(Strasser)	$150.00	DRAGON, INC.	[finished, $450.00]
[$3500.00]				
30"	(Fischner)	$750.00	DREAMSTAR	
72"	(Fischner)	$5,800.00	DREAMSTAR	

Plaques

10x14"	-	$250.00	ROBERT REID	[skull]

Posters

24x36"(Sibbick)	$6.00	MONSTROSITIES	

DIMORPHODON

Life-sized Models

48"	(Braun)	$4,800.00	CYCAD PRODUCTIONS

DIPLODOCUS

Fossil Replicas
Skull

2.5"	(Tskhondin)	$9.95	ANTS r100701110	[fossil color available]
4"	-	$8.99	DINOSAUR FOUNDARY	
16"	-	$400.00	WESTERN	[juvenile]
24"	-	$460.00	ANTIQUARIAN DL02	

Life-sized Models

27m	-	CALL	FLORIDES
85'	(Braun)	$85,000.00	CYCAD PRODUCTIONS

Models and Sculpture

36"	(Fischner)	$600.00	DREAMSTAR	
42"	(McGrady)	$650.00	DINO ART	[fights two Allosaurs]
48"	(Strasser)	$550.00	DRAGON, INC.	[finished, $995.00]

Plastic Figures

15"	(Bos. Mus.)	$22.00	BATTAT MS110
24"	(Carnegie)	$25.00	SAFARI 4010-01

Posters

24x36"(Henderson)	$6.00	MONSTROSITIES

Wooden Toys

34"	-	$8.00	SAFARI 7402-11

DIVINIA

Fossil Replicas
Skull
100mm   - $260.00   GONDWANA

DORYGNATHUS

Fossil Replicas
Skeleton
24"   - $200.00   BLACK HILLS R00765   [on slab]
Life-sized Models
36"   (Braun) $3,600.00   CYCAD PRODUCTIONS

DROMAEOSAURUS

Fossil Replicas
Claw
55mm - $9.00   VALLEY CL41
3"   - $8.00   SECOND NATURE SN02   [manus]
Skeleton
3m   - $12,000.00   GEOLOGICAL VR39
Skull
9"   - $340.00   ANTIQUARIAN JT11
[$1240.00]
Life-sized Models
72"   (Braun) $7,200.00   CYCAD PRODUCTIONS
84"   (Trcic) $39,900.00   TRCIC STUDIO   ["Bird of Prey"]
Models and Sculpture
9"   (Trcic) $1,500.00   TRCIC STUDIO   ["Bird of Prey"]
9.5"   (Tischler) $1,090.00   HUGH ROSE   ['Ambushed']
10"   - $105.00   MONSTROSITIES   [Kaiyodo]
11"   (Trcic) $125.00   TRCIC STUDIO
[$975.00]

DROMICEIOMIMUS

Life-sized Models
11'   (Braun) $11,000.00   CYCAD PRODUCTIONS

DRYOSAURUS

Fossil Replicas
Skulls
8"   - $200.00   NORTH EASTERN RD-140
Life-sized Models
10'   (Braun) $10,000.00   CYCAD PRODUCTIONS
15'   (McGrady) $21,000.00   CM STUDIO

DZUNGARIPTERUS

Fossil Replicas
Skeleton
3m   -   CALL   GONDWANA
Life-sized Models
10'   (Braun) $10,000.00   CYCAD PRODUCTIONS

ECHGINODON

Life-sized Models
24"   (Braun) $2,400.00   CYCAD PRODUCTIONS

EDAPHOSAURUS

Fossil Replicas
Skull
10"   - $225.00   NORTH EASTERN RD-133
Life-sized Models
10'   (Braun) $10,000.00   CYCAD PRODUCTIONS
Models and Sculpture
11"   **(Tischler)**   **$1,250.00**   **HUGH ROSE**   **['Consummate Predator']**
22"   (Strasser) $150.00   DRAGON, INC.   [finished, $450.00]

EDMONTONIA

Fossil Replicas
Skull
2"   (Tskhondin) $9.95   ANTS r100701111   [fossil color available]
Models and Sculpture
10"   (Morales) $124.95   LUNAR MODELS OS09   [fighting Tyrannosaurus]
16"   (Foulkes) $110.00   CRETACEOUS   [finished, $220.00]

Plastic Figures

| 7" | (Bos. Mus.) | $9.00 | BATTAT | |

EDMONTOSAURUS

Fossil Replicas
Feet

| 5.5" | - | $40.00 | BLACK HILLS RD0157 | [ungual] |

Skeleton

14'	-	$44,000.00	BLACK HILLS R00507	[juvenile]
22'	-	$54,000.00	TRIEBOLD	
28'	-	$60,000.00	BLACK HILLS R00505	
28'	-	$12,500.00	CREATIONS E. T.	

Skull

2.5"	(Tskhondin)	$9.95	ANTS r100701112	[fossil color available]
23.5"	-	$1,800.00	BLACK HILLS R00511	
1.3m	-	$750.00	VALLEY S36	[profile]
32"	-	$1200.00	CREATIONS E. T.	
34"	-	$3,495.00	TRIEBOLD	
39"	-	$3,500.00	BLACK HILLS R00509	
43"	-	$1450.00	ANTIQUARIAN DL05	

Skin Impression

| 4x6" | - | $30.00 | BLACK HILLS R00515 | |

Teeth

3"	-	$8.00	SECOND NATURE SN-20	
6"	-	$19.00	PREHISTORIC	[dentary]
13"	-	$125.00	BLACK HILLS R00503	[juvenile dentary]

Life-sized Models

28'	-	$6,500.00	CREATIONS E. T.	
30'	(McGrady)	$41,500.00	CM STUDIO	
43'	(Braun)	$43,000.00	CYCAD PRODUCTIONS	

Models and Sculpture

| 5" | (Fischner) | $45.00 | DREAMSTAR D-17 Sm | [hatchling] |
| 28" | (Fischner) | $575.00 | DREAMSTAR | |

Plaques

| 24x36" | - | $384.00 | ANTIQUARIAN | [skull] |

EFRAASIA

Life-sized Models

| 8' | (Braun) | $8,000.00 | CYCAD PRODUCTIONS | |

EINIOSAURUS

Models and Sculpture

14"	(Krentz)	$120.00	KRENTZ	
18"	(Wenzel)	$325.00	DINOSAUR STUDIO	[finished, $875.00]

ELAPHROSAURUS

Life-sized Models

11'	(Braun)	$11,000.00	CYCAD PRODUCTIONS

ELASMOSAURUS

Fossil Replicas
Skeleton

42'	-	$33,500	ANTIQUARIAN A108
42'	-	$62,500.00	TRIEBOLD

Skull

5"	-	$8.99	DINOSAUR FOUNDRY

Life-sized Models

33'	(McGrady)	$40,000.00	CM STUDIO
46'	(Braun)	$46,000.00	CYCAD PRODUCTIONS

Models and Sculpture

15"	-	$19.95	HORIZON HOR065	
21"	(Geraths)	$165.00	GERATHS	[with calf]
29"	-	$135.00	MONSTROSITIES	[Kaiyodo]

Plaques

9x12"-		$69.99	DINOSAUR FOUNDRY	[skull]

Plastic Figures

10.5"	(Carnegie)	$8.50	SAFARI 4019-01

ELGINIA

Life-sized Models

24"	(Braun)	$2,400.00	CYCAD PRODUCTIONS

ELMISAURUS

Fossil Replicas
Claw

4"	-	$12.00	GASTON DESIGN	[manus]

ENNATOSAURUS

Fossil Replicas
Skeleton
5m   - $3,370.00   GONDWANA

EOCAPTORHINUS

Fossil Replicas
Skull
2.5"   - $36.00   SMITH STUDIOS

EORAPTOR

Fossil Replicas
Skeleton
1m   - $5,500.00   BLACK HILLS
Skull
4"   (Gravino) $60.00   TWO GUYS
4.5"   - $95.00   NORTH EASTERN RD-142
Life-sized Models
40"   (McGrady) $1,600.00   CM STUDIO
Models and Sculpture
11"   (Gerath) $225.00   GERATH   [bust]
36"   (Salas) $1500.00   DINO ART   [with mammal prey]

EOTITANOSUCHUS

Fossil Replicas
Skull
.35m   - $337.00   GONDWANA

EPANTERIAS

Models and Sculpture
20"   (Salas) $120.00   SALAS

ERYTHROSAURUS

Life-sized Models
15'   (Braun) $15,000.00   CYCAD PRODUCTIONS

ESTEMMENOSUCHUS

Fossil Replicas
Skull
.6m   - $985.00   GONDWANA
Models and Sculpture
10"   (Alchemy) $118.98   LINK AND PIN DS05

EUDIMORPHODON

Life-sized Models
24"   (Braun) $2,400.00   CYCAD PRODUCTIONS
Plaque
6"   (Hoeger) $13.00   VALLEY SH08   [skull]

EUOPLOCEPALUS

Fossil Replicas
Skull
2.5"   (Tskhondin) $9.95   ANTS r100701104   [fossil color available]
15"   - $2,499.00   SMITH STUDIOS
Life-sized Models
18'   (Braun) $18,000.00   CYCAD PRODUCTIONS
Models and Sculpture
?   (Krentz)   CALL   KRENTZ
8"   - $97.98   LINK AND PIN R-19   [Kaiyodo]
8"   (Tokugawa) $60.00   MUSASHI
30"   (Fischner) $750.00   DREAMSTAR
Plaques
11x22"(Minott) $100.00   MENTIS GROUP
Plastic Figures
6"   (Bos. Mus.) $8.00   BATTAT

EUPARKERIA

Life-sized Models
24"   (Braun) $2,000.00   CYCAD PRODUCTIONS

EUSTREPTOSPONDYLUS

Life-sized Models
23'   (Braun) $23,000.00   CYCAD PRODUCTIONS

ERHINOSAURUS

Life-sized Models
78" (Braun) $7,200.00 CYCAD PRODUCTIONS

EUHELOPUS

Life-sized Models
49' (Braun) $49,000.00 CYCAD PRODUCTIONS

GALECHIRUS

Life-sized Models
12" (Braun) $1,200.00 CYCAD PRODUCTIONS

GALLIMIMUS

Fossil Replicas
Skeleton
4m - $12,960.00 GONDWANA
Skull
5" (Tskhondin) $21.95 ANTS r100701213 [fossil colored available]
12" - $250.00 NORTH EASTERN RD-138
Life-sized Models
13" (Braun) $13,000.00 CYCAD PRODUCTIONS
Plastic Figures
5.5" (Bos. Mus.) $5.00 BATTAT MS140

GALLODACTYLUS

Life-sized Models
48" (Braun) $4,800.00 CYCAD PRODUCTIONS

GASOSAURUS

Fossil Replicas
Skeleton
4m - CALL GONDWANA
Models and Sculpture
16" (Salas) $140.00 SALAS

GASPARIMOSAURUS

Fossil Replicas
Skull
7cm   (Gravino) $90.00   VALLEY MG10

GASTONIA

Fossil Replicas
Skeleton
12'   -   CALL   GASTON DESIGN   [juvenile]
16'   - $29,500.00   GASTON DESIGN
Skull
10"   - $170.00   GASTON DESIGN   [juvenile, with base]
Models and Sculpture
18"   (McGrady) $125.00   CM STUDIO   [finished, $205.00]

GERMANODACTYLUS

Life-sized Models
48"   (Braun) $4,800.00   CYCAD PRODUCTIONS

GIGANOTOSAURUS

Fossil Replicas
Skeleton
42'   - $120,000.00   ANTIQUARIAN
Skull
8"   - $260.00   ANTIQUARIAN MG01
8"   (Gravino) $175.00   DINOSAUR PRODUCTIONS
23cm   - $249.00   SKULLS UNLIMITED VA-04
72"   - $10,000.00   ANTIQUARIAN LE01
Teeth
7"   - $8.00   ANTIQUARIAN T40
7.5"   - $16.00   BONE ROOM
8"   - $14.99   DINOSAUR PRODUCTIONS
Life-sized Models
45'   (Braun) $45,000.00   CYCAD PRODUCTIONS
Models and Sculpture
14"   (Salas) $120.00   SALAS
21"   (Green) $115.00   CONTINENTAL   [$250.00 finished]
37"   (Musy)   CALL   MARK MUSY
[$1,200.00]

23"	(Salas)	$150.00	DINO ART	
Plaques				
4x8"	(Gravino)	$15.00	VALLEY MG04	[skull]
Plastic Models				
12"	-	$13.00	RESAURUS	[12 moveable joints!]

GNATHOSAURUS

| **_Life-sized Models_** | | | | |
| 60" | (Braun) | $6,000.00 | CYCAD PRODUCTIONS | |

GONIOPHOLIS

| **_Life-sized Models_** | | | | |
| 50' | (Braun) | $50,000.00 | CYCAD PRODUCTIONS | |

GORGONOPSID

Fossil Replicas				
Skull				
16"	-	$137.00	ANTIQUARIAN S16	

GORGOSAURUS

Fossil Replicas				
Claw				
12cm	-	$8.00	VALLEY CL12	
Models and Sculpture				
32"	(Wenzel)	$395.00	DINOSAUR STUDIO	[finished, $945.00]
[$4,800.00]				

GRACILISUCHUS

| **_Life-sized Models_** | | | | |
| 12" | (Braun) | $1,200.00 | CYCAD PRODUCTIONS | |

HADROSAURUS

Fossil Replicas				
Leg				
10'	-	$5,000.00	MT. BLANCO	[world's largest specimen]

Skeleton
12"   (Ignacio) $250.00   DINO ART   [skeleton relief]
Life-sized Models
30'   (Braun) $30,000.00   CYCAD PRODUCTIONS
Models and Sculpture
2"   (Salas) $500.00   DINO ART   [nest with hatchlings]
12"   (Debus) $60.00   HELL CREEK   [with Waterhouse Hawkins!]

HENODUS

Life-sized Models
36"   (Braun) $3,600.00   CYCAD PRODUCTIONS

HERRERASAURUS

Fossil Replicas
Skeleton
3m   - $11,500.00   BLACK HILLS
Skull
5"   (Tskhondin) $25.95   ANTS r100701214   [fossil colored available]
33cm   - $239.000   SKULLS UNLIMITED VA-09
12"   (Gravino) $240.00   VALLEY MG05
12"   - $250.00   NORTH EASTERN RD-139
Life-sized Models
2.5m   - $2,400.00   SALAS GISMONDI

HETERODONTOSAURUS

Life-sized Models
36"   (Braun) $3,600.00   CYCAD PRODUCTIONS
Wooden Toys
48"   - $190.00   DINO WORKS   [skeleton]

HOMALOCEPHLAE

Life-sized Models
10'   (Braun) $10,000.00   CYCAD PRODUCTIONS

HOVASAURUS

Life-sized Models
20"   (Braun) $2,000.00   CYCAD PRODUCTIONS

HYDROTHEROSAURUS

Models and Sculpture
4"   (Tischler) $1,030.00   HUGH ROSE   ['Going Fishing']

HYLAEOSAURUS

Life-sized Models
20'   (Braun) $20,000.00   CYCAD PRODUCTIONS

HYLONOMUS

Life-sized Models
8"   (Braun) $8,000.00   CYCAD PRODUCTIONS

HYPACROSAURUS

Life-sized Models
30'   (Braun) $30,000.00   CYCAD PRODUCTIONS
Models and Sculpture
10"   (Morales) $134.94   LUNAR MODELS OS03   [with Carnotaurus]

HYPERODAEDON

Life-sized Models
48"   (Braun) $4,000.00   CYCAD PRODUCTIONS

HYPSELOSAURUS

Fossil Replicas
Skull
5"   - $145.00   NORTH EASTERN RD-130
Models and Sculpture
12"   (Fischner) $525.00   DREAMSTAR   [hatchling]

HYPSILOPHODON

Fossil Replicas
Skull
2.5"   (Tskhondin) $14.95   ANTS r100701216   [fossil color available]
6"   - $90.00   TWO GUYS

Life-sized Models
1m   -   CALL   GONDWANA   [hatchling]
5'   (Braun) $5,000.00   CYCAD PRODUCTIONS

HYPSOGNATHUS

Life-sized Models
13"   (Braun) $1,300.00   CYCAD PRODUCTIONS

ICHTHYOSAUR

Life-sized Models
77"   (Braun) $7,700.00   CYCAD PRODUCTIONS
Plaques
6x23" - $28.50   ANTIQUARIAN P24
150x580mm   L26.00   GEOU JR 6.7
12x35" $160.00   NORTH EASTERN RD-91
118x268mm   L17.00   GEOU JR 6.0   [skull]
370x170mm   L92.00   GEOU JR 6.6P

IGUANODON

Fossil Replicas
Skeleton
6m   -   CALL   GONDWANA
Skull
2"   (Tskhondin) $5.95   ANTS r100701117   [fossil colored available]
35"   - $3,950.00   SMITH STUDIOS
90cm - $415.00   GONDWANA
Thumb Spike
5.5" - $12.00   BONE ROOM
13cm - $10.00   VALLEY SH04
Teeth
43mm -   L2.25   GEOU CRR 1.01
Life-sized Models
6'   (Braun) $6,000.00   CYCAD PRODUCTIONS   [juvenile]
30'   (Braun) $30,000.00   CYCAD PRODUCTIONS   [male and female available]
Models and Sculpture
7"   (Tokugawa)   Y2,500   TOKUGAWA
10"   (Manit)   CALL   LIVING RESIN
11"   (Braun) $1,100.00   CYCAD PRODUCTION   [Waterhouse Hawkins]
14"   (Braun) $1,400.00   CYCAD PRODUCTIONS   [flayed]
19"   (Foulkes) $95.00   CRETACEOUS   [$200.00 finished]

23"	(Hawkins)	$150.00	VALLEY M24	[Crystal Palace]
28"	(Fischner)	$575.00	DREAMSTAR	
29"	(McGrady)	$200.00	CM STUDIO	[finished, $375.00]

Plastic Figures

| 8" | (Carnegie) | $7.50 | SAFARI 4201-01 | |
| 9" | - | L5.99 | TOYWAY 204 | [Walking with Dinosaurs] |

Posters

| 18x21"(Burian) | $25.00 | MONSTROSITIES | |

INGENIA

Fossil Replicas
Skull

| 10cm | - | $260.00 | GONDWANA |

INOSTRANCEVIA

Fossil Replica
Skeleton

| 84" | - | $12,905.00 | GONDWANA |

KANNEMEYERIA

Life-sized Models

| 10' | (Braun) | $10,000.00 | CYCAD PRODUCTIONS |

KENTROSAURUS

Life-sized Models

| 5m | - | CALL | FLORIDES | |
| 16' | (Braun) | $16,000.00 | CYCAD PRODUCTIONS | |

Models and Sculpture

9"	-	$47.00	MONSTROSITIES	[Kaiyodo]
16"	(Dickens)	$125.00	DINO ART	[swimming]
19"	(Bracco)	$550.00	DINO ART	[swimming]
30"	(Fischner)	$700.00	DREAMSTAR	

KLAMELISAURUS

Fossil Replicas
Skeleton

| 17m | - | CALL | GONDWANA |

KRAMERISAURUS

Fossil Replicas
Skeleton
17m   - $85,000.00   SMITH STUDIOS

KRITOSAURUS

Life-sized Models
7m   - $4,800.00   SALAS GISMONDI
30'   (Braun) $30,000.00   CYCAD PRODUCTIONS

KRONOSAURUS

Life-sized Models
40'   (Braun) $40,000.00   CYCAD PRODUCTIONS
Models and Sculpture
10"   (Dickens) $250.00   DINO ART
14"   (Johnson) $129.95   LUNAR MODELS OS23   [with cuttlefish]
Plastic Figures
13"   (Carnegie) $15.00   SAFARI 4029-01

KUEHNEOSAURUS

Life-sized Models
26"   (Braun) $2,600.00   CYCAD PRODUCTIONS

KUNMINGGOSAURUS

Fossil Replicas
Skeleton
11m   -   CALL   GONDWANA

KWEICHOSAURUS

Fossil Replicas
Skeleton
12"   - $175.00   BLACK HILLS R00750   [on slab]

LABIDOSAURUS

Life-sized Models
27"   (Braun) $2,700.00   CYCAD PRODUCTIONS

LAGOSUCHUS

Life-sized Models
12"   (Braun) $1,200.00   CYCAD PRODUCTIONS
Models and Sculpture
20"   (Salas) $500.00   DINO ART

LAMBEOSAURUS

Life-sized Models
30'   (Braun) $30,000.00   CYCAD PRODUCTIONS
Models and Sculpture
12"   (Wenzel) $85.00   DINOSAUR STUDIO   [finished, $310.00]
25"   (McGrady) $150.00   CM STUDIO
29"   (Strasser) $260.00   DRAGON, INC   [finished, $450.00]
29"   (McGrady) $185.00   CM STUDIO
40"   (Trcic) $8,500.00   TRCIC STUDIO   [with dromaeosaurs]

LANTHANOSUCHUS

Fossil Replicas
Skull
19cm   - $207.00   GONDWANA

LARIOSAURUS

Life-sized Models
24"   (Braun) $2,400.00   CYCAD PRODUCTIONS

LEAELLYNASAURA

Plastic Figures
6"   -   L5.99   TOYWAY 201   [Walking with Dinosaurs]

LEPTOCERATOPS

Life-sized Models
7'   (Braun) $7,000.00   CYCAD PRODUCTIONS
Models and Sculpture
7"   (Jones) $29.98   LINK AND PIN

LESOTHOSAURUS

Life-sized Models
36"   (Braun) $3,600.00   CYCAD PRODUCTIONS

LIOPLEURODON

Fossil Replicas
Teeth
210mm $10.50   GEOU JR 4.01
Life-sized Models
35'   (Braun) $35,000.00   CYCAD PRODUCTIONS
Models and Sculpture
7"   (Dickens) $150.00   INTEGRITY
22"   (Gerath) $165.00   GERATH   [finished, $285.00]

LONGISQUAMA

Life-sized Models
6"   (Braun) $600.00   CYCAD PRODUCTIONS

LOTOSAURUS

Fossil Replicas
Skeleton
3m   -   CALL   GONDWANA

LUFENGGOSAURUS

Fossil Replicas
Skeleton
6.5m   -   CALL   GONDWANA

LYCAENOPS

Life-sized Models
36"	(Braun)	$3,600.00	CYCAD PRODUCTIONS

LYSTROSAURUS

Fossil Replicas
Skeleton
1m	-	$3,988.00	GONDWANA

Life-sized Models
36"	(Braun)	$3,600.00	CYCAD PRODUCTIONS

MACROPLATA

Life-sized Models
15'	(Braun)	$15,000.00	CYCAD PRODUCTIONS

MAIASAURUS

Fossil Replicas
Skeleton
14"	-	$1,600.00	SMITH STUDIOS	[hatchling]
30"	-	$2,400.00	SMITH STUDIOS	[nestling]
7'	-	$12,500.00	ANTIQUARIAN A107	[juvenile]
23'	-	$37,500.00	SMITH STUDIOS	

Skull
12"	-	$289.00	ANTIQUARIAN S017	[juvenile]
30cm		$300.00	VALLEY A107S	[juvenile]
32"	-	$2,200.00	SMITH STUDIOS	

Life-sized Models
30'	(Braun)	$30,000.00	CYCAD PRODUCTIONS
30'	(McGrady)	$30,000.00	CM STUDIO

Models and Sculpture
7"	(Windstone)	$38.00	GRANDIOSITY #308	[hatchling]
11"	-	$34.98	LINK AND PIN MK-03	[Kaiyodo]

Plastic Models
8"	(Carnegie)	$15.00	SAFARI 4027-01	[with nest]
9"	(Bos. Mus.)	$9.50	BATTAT	

MAJUNGASAURUS

Models and Sculpture
9"   (Jones) $149.98   LINK AND PIN   [bust]

MAMENCHISAURUS

Fossil Replicas
Skeleton
25m   - $85,000.00   BLACK HILLS
Life-sized Models
71'   (Braun) $72,000.00   CYCAD PRODUCTIONS
Models and Sculpture
34"   (Morales) $179.95   LUNAR MODELS OS18
36"   (Fischner) $650.00   DREAMSTAR
Plastic Figures
25"   (Kish) $27.00   SAFARI 2602-29
Posters
18x36"(Hallett) $12.00   MONSTROSITIES

MASSETOGNATHUS

Life-sized Models
19"   (Braun) $1,900.00   CYCAD PRODUCTIONS

MASSOSPONDYLUS

Fossil Replicas
Skull
90mm -   L8.00   GEOU TRR 3.1   [juvenile]
220mm   L33.00   GEOU TRR 3.0
8"   - $75.00   TWO GUYS
Life-sized Models
13'   (Braun) $13,000.00   CYCAD PRODUCTIONS

MEGALANIA

Life-sized Models
25'   (Braun) $25,000.00   CYCAD PRODUCTIONS
Models and Sculpture
16"   (Salas) $100.00   SALAS

MEGARAPTOR

Fossil Replicas
Claw
13"   - $60.00   TWO GUYS   [pes]
38cm   - $14.00   VALLEY MG14   [pes]

MEGALOSAURUS

Life-sized Models
30'   (Braun) $30,000.00   CYCAD PRODUCTIONS
Models and Sculpture
7"   - $149.98   LINK AND PIN #11   [Kaiyodo]
18"   (Salas) $109.98   LINK AND PIN
51cm   (Hawkins) $150.00   VALLEY M25   [Crystal Palace]

MEIOLANIA

Life-sized Models
8'   (Braun) $8,000.00   CYCAD PRODUCTIONS
Models and Sculpture
11"   - $214.98   LINK AND PIN #7   [Kaiyodo]

MESENOSAURUS

Fossil Replicas
Skeleton
37cm   - $156.00   GONDWANA   [slab]

MESOSAURUS

Life-sized Models
36"   (Braun) $3,600.00   CYCAD PRODUCTIONS
Plaques
8x13"   - $36.00   ANTIQUARIAN P4

METRICANTHOSAURUS

Models and Sculpture
18"   (Morales) $140.00   DRAGON ATTACK!   [finished, $285.00]

METRIORYHNCHUS

Life-sized Models
10'   (Braun) $10,000.00   CYCAD PRODUCTIONS

MICROCERATOPS

Life-sized Models
24"   (Braun) $2,400.00   CYCAD PRODUCTIONS
Models and Sculpture
3"   (Jones) $29.98   LINK AND PIN
30"   (Jones) $601.98   LINK AND PIN

MILLERETTA

Life-sized Models
24"   (Braun) $2,400.00   CYCAD PRODUCTIONS

MIXOSAURUS

Life-sized Models
36"   (Braun) $3,600.00   CYCAD PRODUCTIONS

MONGOLEMYS

Fossil Replicas
Skeleton
25cm   - $246.00   GONDWANA

MONOLOPHOSAURUS

Fossil Replicas
Skeleton
4.2m   - $22,000.00   SMITH STUDIOS
6m   -   CALL   GONDWANA

Models and Sculpture
12"	(Jones)	$88.98	LINK AND PIN
17"	(Manit)	CALL	LIVING RESIN

MONONYKUS

Models and Sculpture
36"	(Salas)	$1000.00	DINO ART

MONTANOCERATOPS

Life-sized Models
10'	(Braun)	$10,000.00	CYCAD PRODUCTIONS

Models and Sculpture
10"	(Jones)	$89.98	LINK AND PIN

MOSASAURUS

Fossil Replicas
Skeleton
11'	-	$12,500	ANTIQUARIAN

Skull
5"	-	$8.99	DINOSAUR FOUNDRY
114cm	-	L800.00	GEOU MOS 4.0
114cm	-	$950.00	VALLEY S52
45"	-	$944.00	ANTIQUARIAN S52

Teeth
90mm	-	L9.00	GEOU MOS 2.0

Models and Sculpture
7"	(Tokugawa)	Y2,000	TOKUGAWA
9"	(Johnson)	$89.00	ACTION HOBBIES
11.5"	(LoRusso)	$90.00	DINOSAUR STUDIO
18"	(Morales)	CALL	DRAGON ATTACK!
18"	(Dickens)	$170.00	INTEGRITY
20"	(Penkalski)	$150.00	DINO ART
23"	(Salas)	$150.00	SALAS
28"	(Fischner)	$650.00	DREAMSTAR

Plaques
9x12"		$69.99	DINOSAUR FOUNDRY [skull]

Plastic Models
6"	(Carnegie)	$5.00	SAFARI 4020-01

Posters
22x33"	(Stout)	$20.00	MONSTROSITIES

MOSCHOPS

Life-sized Models
16'   (Braun) $16,000.00   CYCAD PRODUCTIONS

MURAENOSAURUS

Life-sized Models
20'   (Braun) $20,000.00   CYCAD PRODUCTIONS

MUSSASAURUS

Life-sized Models
10'   (Braun) $10,000.00   CYCAD PRODUCTIONS

MUTTABURRASAURUS

Life-sized Models
24'   (Braun) $24,000.00   CYCAD PRODUCTIONS

MYMOORAPELTA

Fossil Replicas
Skeleton
144"   (Gaston)   CALL   GASTON DESIGN

NANOSAURUS

Fossil Replicas
Claw
57mm - $6.00   VALLEY CL13
Feet
15cm - $10.00   VALLEY CO6
Skull
15cm   L40.00   GEOU JR 10.0
15cm $40.00   VALLEY S32
Plaques
17x27" $214.00   ANTIQUARIAN PO2

NANOTYRANNUS

Fossil Replicas
Skull

?	-	CALL	ALCHEMY	
5"	-	$45.00	NORTH EASTERN RD-177	
22"	-	$1,500.00	CREATIONS E. T.	

Models and Sculpture

7"	(Jones)	$39.98	LINK AND PIN	
14"	(Dickens)	$159.98	LINK AND PIN	[with Struthiomimus]
19"	(Salas)	$42.00	SALAS	
[$1,300]				
41"	(Finney)	CALL	ALCHEMY	

Posters

20x29"(Glazer)	$24.00	ANTIQUARIAN	

NODOSAURUS

Life-sized Models

18'	(Braun)	$18,000.00	CYCAD PRODUCTIONS

Plaques

8x10"	-	$350.00	ROBERT REID	[skull]

NOTHOSAUR

Life-sized Models

10'	(Braun)	$10,000.00	CYCAD PRODUCTIONS

Plaques

6x9"	-	$56.00	GASTON DESIGN

NYCTIPHRURETUS

Fossil Replicas

33cm	-	$220.00	GONDWANA	[slab]

NYCTOSAURUS

Life-sized Models

9'	(Braun)	$9,000.00	CYCAD PRODUCTIONS

OLIGOKYPHUS

Life-sized Models
20"   (Braun) $2,000.00   CYCAD PRODUCTIONS

OMEISAURUS

Fossil Replicas
Skeleton
20m   -   CALL   GONDWANA
Models and Sculpture
15"   (Salas) $109.98   LINK AND PIN

OPETIOSAURUS

Fossil Replicas
Skeleton
57"   - $275.00   BLACK HILLS R00730   [slab]

OPHIACODON

Life-sized Models
12'   (Braun) $12,000.00   CYCAD PRODUCTIONS

OPISTHIAS

Life-sized Models
24"   (Braun) $2,000.00   CYCAD PRODUCTIONS

OPISTHOCOELICAUDIA

Life-sized Models
40'   (Braun) $40,000.00   CYCAD PRODUCTIONS

OPTHALMOSAURUS

Life-sized Models
11'   (Braun) $11,000.00   CYCAD PRODUCTIONS

ORODROMEUS

Fossil Replicas
Embyro
6.5"   - $53.00   SMITH STUDIOS

ORNITHOCHERIUS

Life-sized Models
8'   (Braun) $8,000.00   CYCAD PRODUCTIONS

ORHITHOLESTES

Life-sized Models
6'   - $8,500.00   JONAS STUDIOS
Models and Sculpture
7.5"   - $375.00   JONAS STUDIOS

ORNITHOMIMUS

Fossil Replicas
Claw
2"   - $6.00   SECOND NATURE SN-14   [manus]
3"   - $8.00   SECOND NATURE SN-15   [manus]
3"   - $8.00   SECOND NATURE SN-16   [pes]
90mm - $6.00   VALLEY CL20
5"   - $50.00   TAYLOR STUDIOS F005   [manus]

ORNITHOSUCHUS

Fossil Replicas
Skull
10"   - $275.00   NORTH EASTERN RD-134
Life-sized Replicas
13'   (Braun) $13,000.00   CYCAD PRODUCTIONS

ORNITHOMIMUS

Life-sized Models
11'   (Braun) $11,000.00   CYCAD PRODUCTIONS
Models and Sculpture
22"   (McGrady) $125.00   CM STUDIO   [base, $15.00]

OTHNIELIA

Fossil Replica
Feet
6.5"	-	$37.00	GASTON DESIGN	[with base]

Leg
25"	-	$79.00	GASTON DESIGN	[with stand]

Skeleton
72"	-	CALL	GASTON DESIGNS

Skull
5.5"	-	$39.00	PREHISTORIC	[profile]

Life-sized Models
48"	(Braun)	$4,800.00	CYCAD PRODUCTIONS

OURANOSAURUS

Life-sized Models
23'	(Braun)	$23,000.00	CYCAD PRODUCTIONS

Models and Sculpture
16"	(Strasser)	$125.00	DRAGON, INC.	[finished, $250.00]

Plastic Figures
7"	(Bos. Mus.)	$8.00	BATTAT

OVIRAPTOR

Fossil Replicas
Claw
6"	-	$20.00	SECOND NATURE SN-06	[manus]

Skull
3"	(Tskhondin)	$21.95	ANTS r100701208	[fossil color available]
4"	(Harvey)	$79.00	WICCART	

Life-sized Models
6'	(Braun)	$6,000.00	CYCAD PRODUCTIONS
8'	-	$1,600.00	CREATIONS E. T.
9'	(McGrady)	$7,200.00	CM STUDIO

Models and Sculpture
14"	(McGrady)	$85.00	CM STUDIO	[base, $35.00]
16"	(Gerath)	$164.98	LINK AND PIN	[on nest]

Posters
13x18"(Sibbick)	L15.00	SIBBICK	

PACHYCEPHALOSAURUS

Fossil Replicas
Claw

60mm	-	$6.00	VALLEY CL14

Skeleton

10'	-	$29,000.00	TRIEBOLD
13'	-	$34,000.00	ANTIQUARIAN

Skull

6"	-	$24.95	EARTHLORE
20"	-	$2,800.00	BLACK HILLS RD0523
23"	-	$2,600.00	TRIEBOLD

Life-sized Models

15'	(Braun)	$15,000.00	CYCAD PRODUCTIONS

Models and Sculpture

7"	-	$189.98	LINK AND PIN R-13	[Kaiyodo, a pair]
8"	**(Tischler)**	**$1,250.00**	**HUGH ROSE**	**['Battering Rams']**
13"	(Strasser)	$100.00	DRAGON, INC.	[finished, $250.00]
28"	(Fischner)	$575.00	DREAMSTAR	

Plaques

12x22"	(Minott)	$95.00	MENTIS GROUP

Plastic Figures

5.5"	(Wild Safari)	$4.00	SAFARI 2785-29
6"	(Bos. Mus.)	$7.50	BATTAT
7.5"	(Carnegie)	$6.00	SAFARI 4018-01

Posters

11x17"	(Cox)	$5.00	COX

PACHYOPHIS

Fossil Replicas
Skeleton

7"	-	$125.00	BLACK HILLS R00770

PACHYPLEUROSAURUS

Fossils Replicas
Skeleton

12"	-	$175.00	BLACK HILLS R00745

PACHYRHACHIS

Life-sized Models
36"   (Braun) $3,600.00   CYCAD PRODUCTIONS

PACHYRHINOSAURUS

Life-sized Models
18'   (Braun) $18,000.00   CYCAD PRODUCTIONS
Models and Sculpture
6"   (LoRusso) $85.00   DINOSAUR STUDIO   [bust]
[$150.00]
6.5"   (LoRusso) $165.00   DINOSAUR STUDIO   [juvenile, finished, $715.00]
8"   (Green) $50.00   CONTINENTAL
15"   (Morales) $149.95   LUNAR MODELS OS18   [two models plus base]
22"   (LoRusso) $345.00   DINOSAUR STUDIO   [finished, $895.00]
[$4,200.00]

PALAEOTIONYX

Life-sized Models
18"   (Braun) $1,800.00   CYCAD PRODUCTIONS

PALEOSANIWA

Life-sized Models
10'   (Braun) $10,000.00   CYCAD PRODUCTIONS

PANOPLOSAURUS

Life-sized Models
15'   (Braun) $15,000.00   CYCAD PRODUCTIONS

PARASAUROLOPHUS

Fossil Replicas
Skeleton
30'   - $12,500.00   CREATIONS E. T.
Skull
5'   - $8.99   DINOSAUR FOUNDARY
6"   (Mendoza) $85.00   ANTIQUARIAN HM09
56"   - $1,500.00   CREATIONS E. T.

Life-sized Models

33'	(Braun)	$33,000.00	CYCAD PRODUCTIONS	

Models and Sculpture

1/35	-	$30.00	TAMIYA	
5"	**(Holmes)**	**$172.00**	**ATTICA**	**[bust]**
9.5"	**(Tischler)**	**$1,090.00**	**HUGH ROSE**	**['Ambushed']**
14"	-	$47.00	MONSTROSITIES	[Kaiyodo]
20"	(Foulkes)	$110.00	CRETACEOUS	[finished, $220.00]
28"	(Fischner)	$600.00	DREAMSTAR	

Plaques

230x320mm	L40.00	EDDY DNHR001	[skeleton]

Plastic Figures

6.5"	(Wild Safari)	$4.00	SAFARI 2786-29
7.5"	(Carnegie)	$9.00	SAFARI 4005-01
9"	(Bos. Mus.)	$7.00	BATTAT

Wooden Toys

15"	-	$5.00	ACTION 18151	[skeleton]

PAREIASAURUS

Life-sized Models

8'	(Braun)	$8,000.00	CYCAD PRODUCTIONS

PARKSOSAURUS

Life-sized Models

8'	(Braun)	$8,000.00	CYCAD PRODUCTIONS

PAWPAWSAURUS

Fossil Replicas
Skull

10"	-	$250.00	CAMPBELL

PENTACERATOPS

Life-sized Models

20'	(Braun)	$20,000.00	CYCAD PRODUCTIONS

Models and Sculpture

9"	(Jones)	CALL	ALCHEMY	[bust]
9"	(Green)	$50.00	CONTINENTAL	[two poses available]
14"	**(Merrithew)**	**$2,800.00**	**MERRITHEW**	**[three juveniles]**
16"	(McVey)	$700.00	MENAGERIE	

19"	(Foulkes)	$95.00	CRETACEOUS	[finished, $220.00]
26"	(Fischner)	$650.00	DREAMSTAR	
37"	**(Merrithew)**	**$6,000.00**	**MERRITHEW**	**[bites Tyrannosaur foot!]**

PETEINOSAURUS

Life-sized Models
| 24" | (Braun) | $2,400.00 | CYCAD PRODUCTIONS |

PETROLACOSAURUS

Life-sized Models
| 16" | (Braun) | $1,600.00 | CYCAD PRODUCTIONS |

PHTHINOSUCHUS

Life-sized Models
| 60" | (Braun) | $6,000.00 | CYCAD PRODUCTIONS |

PISANOSAURUS

Life-sized Models
| 36" | (Braun) | $3,600.00 | CYCAD PRODUCTIONS |

PISTOSAURUS

Life-sized Models
| 10' | (Braun) | $10,000.00 | CYCAD PRODUCTIONS |

PLACOCHELYS

Life-sized Models
| 36" | (Braun) | $3,600.00 | CYCAD PRODUCTIONS |

PLACODUS

Life-sized Models
| 72" | (Braun) | $7,200.00 | CYCAD PRODUCTIONS |

PLANOCEPHALOSAURUS

Life-sized Models
8"   (Braun) $8,000.00   CYCAD PRODUCTIONS

PLATECARPUS

Fossil Replicas
Skeleton
15.5'   - $17,500.00   TRIEBOLD
Skull
8"   (Harbey) $89.00   WICCART   [finished, $199.00]
19"   - $1,100.00   TRIEBOLD
Life-sized Models
14'   (Braun) $14,000.00   CYCAD PRODUCTIONS
18'   (McGrady) $28,000.00   CM STUDIO

PLATEOSAURUS

Fossil Replicas
Skull
4"   (Tskhondin) $25.95   ANTS r100701219   [fossil color available]
Life-Sized Models
32'   (Braun) $23,000.00   CYCAD PRODUCTIONS
Models and Sculpture
6"   - $58.98   LINK AND PIN DS33   [after Zallinger]

Plastic Figures
7.5"   (Carnegie) $7.00   SAFARI 4025-01

PLATYOPOSAURUS

Fossil Replicas
Skull
.37m   - $389.00   GONDWANA

PLEONEUSTES

Life-sized Models
10'   (Braun) $10,000.00   CYCAD PRODUCTIONS

PLESIOSAURUS

Fossil Replicas
Skull
22"   - $980.00   ANTIQUARIAN S108
Life-sized Models
7'   (Braun) $7,000.00   CYCAD PRODUCTIONS
Models and Sculpture
13"   - $130.00   MONSTROSITIES   [Kaiyodo]
17"   (Fischner) $575.00   DREAMSTAR
Plaques
29x31" $390.00   TAYLOR STUDIO F050   [juvenile]
Wooden Toys
19"   - $5.00   ACTION 18143   [skeleton]

PLEUROCOELUS

Posters
25x38"(Montgomery) $9.95   TEXAS PARKS

PLEURUSAURUS

Life-sized Models
24"   (Braun) $2,400.00   CYCAD PRODUCTIONS

PLIOPLATECARPUS

Fossil Replicas
Skeleton
18'   - $30,000.00   BLACK HILLS RR0771
Skull
22.5"   - $2,000.00   BLACK HILLS R00705

PLOTOSAURUS

Life-sized Models
30'   (Braun) $30,000.00   CYCAD PRODUCTIONS

POLACANTHUS

Fossil Replicas
Dermal Scute
80mm - L.5.00 GEOU CRR 11.2
Life-sized Models
13' (Braun) $13,000.00 CYCAD PRODUCTIONS
Models and Sculpture
23" (Fischner) $650.00 DREAMSTAR
Plastic Figures
9.5" - L.5.99 TOYWAY 203 [Walking with Dinosaurs]

POSTOSUCHUS

Life-sized Models
10' (McGrady) $11,000.00 CM STUDIO
Models and Sculpture
15" (Alchemy) $179.98 LINK AND PIN DS04 [with Desmatosuchus]
18" (McGrady) $225.00 CM STUDIO [finished, $490.00]
Plastic Figures
10.5" - L.5.99 TOYWAY 206 [Walking with Dinosaurs]

PRENOCEPHALE

Fossil Replicas
Skull
.23cm - $285.00 GONDWANA
Life-sized Models
8' (Braun) $8,000.00 CYCAD PRODUCTIONS

PRISICHAMPSUS

Life-sized Models
10' (Braun) $10,000.00 CYCAD PRODUCTIONS

PROBACTROSAURUS

Fossil Replicas
Skeleton
5m - $15,552.00 GONDWANA

PROCOMPSOGNATHUS

Life-sized Models
48"   (Braun) $4,800.00   CYCAD PRODUCTIONS

PROCYNOSUCHUS

Life-sized Models
24"   (Braun) $2,400.00   CYCAD PRODUCTIONS

PROSAUROLOPHUS

Fossil Replicas
Skull
90cm   - $500.00   VALLEY S40   [Royal Ontario Museum]
Plaques
24x36" $384.00   ANTIQUARIAN   [skull]

PROTOCERATOPS

Fossil Replicas
Skeleton
1.8m   - $6,739.00   GONDWANA
Skull
2.5"   (Tskhondin) $9.95   ANTS r100701120   [fossil color available]
11"   - $150.00   GASTON DESIGN   [juvenile, with base]
Life-sized Models
1.8m   - $6,000.00   GONDWANA
8'   - $1,650.00   CREATIONS E. T.
9'   (Braun) $9,000.00   CYCAD PRODUCTIONS
Models and Sculpture
6"   (Hunt) $400.00   HUNT STUDIOS
7"   (Windstone) $38.00   GRANDIOSITY #306   [hatchling]
8"   (Manit) $65.00   LIVING RESIN
10"   - $134.95   LUNAR MODELS OS05   [fighting Velociraptor]
12"   (McGrady) $85.00   CM STUDIO   [base, $35.00]
13"   (Jones) $149.98   LINK AND PIN   [Model A]
13"   (Jones) $129.98   LINK AND PIN   [Model B]
27"   (Fischner) $575.00   DREAMSTAR
Wooden Toys
72"   - $300.00   DINO WORKS   [skeleton]

PROTOROSAURUS

Life-sized Models
72"   (Braun) $7,200.00   CYCAD PRODUCTIONS

PROTOSTEGA

Fossil Replicas
Skeleton
30"   - $11,000.00   ANTIQUARIAN A109
Skull
5.5"   - $180.00   ANTIQUARIAN   [juvenile]
18"   - $644.00   ANTIQUARIAN S109
33cm   - $800.00   VALLEY A109S   [Denver Museum]

PROTOSUCHUS

Life-sized Models
36"   (Braun) $3,600.00   CYCAD PRODUCTIONS
Fossil Replicas
Skull
4.5"   - $65.00   NORTH EASTERN RD-181

PSITTACOSAURUS

Fossil Replicas
Skeleton
.4m   - $1,500.00   SMITH STUDIOS
1m   - $5,443.00   GONDWANA
Skull
3"   (Tskhondin) $19.95   ANTS r100701208   [fossil color available]
Life-sized Models
8'   (Braun) $8,000.00   CYCAD PRODUCTIONS
Models and Sculpture
5"   (Jones)   CALL   ALCHEMY
Plastic Figures
6.5"   (Carnegie) $10.00   SAFARI 4034-01

PTERANODON

Fossil Replicas
Skeleton

9"	(Maniscalco)	$275.00	MAXILLA	['The Take Off']
11'	-	$5,400.00	TRIEBOLD	
11'	-	$6,500.00	ANTIQUARIAN TB05	
12'	-	$6,000.00	SMITH STUDIOS	
20'	-	$11,500.00	SMITH STUDIOS	

Skull

8"-		$8.99	DINOSAUR FOUNDRY	
34"	-	$650.00	TRIEBOLD	
34"	-	$850.00	ANTIQUARIAN TB06	

Life-sized Models

23'	(Braun)	$23,000.00	CYCAD PRODUCTIONS	
24'	(Watson)	$16,350.00	WATSON SCULPTURE	

Models and Sculpture

4"	(Fischner)	$45.00	DREAMSTAR D18-Sm	[hatchling]
4"	-	$38.98	LINK AND PIN DS34	[after Zallinger]
6"	(Dickens)	$50.00	INTEGRITY	
13"	**(Tischler)**	**$950.00**	**HUGH ROSE**	**['Catcher gets Caught']**
16"	-	CALL	ALCHEMY	
23"	(Watson)	$220.00	WADTON SCULPTURE	[two poses]
23"	(Penkalski)	$128.98	LINK AND PIN	
23"	(Neill)	$200.00	NEILL	[finished, $750.00]
[$1,500.00]				

Plastic Figures

4.5"	(Carnegie)	$2.00	SAFARI 4014-01	

Wooden Toys

20"	-	$5.00	ACTION 18146	[skeleton]
29"	-	$14.00	SAFARI 7307-10	[skeleton]
37"	-	$7.00	DINOSAUR PATTERNS	[skeleton]
35"	-	$24.99	DINO BONZ 40102	[skeleton]
60"	-	$34.95	DINO BONZ 40108	[skeleton]
60"	-	$59.00	SAFARI 7389-10	[skeleton]

PTERODACTYLUS

Fossil Replicas
Skull

?	-	$2,100.00	ANTIQUARIAN FL4
10.5"		$200.00	WESTERN

Life-sized Models

24"	(Braun)	$2,400.00	CYCAD PRODUCTIONS

Plaques

5x7"	-	$29.95	HORIZON 11255	[juvenile]
6x9"	-	$89.00	PREHISTORIC	
7x9"	-	$39.95	HORIZON 11251	
13x13"		$89.00	PREHISTORIC	
15x18"		$65.00	TAYLOR STUDIOS F035	

PTERODAUSTRO

Life-sized Models

| 48" | (Braun) | $2,400.00 | CYCAD PRODUCTIONS |

Fossil Replicas
Skull

| 8" | (Gravino) | $270.00 | VALLEY MG11 |
| 9" | - | $18.00 | NORTH EASTERN RD-170 [slab] |

PURUSSAURUS

Fossil Replicas
Skull

| 1.30m | - | $1,450.00 | SALAS GISMONDI |

QUETZALCOATALUS

Life-sized Models

| 34' | (McGrady) | $53,000.00 | CM STUDIOS | |
| 40' | (Braun) | $40,000.00 | CYCAD PRODUCTIONS | |

Models and Sculpture

| 11" | (Tokugawa) | Y2,500 | TOKUGAWA | |
| 14" | (Lunar) | $95.00 | DINO ART | [with Albertosaurus] |

Plastic Figures

| 7" | (Carnegie) | $6.00 | SAFARI 4031-01 |

REBBACHIOSAURUS

Fossil Replicas
Teeth

| 1.5" | - | $6.00 | SECOND NATURE SN-23 |

RHAMPHORHYNCHUS

Fossil Replicas
Skeleton
15"	(Harvey)	$349.00	WICCART	[finished, $749.00]

[$1,500.00]
Skull
2.5"	(Harvey)	$59.00	WICCART
5"	-	$24.95	EARTHLORE

Life-sized Models
36"	(Braun)	$3,600.00	CYCAD PRODUCTIONS

Plaques
4x6"	(Hoeger)	$13.00	VALLEY SH09	[skull]
9x13"		$89.00	PREHISTORIC	
11x5"		$39.95	HORIZON 11253	
13x13"		$89.00	PREHISTORIC	
13x28"		$139.00	PREHISTORIC	

RIOJASUCHUS

Fossil Replicas
Skull
5"	(Harvey)	$69.00	WICCART	[finished, $149.00]

Life-sized Models
35'	(Braun)	$35,000.00	CYCAD PRODUCTIONS

ROBERTIA

Life-sized Models
18"	(Braun)	$1,800.00	CYCAD PRODUCTIONS

RUTDIODON

Life-sized Models
10'	(Braun)	$10,000.00	CYCAD PRODUCTIONS
12'	(McGrady)	$12,000.00	CM STUDIO

Models and Sculpture
22"	(McGrady)	$400.00	CM STUDIO	[a pair]

SAICHANIA

Life-sized Models
23'   (Braun) $23,000.00   CYCAD PRODUCTIONS
Models and Sculpture
11"   - $131.98   LINK AND PIN R-04   [Kaiyodo]

SALTASAURUS

Life-sized Models
39'   (Braun) $39,000.00   CYCAD PRODUCTIONS
Models and Sculpture
11"   (Salas) $89.98   LINK AND PIN
23"   - $59.00   MONSTROSITIES   [Kaiyodo]
Plastic Figures
11.5"   (Carnegie) $9.00   SAFARI 4030-01

SALTOPUS

Life-sized Models
24"   (Braun) $2,400.00   CYCAD PRODUCTIONS

SAUROLOPHUS

Life-sized Models
30'   (Braun) $30,000.00   CYCAD PRODUCTIONS
Posters
24x36"(Henderson) $6.00   MONSTROSITIES   [with Tarbosaurus]

SAURONITHOLESTES

Fossil Replicas
Claw
30mm - $6.00   VALLEY CL40
Life-sized Models
6'   (Braun) $6,000.00   CYCAD PRODUCTIONS
6'   (McGRady) $4,500.00   CM STUDIO

SAUROPELTA

Life-sized Models
25'   (Braun) $25,000.00   CYCAD PRODUCTIONS

SAURORNITHOIDES

Life-sized Models
6'   (Braun) $6,000.00   CYCAD PRODUCTIONS

SCAPHOGNATHUS

Life-sized Models
36"   (Braun) $3,600.00   CYCAD PRODUCTIONS

SCELIDOSAURUS

Life-sized Models
13'   (Braun) $13,000.00   CYCAD PRODUCTIONS

SCUTELLOSAURUS

Life-sized Models
48"   (Braun) $4,800.00   CYCAD PRODUCTIONS

SCUTOSAURUS

Life-sized Models
8'   (Braun) $8,000.00   CYCAD PRODUCTIONS
Fossil Replicas
Skeleton
1.5m   - $2,955.00   GONDWANA

SEISMOSAURUS

Models and Sculpture
40"   (Salas) $189.98   LINK AND PIN
Posters
11x26"(Hallet) $16.50   ANTIQUARIAN

SEYMOURIA

Fossil Replicas
Skeleton
23"   - $420.00   TAYLOR STUDIOS F046

Models and Sculpture
3"   - $175.00   JONAS STUDIOS

SHAMOSUCHUS

Fossil Replicas
Skull
.59m - $518.00   GONDWANA

SHANTUNGOSAURUS

Life-sized Models
43'   (Braun) $43,000.00   CYCAD PRODUCTIONS
45'   - $5,500.00   CREATIONS E. T.
Models and Sculpture
1/24 (Green)   CALL   CONTINENTAL

SHONISAURUS

Life-sized Models
35'   - $8,700.00   CREATIONS E. T.
45'   (Braun) $45,000.00   CYCAD PRODUCTIONS
Models and Sculpture
22.5" (Green) $160.00   CONTINENTAL

SHUNOSAURUS

Fossil Replicas
Skeleton
9m   - $58,000.00   SMITH STUDIOS
11m   -   CALL   GONDWANA
Models and Sculpture
13"   (Salas) $120.00   SALAS

SILVISAURUS

Life-sized Models
11'   (Braun) $11,000.00   CYCAD PRODUCTIONS

SINOKANNEMEYERIA

Fossil Replicas
Skeleton
1.8m   - $8,000.00   SMITH STUDIOS

SINOSAUROPTERYX

Model and Sculptures
18"   (Bowman) $99.00   BOWMAN ARTS

SINRAPTOR

Fossil Replicas
Skull
10cm   (Gravino) $90.00   VALLEY MG07

SIORNTHOIDES

Models and Sculpture
7"   (Dickens) $35.00   INTEGRITY

SORDES

Life-sized Models
12"   (Braun) $1,200.00   CYCAD PRODUCTIONS

SPHENACODON

Life-sized Models
10'   (Braun) $10,000.00   CYCAD PRODUCTIONS

SPINOSAURUS

Fossil Replicas
Teeth
3"   - $8.00   ANTIQUARIAN T31
3"   - $8.00   SECOND NATURE SN-25
5"   - $12.00   SECOND NATURE SN-24
Life-sized Models
39'   (Braun) $39,000.00   CYCAD PRODUCTIONS

Models and Sculpture

14"	(Salas)	$234.98	LINK AND PIN	
15"	(Debus)	$105.00	HELL CREEK	[munching on plesiosaur!]
26"	(Fischner)	$650.00	DREAMSTAR	
30"	(Strasser)	$225.00	DRAGON, INC.	[finished, $500.00]

Plastic Figures

8.5"	(Carnegie)	$13.00	SAFARI 4022-01

Wooden Toys

17"	-	$8.00	SAFARI 7009-11	[skeleton]
17"	-	$7.00	ACTION 18148	[skeleton]
28"	-	$7.00 .	DINOSAUR PATTERNS	[skeleton]

STAGONOLEPIS

Life-sized Models

10'	(Braun)	$10,000.00	CYCAD PRODUCTIONS

STEGOCERAS

Fossil Replicas
Skeleton

2m	-	$7,000.00	BLACK HILLS	

Skull

3cm	(Tskhondin)	$25.95	ANTS r100701522	[fossil color available]
8"	-	$350.00	NORTH EASTERN RD-92	

Life-sized Models

6'	(Braun)	$6,000.00	CYCAD PRODUCTIONS

Models and Sculpture

22"	(McGrady)	$100.00	CM STUDIO	[finished, $175.00]

STEGOSAURUS

Fossil Replicas
Dorsal Plates

4"	-	$20.00	WESTERN	
7"	-	$26.50	SMITH STUDIOS	
14"	-	$30.00	ANTIQUARIAN M08	
350mm		L26.00	GEOU JR 11.1	
18.5"	-	$150.00	GASTON DESIGN	[with base]

Skull

2"	(Tskhondin)	$5.95	ANTS r100701105	[fossil color available]
4"	(Kronen)	$30.00	BONE CLONES KO-S01	

13"	-	$700.00	WESTERN	
16"	-	$220.00	ANTIQUARIAN DL06	
18.5"	-	$25.00	WESTERN	
33"	-	$100.00	WESTERN	
Spike				
20"	-	$30.00	ANTIQUARIAN	
500mm		L26.00	GEOU JR 11.0	
21"	(Kronen)	$95.00	BONE CLONES KO-015	
Life-sized Models				
26'	-	$42,000.00	JONAS STUDIOS	[1964 World's Fair]
30'	(Braun)	$30,000.00	CYCAD PRODUCTIONS	
Models and Sculpture				
4.5"	-	$58.00	MONSTROSITIES	[Kaiyodo]
5"	(Fischner)	$45.00	DREAMSTAR D-15-Sm	[hatchling]
6"	-	$95.00	JONAS STUDIOS	[1964 World's Fair]
6.5"	-	$19.95	HORIZON HOR028	
7"	(Windstone)	$40.00	GRANDIOSITY #305	[hatchling]
10"	(Morales)	$144.95	LUNAR MODELS OS08	[fighting Ceratosaurus]
11"	(Delgado)	$50.00	LESSER	[film prop]
8.5"	(LoRusso)	$85.00	DINOSAUR STUDIO	[finished, $310.00]
10"	**(Tischler)**	**$1,250.00**	**HUGH ROSE**	**['Confrontation']**
10"	-	$67.95	LUNAR MODELS OS25C	[after Zallinger]
15"	**(Merrithew)**	**$3,700.00**	**MERRITHEW**	**[two Stegos on stand]**
17"	(Furuya)	$158.00	FURUYA STUDIO	[finished, $518.00]
18"	(McGrady)	$185.00	CM STUDIO	[base, $15.00]
20"	(McVey)	$700.00	MENAGERIE	
24"	(Holmes)	L1,950	HOLMES	
28"	(Fischner)	$750.00	DREAMSTAR	
31.5"	-	$2,250.00	JONAS STUDIOS	[1964 World's Fair]
Plaques				
230x320mm		L40.00	EDDY DNST004	[skeleton]
11x14"	-	$35.00	HOWARD	
13x24"	(Minott)	$100.00	MENTIS GROUP	
Plastic Figures				
5.5"	(Wild Safari)	$4.00	SAFARI 2787-29	
6"	(Carnegie)	$9.00	SAFARI 4000-01	
7"	(Bos. Mus.)	$8.00	BATTAT MS150	
10"	-	$13.00	RESAURUS	[12 moveable joints!]
Posters				
12x36"	-	$2.95	NATURE SOURCE W2140	
33x55"	-	$12.95	OMNI 99-0312	[glow in the dark]
Wooden Toys				
17"	-	$8.00	SAFARI 7005-11	[skeleton]
17"	-	$5.00	ACTION 18144	[skeleton]
30"	-	$7.00	DINOSAUR PATTERNS	[skeleton]

31"	-	$26.00	SAFARI 7305-10	[skeleton]
32"	-	$15.00	B. C. BONZ S-SML	[skeleton]
46"	-	$25.00	B. C. BONZ S-MED	[skeleton]
64"	-	$40.00	B. C. BONZ S-LRG	[skeleton]

STENEOSAURUS

Fossil Replicas
Skeleton
| 47" | - | $600.00 | BLACK HILLS R00735 | [on slab] |

STENONYCHOSAURUS

Fossil Replicas
Claw
| 35mm - | $6.00 | VALLEY CL17 |

STENOPTERYGIUS

Life-sized Models
| 10' | (Braun) | $10,000.00 | CYCAD PRODUCTIONS |

Fossil Replicas
Skeleton
| 60" | - | CALL | BLACK HILLS R00755 |

STENOSAURUS

Plaques
| 18x18" | - | $69.00 | PREHISTORIC | [ichthyosaur] |

STRUTHIOMIMUS

Fossil Replicas
Arm
| 23" | - | $625.00 | BLACK HILLS RD0528 |

Claw
66mm	-	$6.50	VALLEY CL18	
3"	-	$20.00	BLACK HILLS R00519	[pes]
4.5"	-	$25.00	BLACK HILLS R00517	[manus]

Feet
| 23" | - | $600.00 | BLACK HILLS R00519 |

Hand

15"	-	$250.00	BLACK HILLS RD0527	
Skeleton				
13"	**(Maniscalco)**	**$225.00**	**MAXILLA**	**['Speedy']**
8'	-	$16,000.00	BLACK HILLS RD0526	[slab]
16'	-	$45,000.00	BLACK HILLS RD0525	
Life-sized Models				
9'	-	$14,500.00	JONAS STUDIOS	
11'	(Braun)	$11,000.00	CYCAD PRODUCTIONS	
Models and Sculpture				
5"	(Fischner)	$45.00	DREAMSTAR	[hatchling]
10"	-	$650.00	JONAS STUDIOS	[1964 World's Fair]
15"	(Finney)	$149.98	LINK AND PIN	
18"	(Dickens)	$159.98	LINK AND PIN	
28"	(Fischner)	$575.00	DREAMSTAR	
36"	(Finney)	$294.98	LINK AND PIN	

STRUTHIOSAURUS

Life-sized Models			
72"	(Braun)	$6,000.00	CYCAD PRODUCTIONS

STUPENDEMYS

Life-sized Models			
72"	(Braun)	$7,200.00	CYCAD PRODUCTIONS

STYGIMOLOCH

Models and Sculpture				
5.5"	**(Holmes)**	**$172.00**	**ATTICA**	**[bust]**
25"	(Jones)	$179.98	LINK AND PIN	

STYRACOSAURUS

Fossil Replicas				
Skeleton				
19"	**(Maniscalco)**	**$1,200.00**	**MAXILLA**	**['The Charge']**
Skull				
7"	**(Maniscalco)**	**$165.00**	**MAXILLA**	
8.5"	(Harvey)	$89.00	WICCART	
Life-sized Models				
17'	(Braun)	$17,000.00	CYCAD PRODUCTIONS	

SUCHOMIMUS

Models and Sculpture

4"	(Wenzel)	$85.00	DINOSAUR STUDIO	[bust, bronzed, $150.00]
6"	(Green)	$50.00	CONTINENTAL	
11"	-	$59.98	LINK AND PIN LK-11	[Kaiyodo]
11"	(Delgado)	$50.00	LESSER	[film prop]
12"	(Trcic)	$125.00	TRCIC STUDIO	[wall mount bust]
12"	(McGrady)	$85.00	CM STUDIO	
19"	(Wenzel)	$325.00	DINOSAUR STUDIO	[finished, $875.00]
22"	(Darga)	CALL	HORIZON 55704	
27"	(Fischner)	$675.00	DREAMSTAR	

Plastic Figures

6"	(Wild Safari)	$4.00	SAFARI 2788-29	
6"	(Bos. Mus.)	$7.00	BATTAT	
10"	-	$13.00	RESAURUS	[12 moveable joints!]

Wooden Toys

18"	-	$5.00	ACTION 18150	[skeleton]
32"	-	$7.00	DINOSAUR PATTERNS	[skeleton]
40"	-	$29.95	DINO BONZ 40105	[skeleton]

SUCHOMIMUS

Models and Sculpture

1/35	(Jones)	CALL	MIKE JONES	
21"	(Strasser)	$149.98	DRAGON, INC	[finished, $400.00]
36"	(McGrady)	$285.00	CM STUDIO	[finished, $395.00]

SUMINIA

Fossil Replicas
Skeleton

13"	-	$120.00	FOSSILNET	[on slab]

SUPERSAURUS

Fossil Replicas
Scapula

1.7m	-	$2,500.00	VALLEY BD05

SYNTARSUS

Fossil Replicas
Skull

8"	-	$35.00	NORTH EASTERN RD-157

SZECHHUANOSAURUS

Fossil Replicas
Skeleton
5m   -   CALL   GONDWANA

TALARURUS

Fossil Replicas
Skeleton
4.5m   - $21,760.00   GONDWANA
Life-sized Models
16'   (Braun) $16,000.00   CYCAD PRODUCTIONS

TANYSTROPHEUS

Life-sized Models
10'   (Braun) $10,000.00   CYCAD PRODUCTIONS
6m   -   CALL   FLORIDES

TAPAJARA

Fossil Replicas
Skull
9"   - $175.00   NORTH EASTERN RD-136

TARBOSAURUS

Fossil Replicas
Skeleton
7m   - $62,208.00   GONDWANA
Teeth
3"   - $8.00   SECOND NATURE SN-17
Life-sized Models
45'   (Braun) $45,000.00   CYCAD PRODUCTIONS
Posters
24x36"(Henderson) $8.99   ALLWALL.COM 1000-2484A

TARCHIA

Fossil Replicas
Skull
.35m   - $985.00   GONDWANA

TELEOSAURUS

Life-sized Models
10'   (Braun) $10,000.00   CYCAD PRODUCTIONS

TENODONTOSAURUS

Fossil Replicas
Claw
75mm - $6.00   VALLEY CL19
Life-sized Models
30'   (Braun) $30,000.00   CYCAD PRODUCTIONS

TERRESTRISUCHUS

Life-sized Models
20"   (Braun) $2,000.00   CYCAD PRODUCTIONS

TESTUDO

Life-sized Models
8'   (Braun) $8,000.00   CYCAD PRODUCTIONS

TENOTOSAURUS

Life-sized Models
24'   (Braun) $24,000.00   CYCAD PRODUCTIONS

THADEOSAURUS

Life-sized Models
24"   (Braun) $2,400.00   CYCAD PRODUCTIONS

THALASSOMEDON

Fossil Replicas
Skeleton
42'   -   CALL   VALLEY   [Denver Museum]
Skull
57cm - $800.00   VALLEY A108S   [Denver Museum]
Life-sized Models
12m   -   CALL   FLORIDES

THECELOSAURUS

Life-sized Models
11'   (Braun) $11,000.00   CYCAD PRODUCTIONS

THECODONTOSAURUS

Life-sized Models
7'   (Braun) $7,000.00   CYCAD PRODUCTIONS

THERIZINOSAURUS

Fossil Replicas
Claw
3.5"   - $12.00   GASTON DESIGN   [pes]
23"   - $34.00   ANTIQUARIAN SH10   [manus]
26"   - $45.00   BONE ROOM   [manus]
70cm - $156.00   GONDWANA   [manus]
Life-sized Models
15'   (McGrady) $21,000.00   CM STUDIO
Models and Sculpture
17"   (McGrady) $100.00   CM STUDIO   [finished, $175.00]
48"   (Graham) $502.98   LINK AND PIN
Plastic Figures
6.5"   (Kish) $12.00   SAFARI 2601-29   [with background]

THESCELOSAURUS

Fossil Replicas
Claw
2"   - $6.00   SECOND NATURE SN-13 [pes]

TICINOSUCHUS

Life-sized Models
10'   (Braun) $10,000.00   CYCAD PRODUCTIONS

TITANOSAURUS

Life-sized Models
7m   - $4,000.00   SALAS GISMONDI

TITANOSUCHUS

Life-sized Models
8'   (Braun) $8,000.00   CYCAD PRODUCTIONS
Models and Sculpture
9"   (Jones) $44.98   LINK AND PIN

TOJIANGASAURUS

Fossil Replicas
Skeleton
4.7m   - $23,000.00   SMITH STUDIOS

TOROSAURUS

Fossil Replicas
Teeth
8"   - $20.00   WESTERN
Life-sized Models
24'   (Braun) $24,000.00   CYCAD PRODUCTIONS
26'   - $5,900.00   CREATIONS E. T.
Models and Sculpture
13"   (Green) $84.98   LINK AND PIN
24"   (LoRusso) $425.00   DINOSAUR STUDIO
Plastic Figures
9"   -   L5.99   TOYWAY 202   [Walking with Dinosaurs]

TOXOCHELYS

Fossil Replicas
Skeleton
9.5"   - $650.00   TRIEBOLD

| 35" | - | $3,500.00 | BLACK HILLS R00721 | [panel mount] |
| 35" | - | $8,500.00 | BLACK HILLS R00720 | |

TRACHODON

Life-sized Models
| 23' | - | $37,500.00 | JONAS STUDIOS | [1964 World's Fair] |

Models and Sculpture
6"	-	$68.98	LINK AND PIN DS39	[after Zallinger]
7"	-	$145.00	JONAS STUDIOS	[1964 World's Fair]
27"	-	$1,950.00	JONAS STUDIOS	[1964 World's Fair]

TRICERATOPS

Fossil Replicas
Feet
| 3.5" | - | $30.00 | BLACK HILLS RD0541 | [ungual] |

Horn
9"	(Monteleone)	**$400.00**	**LOST ART**	**[horn cores]**
13"	-	$120.00	BLACK HILLS R00529	[nasal]
17"	-	$125.00	TAYLOR STUDIOS F029	
31"	-	$250.00	BLACK HILLS R00531	[supraorbital]

Skeleton
20"	-	$325.00	MONSTROSITIES	[Kaiyodo]
17'	-	$21,300.00	ANTIQUARIAN V37	
21'	-	$54,000.00	TRIEBOLD	

Skull
6"	-	$24.95	EARTHLORE	
6"	(Tskhondin)	$49.95	ANTS r100701101	[fossil color available]
6"	(Mendoza)	$135.00	ANTIQUARIAN HM10	
7"	(Comiskey)	$25.00	SKULLS OF ANTIQUITY	
10"	(Mjos)	$129.95	NATURAL CANVAS	
17"	(Williams)	$299.00	SKULLDUGGERY 0242	
66"	-	$5,500.00	TRIEBOLD	
78"	-	$4,900.00	ANTIQUARIAN AF555	
80"	-	$7,500.00	BLACK HILLS R00533	
80"	-	$8,500.00	BLACK HILLS R00525	[mounted]

Teeth
1"	-	$5.00	ANTIQUARIAN T34	
2"	-	$12.00	BLACK HILLS R00527	
2.5"	-	$8.00	SECOND NATURE SN-18	[with root]

Life-sized Models
| 10" | - | $750.00 | JONAS STUDIOS | [juvenile] |
| 26' | - | $39,500.00 | JONAS STUDIOS | [1964 World's Fair] |

Size	(Artist)	Price	Maker	Notes
28'	-	$8,500.00	CREATIONS E. T.	
30'	(Braun)	$30,000.00	CYCAD PRODUCTIONS	

Models and Sculpture

Size	(Artist)	Price	Maker	Notes
?	(Furuya)	CALL	FURUYA	
3"	-	$36.00	TAMIYA	
5"	(Fischner)	$45.00	DREAMSTAR D-14-Sm	[hatchling]
7"	(Windstone)	$40.00	GRANDIOSITY #301	[hatchling]
7"	(Fischner)	$65.00	DREAMSTAR D-11-Lg	[hatchling]
7"	**(Tischler)**	**$950.00**	**HUGH ROSE**	**['Mother and Baby']**
7"	-	$95.00	JONAS STUDIOS	[1964 World's Fair]
9"	-	$39.98	LINK AND PIN MK-02	[Kaioydo]
10"	(Wenzel)	$85.00	DINOSAUR STUDIO	[finished, $310.00]
10"	(Trcic)	$135.00	TRCIC STUDIO	
[$1,350.00]				
11"	(Watson)	$275.00	WATSON SCULPTURE	[with Tyrannosaur]
[$1,250.00]				
11"	(Laudati)	$70.00	X-O-FACTO	[with Tyrannosaur]
11"	**(Trcic)**	**$1,350.00**	**TRCIC STUDIO**	**[wall mount bust]**
14"	-	$59.98	LINK AND PIN LK-02	[Kaiyodo]
18"	-	$144.95	LUNAR MODELS OS13C	[after Knight; fights T. rex]
20"	(McVey)	$760.00	MENAGERIE	
20"	**(Van Howd)**	**$3,750.00**	**SIERRA SCULPTURE**	**[with Tyrannosaurus]**
24"	-	$194.95	LUNAR MODELS F669	[with girl in tree]
24"	(Strasser)	$324.98	DRAGON, INC	[$650.00 finished]
24"	(Jones)	$501.98	LINK AND PIN	[bust]
25"	(Fischner)	$675.00	DREAMSTAR	
26"	(McGrady)	$600.00	CM STUDIO	[finished, $1,050.00]
30"	(Darga)	$120.00	HORIZON 55705	
32"	-	$2,000.00	JONAS STUDIOS	[1964 World's Fair]
36"	(Holmes)	L2,400	HOLMES	

Plaques

Size	(Artist)	Price	Maker	Notes
100x130mm		L5.50	GEOU CRR 23.7	[skull]
9x12"	-	$69.99	DINOSAUR FOUNDRY	[skull]
11x14"		$35.00	HOWARD	
12x19"	(Minott)	$100.00	MENTIS GROUP	

Plastic Figures

Size	(Artist)	Price	Maker	Notes
7"	(Carnegie)	$7.00	SAFARI 4006-01	
7"	(Wild Safari)	$4.50	SAFARI 2790-29	
7.5"	(Bos. Mus.)	$10.00	BATTAT MS120	
10"	-	$13.00	RESAURUS	[12 moveable joints!]

Posters

Size	(Artist)	Price	Maker	Notes
11x17"	(Cox)	$5.00	COX	
24x36"	(Hallett)	$6.00	MONSTROSITIES	
33x55"	-	$12.95	OMNI 99-8314	[glow in the dark]

Wooden Toys

13"	-	$5.00	ACTION 18141	[skeleton]
15"	-	$8.00	SAFARI 7002-11	[skeleton]
29"	-	$19.50	SAFARI 7302-10	[skeleton]
32"	-	$7.00	DINOSAUR PATTERNS	[skeleton]
40"	-	$29.95	DINO BONZ 40104	

TRINACROMERUM

Life-sized Models
18'   (McGrady) $28,000.00   CM STUDIO

TRINAXODON

Life-sized Models
20"   (Braun) $2,000.00   CYCAD PRODUCTIONS
Models and Sculpture
13"   (Salas) $200.00   SALAS   [$400.00 finished]

TROODON

Fossil Replicas
Claw
2.5"   - $8.00   SECOND NATURE SN-01   [pes]
Life-sized Models
6'   (Braun) $6,000.00   CYCAD PRODUCTIONS
9'   (McGrady)   CALL   CM STUDIO
Models and Sculpture
16"   (Salas) $500.00   DINO ART   [five poses]

TROPEOGNATHUS

Fossil Replicas
Skull
117cm - $349.00   SKULLS UNLIMITED VA-026
Life-sized Models
3.5m   - $2,500.00   SALAS GISMONDI
Models and Sculpture
42"   (Weisgerber) $295.00   VALLEY JW01
Plaques
8x25"   (Hoeger) $100.00   VALLEY SH12   [skull]

TSINTAOSAURUS

Fossil Replicas
Skeleton

7m	-	CALL	GONDWANA
9m	-	$32,000.00	SMITH STUDIOS
27'	-	$40,000.00	TREASURES

Life-sized Models

33'	(Braun)	$33,000.00	CYCAD PRODUCTIONS

TUOJIANGASAURUS

Fossil Replicas

7m	-	CALL	GONDWANA

Life-sized Models

23'	(Braun)	$23,000.00	CYCAD PRODUCTIONS

Models and Sculpture

8"	(Finney)	$60.00	FINNEY

TYRANNOSAURUS

Fossil Replicas
Arm

30"	-	$1,200.00	BLACK HILLS RD0560	[Sue]

Brain Cast

7"	-	$14.00	BONE ROOM

Claw

1.5"	-	$8.00	GASTON DESIGN	[manus]
2.5"	-	$20.00	BLACK HILLS R00555	[manus]
3.5"	-	$25.00	BLACK HILLS R00551	[manus]
3.5"	-	$20.00	BONE ROOM	[manus]
4"	-	$25.00	BLACK HILLS R00549	[manus]
7"	-	$21.95	SKULLDUGGERY 0224	
7"	-	$36.00	SMITH STUDIOS	[pes]
7"	-	$45.00	BLACK HILLS R00537	[pes]
7.5"	-	$95.00	TAYLOR STUDIOS F004	[pes]
23cm	-	$18.00	VALLEY SH02	[pes]
9.5"	-	$30.00	SECOND NATURE SN-07	[pes]

Dentary

27.5"	-	$550.00	ANTIQUARIAN
39.5"	-	$990.00	BLACK HILLS RD0551

Feet

39"	-	$1,750.00	BLACK HILLS RD0547

114cm	-	$500.00	VALLEY M99	
48"	-	$744.00	ANTIQUARIAN	
Maxilla				
6"	(Monteleone)	**$425.00**	**LOST ART**	**[left]**
76cm		L220.00	GEOU CRR 23.0	
76cm	-	$200.00	VALLEY ANATOMICAL	
30"	-	$244.00	ANTIQUARIAN	
Skeleton				
27"	-	$350.00	MONSTROSITIES	[Kaiyodo]
35"	(Tippmann)	$1,000.00	TIPPMANN 1008	[Sue dig site]
48"	(Tippmann)	$600.00	TIPPMANN 1002	[Stan; finished, $1,500.00]
[$6,000.00]				
48"	-	$584.00	ANTIQUARIAN JT01	[finished, $1,340.00]
[$6800.00]				
51"	(Tippmann)	$600.00	TIPPMANN 1005	[Sue; assembled, $1,500.00]
[$4,800.00]				
55"	-	$1,100.00	BLACK HILLS SR0105	[Sue]
38'	-	$75,000.00	SMITH STUDIOS	[MOR555 specimen]
40'	-	$25,000.00	CREATIONS E. T.	
40'	-	$100,000.00	BLACK HILLS R00543	[Stan]
Skull				
4"	-	$8.99	DINOSAUR FOUNDRY	
4"	(Groman)	$30.00	ESPI	
4"	(Tippmann)	$75.00	TIPPMANN 1006	
[$200.00]				
5.5"	(Tskhondin)	$49.95	ANTS r100701123	[fossil color available]
5.5"	(McVey)	$46.50	MENAGERIE	
6"	(Gravino)	$270.00	VALLEY MG06	
6"	-	$24.95	EARTHLORE	
6"	-	$18.00	SAFARI 3531-40	
6"	(Tippmann)	$120.00	BLACK HILLS R005	[Stan]
6.5"	(McVey)	$60.00	MENAGERIE	[two bookends!]
7"	-	$120.00	BLACK HILLS RDSR0106	
7"	**-**	**$480.00**	**ANTIQUARIAN JT10**	
10"	(Williams)	$135.00	SKULLDUGGERY 0241	[with stand, $31.95]
10"	**-**	**$580.00**	**ANTIQUARIAN JT11**	**[with 12 neck vertebrae]**
12"	**(Monteleone)**	**$3200.00**	**LOST ART**	
13"	(Pinney)	$225.00	SKULLDUGGERY 0239	
20"	(Auger)	$695.00	CRETACEOUS (Cdn)	
28"	(Hutton)	$550.00	STUDIO SCULPTURE	
[$9000.00]				
38"	-	$4,250.00	SMITH STUDIOS	
48"	-	$4,000.00	BLACK HILLS R00553	[Duffy, half-skull]
58"	-	$5,750.00	BLACK HILLS RD0553	[Stan, half skull]
58"	-	$9,500.00	BLACK HILLS R00541	

Size	(Sculptor)	Price	Company	Notes
60"	-	$8,440.00	ANTIQUARIAN	
78"	-	$15,000.00	BLACK HILLS RD0552	[with neck]
Teeth				
2.5"	-	$15.00	BLACK HILLS R00547	
2.5"	-	$16.00	GASTON DESIGN	
3"	-	$11.50	SMITH STUDIOS	
3.5"	-	$8.00	SECOND NATURE SN-08	
4"	-	$45.00	TAYLOR STUDIOS F039	
4.5"	-	$25.00	BLACK HILLS R00545	
4.5"	-	$17.00	SMITH STUDIOS	
5.5"	-	$12.00	ANTS r100403100	
5.5"	-	$10.00	WESTERN	
7"	-	$19.00	PREHISTORIC	
7.5"	-	$15.00	BONE ROOM	
190mm		L9.00	GEOU CRR 23.1	
11"	-	$32.95	SKULLDUGGERY 0216	[with stand, $42.95]
11.5"	-	$75.00	BLACK HILLS R00535	
Life-sized Models				
1/1	(Geraths)	CALL	GERATHS	[bust, juvenile]
70"	-	$4,500.00	TIME TRAVEL	[bust]
84"	(Trcic)	$22,000.00	TRCIC	[bust]
[$45,000.00]				
29'	-	$52,500.00	JONAS STUDIOS	[1964 World's Fair]
40'	-	$9,500.00	CREATIONS E. T.	
49'	(Braun)	$49,000.00	CYCAD PRODUCTIONS	
Models and Sculpture				
?	(Krentz)	CALL	KRENTZ	
5"	(Neill)	$50.00	NEILL	[cup topper]
6"	(Fischner)	$45.00	DREAMSTAR D-13-Sm	[hatchling]
6"	-	$67.95	LUNAR MODELS OS14C	[after Zallinger]
7"	-	$145.00	JONAS STUDIOS	[1964 World's Fair]
7"	(Fischner)	$65.00	DREAMSTAR D-12-Lg	[hatchling]
8"	-	$49.95	VITTETOE	[bust]
8"	(Trcic)	$135.00	TRCIC STUDIO	
[$1,350.00]				
9"	**(Monteleone)**	**$1,200.00**	**LOST ART**	**[running]**
10"	(Trcic)	$125.00	TRCIC STUDIO	[profile bust]
[$995.00]				
10"	(Morales)	$124.95	LUNAR MODELS OS09	[fighting Edmontonia]
10.5"	**(Tischler)**	**$950.00**	**HUGH ROSE**	
11"	(Laudati)	$70.00	X-O-FACTO	[and Triceratops]
11"	(Alfrey)	$85.00	MENTAL MISCHIEF	
12"	(Morales)	$144.95	LUNAR STUDIOS 0S04	[with Velociraptors]
13"	(Weigler)	$69.98	LINK AND PIN	[hatchling]
13"	(Debus)	$69.00	HELL CREEK	

Size	(Sculptor)	Price	Company	Notes
13"	(Monteleone)	$2950.00	LOST ART	[juvenile]
14"	(Schultz)	$85.00	CREATION SCIENCE	[bust]
14"	(Salas)	$120.00	SALAS	[male and female]
16"	-	$144.95	LUNAR MODELS OS26C	[Burian, with Trachodon]
16"	(McVey)	$100.00	MENAGERIE	['Running']
16"	(McVey)	$100.00	MENAGERIE	['In Pursuit']
16"	-	$50.00	MONSTROSITIES	[Kaiyodo]
17"	(McGrady)	$100.00	CM STUDIO	[finished, $175.00]
17"	(Darga)	$59.95	HORIZON 55701	[hatchling]
18"	-	$37.00	MONSTROSITIES	[Kaiyodo]
18"	-	$144.95	LUNAR MODELS OS13C	[Knight, with Triceratops]
19"	(Watson)	$245.00 [$1,500.00]	WATSON SCULPTURE	[with Triceratops]
19"	-	$70.00	MONSTROSITIES	[Kaiyodo]
20"	(Van Howd)	$3,750.00	SIERRA SCULPTURE	[with Triceratops]
22"	(Smith)	$350.00 [$1,500.00]	SMITH STUDIOS	
22"	(McGrady)	$140.00	CM STUDIO	[finished, $215.00]
24"	(Furuya)	$218.99	FURUYA STUDIO	[finished, $518.00]
25"	-	$78.00	MONSTROSITIES	[Kaiyodo, striding]
25"	-	$78.00	MONSTROSITIES	[Kaiyodo, roaring]
25"	(McVey)	$1000.00	DINO ART	[bust]
27"	(Sorton)	$350.00	DINO ART	
28"	(Fischner)	$750.00	DREAMSTAR	
29"	(Auger)	$1,550.00	CRETACEOUS (Cdn)	[bust]
30"	(Manit)	CALL	LIVING RESIN	
31"	(Lunar)	$305.98	LINK AND PIN DS27	
34"	(Darga)	$120.00	HORIZON 55703	
35"	-	$3,250.00	JONAS STUDIOS	[1964 World's Fair]
36"	(Holmes)	L2,200	HOLMES	
36"	(McGrady)	$450.00	CM STUDIO	[base, $35.00]
36"	(Strasser)	$450.00	DRAGON, INC.	[finished, $745.00]
37"	(Musy)	CALL	MARK MUSY	
37"	(Merrithew)	$5,600.00	MERRITHEW	[Pentaceratops bites foot!]
38"	(Ovenshire)	$300.00	FANTASY CREATIONS	
46"	(Merrithew)	$7,000.00	MERRITHEW	[attacks Deinonychus pack]
48"	(McVey)	$4,500.00	MENAGERIE	
48"	(McGrady)	$900.00	CM STUDIO	[finished, $1,425.00]
51"	(Tippmann)	$1,500.00 [$6,000.00]	TIPPMANN 1003	[Sue]
60"	(Trcic)	CALL	TRCIC STUDIO	
60"	(McGrady)	$1,600.00	CM STUDIO	[finished, $2,800.00]
84"	(Weigler)	$3,000.00	DINO ART	[sitting]
96"	(McVey)	$5500.00	DREAMS TO REALITY	

Plaques

3x6"	(Hoeger)	$7.00	VALLEY SH03	[skull]
9x11"	(Hoffman)	$35.00	S. G. HOFFMAN	[Tyrannosaur and offspring]
9x12"	-	$69.99	DINOSAUR FOUNDRY	[skull]
11x14"		$35.00	HOWARD	
230x320mm		L40.00	EDDY DNTY003	[skeleton]

Plastic Figures

7"	(Wild Safari)	$5.00	SAFARI 2789-29	
10"	(Carnegie)	$10.00	SAFARI 4035-01	[10th Anniversary]
11"	(Carnegie)	$7.50	SAFARI 4001-01	
12"	(Bos. Mus.)	$15.00	BATATT MS130	
12"	-	$13.00	RESAURUS	[12 moveable joints]

Posters

11x17"(Cox)		$5.00	COX	
13x18"(Sibbick)		L15.00	SIBBICK	
18x22"(Penny)		$6.00	PENNY	
19x24"(Tucciarone)		$25.00	NOVAGRAPHICS 0509-P	
24x36"(Hallett)		$6.00	MONSTROSITIES	
24x36"(Moravec)		$14.95	PREHISTORIC	[with babies]
33x55"-		$12.95	OMNI 99-8316	[glow in the dark]

Wooden Toys

13"	-	$8.00	SAFARI 7060-11	[skeleton]
13"	-	$5.00	ACTION 18140	[skeleton]
26"	-	$14.00	SAFARI 7300-10	[skeleton]
27"	-	$19.95	DINO BONZ 40107	[skeleton]
31"	-	$7.00	DINOSAUR PATTERNS	[skeleton]
36"	-	$59.00	SAFARI 7380-10	[skeleton]
40"	-	$15.00	B. C. BONZ T-SML	[skeleton]
47"	-	$29.95	DINO BONZ 40401	[skeleton]
60"	-	$25.00	B. C. BONZ T-MED	[skeleton]
80"	-	$40.00	B. C. BONZ T-LRG	[skeleton]
120"	-	$125.00	B. C. BONZ T-XLG	[skeleton]
160"	-	$750.00	B. C. BONZ T-XXL	[skeleton]

TYLOSAURUS

Fossil Replicas
Skeleton

45'	-	$64,000.00	TRIEBOLD

Skull

60"	-	$4,500	TRIEBOLD

Models and Sculpture

1/35	(Jones)	CALL	MIKE JONES	
11"	-	$149.98	LINK AND PIN R-21	[Kaiyodo]

| 13" | (Tischler) | $950.00 | HUGH ROSE | ['Catcher gets Caught'] |
| 28" | (Fischner) | $650.00 | DREAMSTAR | |

UTAHRAPTOR

Fossil Replicas
Claw

6"	-	$7.50	ANTIQUARIAN CL33	[manus]
120mm		$7.00	VALLEY SH01	
7"	-	$21.00	GASTON DESIGN	[manus]
9"	-	$20.95	SKULLDUGGERY 0235	[pes, with stand, $30.95]
10"	-	$30.00	GASTON DESIGN	[manus]
12"	-	$30.00	GASTON DESIGN	[pes]

Fingers

| 12" | - | $30.00 | GASTON DESIGN | [2nd digit] |

Hands

| 15.5" | - | $160.00 | GASTON DESIGN | [with base] |

Legs

| 50" | - | $425.00 | GASTON DESIGN | [with armature] |

Life-sized Models

| 15' | (McGrady) | $18,000.00 | CM STUDIO | |

Models and Sculpture

7"	(Finney)	$35.98	LINK AND PIN	[four different poses]
17"	(Watson)	$245.00	WATSON SCULPTURES	
24"	(McGrady)	$225.00	CM STUDIOS	[finished, $395.00]

Plastic Figures

4.5"	(Bos. Mus.)	$6.00	BATTAT	
6"	(Wild Safari)	$3.50	SAFARI 2791-29	
11"	-	L5.99	TOYWAY 201	[Walking with Dinosaurs]

Posters

| 20x29"(Glazer) | | $24.00 | ANTIQUARIAN | |

VARANOSAURUS

Life-sized Models

| 60" | (Braun) | $6,000.00 | CYCAD PRODUCTIONS | |

VECTISAURUS

Life-sized Models

| 13' | (Braun) | $13,000.00 | CYCAD PRODUCTIONS | |

VELOCIRAPTOR

Fossil Replica
Claw

2"	-	$7.00	ANTIQUARIAN CL34	[manus]
3"	-	$30.00	NORTH EASTERN RD-151	[pes, part of set]
75mm	-	$6.00	VALLEY SH05	
80mm	-	L3.75	GEOU CRR 24.0	
3.5"	-	$10.00	SECOND NATURE SN-03	[pes]

Foot

7"	-	$70.00	TAYLOR STUDIOS F041
8"	**(Monteleone)**	**$375.00**	**LOST ART**

Skull

4"	-	$8.99	DINOSAUR FOUNDRY	
6"	-	$24.95	EARTHLORE	
7"	-	$75.00	TWO GUYS	
8"	-	$90.00	ANTIQUARIAN SH15	
8"	(Auger)	$22.95	CRETACEOUS (Cdn)	[half skull]
9"	-	$199.98	LINK AND PIN S-01	[Kaiyodo]
9"	(Gerath)	$185.00	GERATH	[painted, $245.00]
9"	(Knuth)	$75.00	KNUTH	
[$200.00]				
12.5"	(Hoeger)	$120.00	VALLEY SH15	
21cm	-	$119.00	SKULLS UNLIMITED VA-07	
220mm	-	$259.00	GONDWANA	
.32m	-	$280.00	SALAS GISMONDI	

Life-sized Models

84"	-	$6,000.00	GONDWANA
5'	(Knuth)	CALL	KNUTH
6'	(Braun)	$6,000.00	CYCAD PRODUCTIONS
3m	-	$2,500.00	SALAS GISMONDI
7'	(McGrady)	$5,600.00	CM STUDIO
12'	-	$2,500.00	CREATIONS E. T.

Models and Sculpture

1.5"	-	$18.00	TAMIYA	[pack of six]
6"	**(Hunt)**	**$350.00**	**HUNT STUDIOS**	
7"	(Fischner)	$54.98	LINK AND PIN	[hatchling]
7"	-	$136.98	LINK AND PIN R-01	[Kaiyodo; in tree!]
7"	(Windstone)	$52.00	GRANDIOSITY #309	[hatchling]
9"	(Tokugawa)	$30.00	MUSASHI	
12"	(Kelley)	$119.98	LINK AND PIN	
12"	(Lunar)	$95.00	DINO ART	[fighting Protoceratops]
13"	(Bowman)	$99.00	BOWMAN ARTS	[feathered!]
[$250.00]				

14"	(McGrady)	$85.00	CM STUDIO	[Protoceratops base, $45.00]
16"	-	$145.00	MONSTROSITIES	[feasting on Protoceratops]
18"	(McGrady)	$150.00	DINO ART	[bust]
24"	(Dickens)	$195.00	INTEGRITY	
26"	(McGrady)	$225.00	CM STUDIO	[feathered!]
27"	(Fischner)	$750.00	DREAMSTAR	
30"	(Darga)	$69.95	HORIZON 55702	
65"	(Bowman)	$750.00	BOWMAN ARTS	[feathered!]
[$12,000.00]				
84"	(Burnett)	$750.00	BURNETT	[finished, $3000.00]

Plaques

| 11x14" | | $35.00 | HOWARD | |
| 16x27"(Minott) | | $110.00 | MENTIS GROUP | |

Plastic Figures

| 12" | (Kish) | $15.00 | SAFARI 2500-29 | |
| 12" | - | $13.00 | RESAURUS | [12 moveable joints!] |

Posters

| 17x21"(Barlowe) | | $25.00 | MONSTROSITIES | |

Wooden Toys

21"	-	$8.00	SAFARI 7400-11	[skeleton]
34"	-	$7.00	DINOSAUR PATTERNS	[skeleton]
36"	-	$15.00	B. C. BONZ V-SML	[skeleton]
51"	-	$25.00	B. C. BONZ V-MED	[skeleton]
69"	-	$40.00	B. C. BONZ V-LRG	[skeleton]
105"	-	$125.00	B. C. BONZ V-XLG	[skeleton]
180"	-	$750.00	B. C. BONZ V-XXL	[skeleton]

WUERHOSAURUS

Life-sized Models

| 20' | (Braun) | $20,000.00 | CYCAD PRODUCTIONS | |

YANGCHUANOSAURUS

Fossil Replicas
Skeleton

| 10m | - | $35,000.00 | BLACK HILLS | |

Life-sized Models

| 33' | (Braun) | $33,000.00 | CYCAD REPRODUCTIONS | |

Models and Sculpture

| 13" | (Salas) | $120.00 | SALAS | |
| 25" | (Dickens) | $160.00 | MONSTROSITIES | |

Plastic Figures

| 6.5" | (Kish) | $12.00 | SAFARI 2600-29 | |

MAMMALS
(AND OTHER SECOND-CLASS CITIZENS...)

AEPYORNIS

Life-sized Models
10'   (Braun) $10,000.00   CYCAD PRODUCTIONS

ALTICAMELUS

Models and Sculpture
10"   - $950.00   JONAS STUDIOS

AMBELODON

Models and Sculpture
6"   (Holmes)   **$384.00**   ATTICA   [bust]

AMERICAN LION

Fossil Replicas
Skull
18"   - $299.00   SKULLDUGGERY 0227
19"   (Kronen) $390.00   BONE CLONES BC-19A   [also tarpit finish]

ANCHTHERIUM

Plastic Figures
4"   - $8.00   BULLYLAND 58360

ANDREWSARCHUS

Models and Sculpture
7"   (Cooper) $60.00   PALEOCRAFT
Plastic Figures
7"   - $11.50   BULLYLAND 58353

ARCHAEOTHERIUM

Fossil Replicas
Skull
20"   - $237.00   ANTIQUARIAN S44

ARSINOTHERIUM

Models and Sculpture
12"   (Alchemy) $158.98   LINK AND PIN DS22   [with Dire Wolf]

BASILOSAURUS

Models and Sculpture
1/35   (Salas)   CALL   SALAS
12"   (Jonas) $450.00   JONAS STUDIOS

BISON

Models and Sculpture
20"   (McGrady) $400.00   CM STUDIO   [finished, $650.00]

BRONTOPS

Models and Sculpture
25"   (Morales)   CALL   DRAGON ATTACK!

BRONTOTHERIUM

Fossil Replicas
Jaw
24"   - $175.00   TAYLOR STUDIOS F031
25"   - $825.00   BLACK HILLS RM0625
Models and Sculpture
12"   (Morales) $120.00   DRAGON ATTACK!   [finished, $220]
12"   (Davis) $800.00   DAVIS
13"   (Debus) $65.00   HELL CREEK

CASTOROIDES

Fossil Replicas
Skull
10"   - $450.00   TAYLOR STUDIOS F048
Models and Sculpture
5.5"   - $350.00   JONAS STUDIOS

CACOPS

Posters
24x36"(Sibbick) $6.00   MONSTROSITIES   [with Casea and Varanops]

CAVE BEAR

Fossil Replicas
Skull
19"   - $234.00   ANTIQUARIAN AF50
21"   - $299.00   ANTIQUARIAN AF51   [largest known specimen]
Plastic Replicas
3"   - $6.50   BULLYLAND 58352

CERVELCES

Models and Sculpture
13.5" - $950.00   JONAS STUDIOS

CHALICOTHERE

Fossil Replicas
Skeleton
8'   - $18,500.00   ANTIQUARIAN A106   [Moropus]
Plastic Figures
5.5"   - $12.00   BULLYLAND 58357

CHILOTHERIUM

Fossil Replicas
Skeleton
2.3m   - $7,000.00   SMITH STUDIOS

COELACANTH

Models and Sculpture
8"   - $59.00   MONSTROSITIES   [Kaiyodo]

COLUMBIAN ELEPHANT

Models and Sculpture
26"   - $1,950.00   JONAS STUDIOS

CREODONT

Fossils Replicas
Skull
10"   - $244.00   ANTIQUARIAN DL106   [Patriofelis]
11"   - $134.00   ANTIQUARIAN S46   [Hyaeodon]

DEINOTHERIUM

Plastic Figures
9"   - $19.00   BULLYLAND 58351

DIATRYMA

Life-sized Models
7'   (Braun) $7,000.00   CYCAD PRODUCTIONS

DINICTIS

Fossil Replicas
Skull
6"   - $175.00   BLACK HILLS RM0605
7"   (Kronen) $170.00   BONE CLONES BC-30

DINOHYUS

Models and Sculpture
?   (Cooper) $65.00   PALEOCRAFT
9"   (Wood)   CALL   WOOD

DINORNIS

<u>Life-sized Models</u>
11'   (Braun) $11,000.00   CYCAD PRODUCTIONS

DIPLOCAULUS

<u>Fossil Replicas</u>
Skull
6"   - $145.00   SMITH STUDIOS
<u>Models and Sculpture</u>
6"   (Dickens) $30.00   INTEGRITY
33"   (Fischner) $550.00   DREAMSTAR

DIRE WOLF

<u>Fossil Replicas</u>
Skull
12.5"   (Kronen) $180.00   BONE CLONES BC-20A   [also tarpit finish]
12.5"   - $200.00   ANTS
<u>Models and Sculpture</u>
7.5"   - $475.00   JONAS STUDIOS
<u>Plastic Figures</u>
4"   - $9.00   BULLYLAND 58374

DIATRYMA

<u>Plastic Figures</u>
4"   - $9.00   BULLYLAND 58356

DODO

<u>Life-sized Models</u>
31"   (Holmes)   L3,400   HOLMES

DROMORNIS

<u>Fossil Replicas</u>
Skeleton
3.2m   -   CALL   GONDWANA

DUNKLEOSTEUS

Models and Sculpture
11.5"	(Harvey)	$129.99	WICCART	[finished, $199.00]
32"	(McGrady)	$600.00	CM STUDIO	[finished, $1,025.00]

ELASMOTHERIUM

Models and Sculpture
10"	-	$102.95	LUNAR MODELS OS12
11"	(Green)	$108.00	CONTINENTAL

EMEUS

Life-sized Models
60"	(Braun)	$6,000.00	CYCAD PRODUCTIONS

EOGYRINUS

Life-sized Models
15'	(Braun)	$15,000.00	CYCAD PRODUCTIONS

EOHIPPUS

Models and Sculpture
2.5"	-	$350.00	JONAS STUDIOS

ERYOPS

Fossil Replicas
Claw
19mm	-	$5.00	VALLEY CL11

Skeleton
5.5'	-	CALL	VALLEY

Skull
13.5"	-	$344.00	ANTIQUARIAN S55
33cm	-	$440.00	VALLEY SO55

EUSMILUS

Fossil Replicas
7"	(Kronen)	$300.00	BONE CLONES CB-7PR

Plastic Figures
4"	-	$7.50	BULLYLAND 58359

GIGANTOPITHICUS

Fossil Replicas
Skull
7"	(Wood)	CALL	WOOD
12"	-	$294.00	ANTIQUARIAN

GLYPTODONT

Models and Sculpture
10"	(Salas)	$118.98	LINK AND PIN

GREERERPETON

Life-sized Models
60"	(Braun)	$6,000.00	CYCAD PRODUCTIONS

HARPAGORNIS

Life-sized Models
36"	(Braun)	$3,600.00	CYCAD PRODUCTIONS

HESPERORNIS

Fossil Replicas
Skeleton
43"	-	$4,000.00	BLACK HILLS RB0570

Life-sized Models
72'	(Braun)	$6,000.00	CYCAD PRODUCTIONS

HOLMESINIA

Fossil Replicas
Skeleton
7'	-	CALL	FOSSILNET

Skull
13"	-	$450.00	FOSSILNET

HOLOPHONEUS

Fossil Replicas
Skull
7"	-	$167.00	SKULLDUGGERY 0219
7.5"	-	$227.00	ANTIQUARIAN AF121
8"	-	$225.00	BLACK HILLS RM0606
9.5"	-	$325.00	BLACK HILLS RM0607
8.5"	(Kronen)	$350.00	BONE CLONES CB-19MP
10"	(Kronen)	$325.00	BONE CLONES CB-18CPR

HYRACOTHERIUM

Life-sized Models
23"	(Holmes)	L3,300	HOLMES

INDRICOTHERIUM

Models and Sculpture
8"	(Cooper)	$65.00	PALEOCRAFT

ICHTHYORNIS

Life-sized Models
8"	(Braun)	$800.00	CYCAD PRODUCTIONS

KUBANOCHOERUS

Fossil Replicas
Skeleton
2m	-	$9,500.00	SMITH STUDIOS

LEPTOMEYRX

Fossil Replicas
| 23" | - | $425.00 | BLACK HILLS RM0615 | [on slab] |

MACHAIRODUS

Fossil Replicas
Teeth
| 4.5" | - | $12.00 | SMITH STUDIOS |

MAMMOTH

Fossil Replicas
Teeth
| 8" | - | $300.00 | TAYLOR STUDIOS F002 |
| 9" | - | $32.95 | SKULLDUGGERY 0214 |

Life-sized Models
| 5' | (Braun) | $5,000.00 | CYCAD PRODUCTIONS | [juvenile] |
| 13' | (Braun) | $13,000.00 | CYCAD PRODUCTIONS | |

Wooden Toys
| 17" | - | $5.00 | ACTION 18145 | [skeleton] |

MASTODON

Fossil Replicas
Skull
| 44" | - | $1700.00 | ANTIQUARIAN S21 |

Teeth
| 7" | - | $40.00 | BONE ROOM |
| 7" | - | $300.00 | TAYLOR STUDIOS F001 |

Life-sized Models
| 11' | (Braun) | $11,000.00 | CYCAD PRODUCTIONS | |
| 21' | - | $35,000.00 | JONAS STUDIOS | |

Models and Sculpture
5"	-	$550.00	LINK AND PIN	[Jonas, calf]
22.5"	-	$1,750.00	LINK AND PIN	[Jonas; cow]
26.5"	-	$1,750.00	JONAS STUDIOS	[bull]
27"	(Braun)	$2,700.00	CYCAD PRODUCTIONS	

Plastic Figures
| 7.5" | - | $19.00 | BULLYLAND 58373 |

MEGACHOERUS

Fossils Replica
Skull
32"   - $975.00   BLACK HILLS RM0620

MEGALOCERAS

Life-sized Models
12'   - $6,200.00   CREATIONS E. T.
Models and Sculpture
7"   (Cooper) $65.00   PALEOCRAFT
13"   - $950.00   JONAS STUDIOS
Plastic Figures
4"   - $9.00   BULLYLAND 58358

MEGALODON

Fossil Replicas
Jaws
4x5'   - $8,000.00   J & S FOSSILS
5x6.5' $12,000.00   J & S FOSSILS
7x8'   -   CALL   NATURAL CANVAS
7x8' $20,000.00   J & S FOSSILS
8x10' $25,000.00   J & S FOSSILS
Teeth
5"   - $14.95   EARTHLORE
5.5"   - $30.00   GASTON DESIGN
5.5"   - $32.95   SKULLDUGGERY 0215
5.5"   - $31.00   SMITH STUDIOS
6"   - $15.00   BONE ROOM
6"   - $25.00   BONE CLONES KO-218
6"   - $80.00   TAYLOR STUDIOS F003
6.5"   - $29.95   ANTIQUARIAN AF207
7"   - $64.00   BONE CLONES KO-008
Models and Sculpture
1/35   (Finney) $99.98   LINK AND PIN

MEGATHERIUM

Fossil Replicas
Claw
12"   - $32.95   SKULLDUGGERY 0252   [with stand, $42.95]

| 17" | - | $120.00 | TAYLOR STUDIOS F030 | |
| 30" | - | $744.00 | ANTIQUARIAN S34 | [Eremotherium] |

Skeleton

| 20' | - | $33,500.00 | ANTIQUARIAN A101 | |

Models and Sculpture

| ? | (Cooper) | $65.00 | PALEOCRAFT | |
| 14" | - | $1,100.00 | JONAS STUDIOS | [with calf, $1,300.00] |

Plastic Figures

| 8" | - | $19.00 | BULLYLAND 58354 | |

MERYCHIPPUS

Fossil Replicas
Skeleton

| 60" | - | $6,000.00 | BLACK HILLS RM0630 |

Skull

| 12" | - | $375.00 | BLACK HILLS RM0631 |

MESOHIPPUS

Fossil Replica
Skeleton

| 48" | - | $3,900.00 | BLACK HILLS RM0640 |

Skull

| 7" | - | $150.00 | BLACK HILLS RM0641 |

Models and Sculpture

| 4" | - | $425.00 | JONAS STUDIOS |

METOPOSAUR

Fossil Replicas
Skull

| 20" | - | $300.00 | MT. BLANCO |

Life-sized Models

| 7' | (McGrady) | $6,500.00 | CM STUDIO |

MYLODON

Models and Sculpture

| 9.5" | - | $850.00 | JONAS STUDIOS |

PACHYRHIZODUS

Fossil Replicas
Skeleton
72"   - $9,500.00   TRIEBOLD
Skull
15"   - $1,500.00   TRIEBOLD

PALEONOLOXODON

Fossil Replicas
Skeleton
8m   - $25,000.00   SMITH STUDIOS

PALEOSPHENISCUS

Fossil Replicas
Skeleton
33"   - $3,500.00   BLACK HILLS RB0575

PANTYLUS

Fossil Replicas
Skull
2"   - $26.00   SMITH STUDIOS

PARAMERYCOIDODON

Fossil Replicas
24"   - $875.00   BLACK HILLS R00645

PHORORACUS

Models and Sculpture
10"   (Salas) $108.98   LINK AND PIN
12"   (McGrady) $200.00   CM STUDIO   [finished, $350.00]

PLATYBELODON

Fossil Replicas
Skeleton

5.8m	-	$15,000.00	SMITH STUDIOS	
7m	-	CALL	GONDWANA	

Models and Sculpture

12"	(Morales)	$179.95	LUNAR MODELS OS07	[diorama]

RAPHUS

Life-sized Models

36"	(Braun)	$3,600.00	CYCAD PRODUCTIONS

SHANSITHERIUM

Fossil Replicas
Skeleton

2m	-	$12,000.00	SMITH STUDIOS

SHORT-FACED BEAR

Models and Sculpture

7"	(Finney)	$60.00	FINNEY

SINOMASTODON

Fossil Replicas
Skeleton

5.3m	-	CALL	GONDWANA

SMILODON

Fossil Replicas
Skeleton

60"	(Kronen)	$8,950.00	BONE CLONES SC-18B	[custom mount, $10,950]

Skull

4"	-	$8.99	DINOSAUR FOUNDRY	
7"	-	$18.00	SAFARI 3523-40	
13"	-	$224.00	SKULLDUGGERY 0204	[display case, $146.00]
13.5"	-	$225.00	SMITH STUDIOS	
14"	(McGrady)	$140.00	CM STUDIO	[finished, $250.00]

16"	(Kronen)	$300.00	BONE CLONES BC-18TA	[also, tarpit finish]
16"	-	$595.00	TAYLOR STUDIOS F032	
16"	-	$300.00	BLACK HILLS R00660	

Teeth

| 11" | - | $21.95 | SKULLDUGGERY 0236 | |
| 11" | - | $30.00 | BONE CLONES KO-212P | [pair] |

Models and Sculpture

?	(Cooper)	$65.00	PALEOCRAFT	
4"	(Finney)	$25.00	FINNEY	[with caveman, $45.00]
4"	(Silver)	$50.00	BONE CLONES	[ivory finish, $76.00]
6"	(Harryhausen)	$119.95	MONSTERS IN MOTION	
7"	**(Holmes)**	**$516.00**	**ATTICA**	**[bust]**
10.5"	-	$1,150.00	JONAS STUDIOS	[snarling]
11.5"	-	$795.00	JONAS STUDIOS	
14"	(McGrady)	$140.00	CM STUDIO	

Plastic Models

| 5" | - | $7.50 | BULLYLAND 58372 | |
| 6.5" | - | $9.00 | SAFARI 3405-61 | |

STEGODON

Fossil Replicas

Skeleton

| 8m | - | $33,000.00 | SMITH STUDIOS | |

THOOSUCHUS

Fossil Replicas

Teeth

| 5" | (Kronen) | $40.00 | BONE CLONES BC-40 | |

THYLACOSMILUS

Fossil Replicas

Skull

| 8" | - | $187.00 | ANTIQUARIAN AF101 | |

Models and Sculpture

| 14" | (Salas) | $108.98 | LINK AND PIN | |

UINTATHERIUM

Fossil Replicas
Skeleton
9.5"	-	$15,000.00	VALLEY A114	

Skull
29"	-	$500.00	VALLEY S114	

Models and Sculpture
11"	-	$112.95	LUNAR MODELS OS24	[with calf]
15"	-	$795.00	JONAS STUDIOS	

WOOLY MAMMOTH

Fossil Replicas
Teeth
7"	-	$40.00	BONE ROOM

Models and Sculpture
18"	(Van Howd)	$3500.00	SIERRA SCULPTURE
23.5"	-	$1,950.00	JONAS STUDIOS
34"	(Fischner)	$750.00	DREAMSTAR

Plastic Figures
3"	-	$4.00	SAFARI 3401-61	[juvenile]
7.5"	-	$19.00	BULLYLAND 58355	
9.5"	-	$15.00	SAFARI 3400-61	

Posters
18x26"(Burian)	$25.00	MONSTROSITIES	

Wooden Toys
32"	-	$29.95	DINO BONZ 40106	[skeleton]

WOOLY RHINOCEROS

Models and Sculpture
1/35	(Finney)	$29.00	FINNEY	
6"	(Cooper)	$65.00	PALEOCRAFT	[with calf]

Plastic Figures
6.5"	-	$12.00	SAFARI 3406-01
7"	-	$11.50	BULLYLAND 58350

XENOSMILUS

Fossil Replicas
Skull
13"	(Kronen)	$650.00	BONE KLONES CB-12P

Whimsical Dinosaurs
Dragons, and Critters Galore

Illustrations by David T. Hubbard

29827 C.R. 22 W. • Elkhart, IN 46517 • (219) 295-6081

All Artwork Copyright © 1999 by David T. Hubbard